Fourth Workshop on Insights from Negative Results in NLP (Insights 2023)

Dubrovnik, Croatia
5 May 2023

ISBN: 978-1-7138-7383-9

Printed from e-media with permission by:

Curran Associates, Inc.
57 Morehouse Lane
Red Hook, NY 12571

Some format issues inherent in the e-media version may also appear in this print version.

Association for Computational Linguistics
209 N. Eighth Street
Stroudsburg, Pennsylvania 18360

Phone: 1-570-476-8006
Fax: 1-570-476-0860

acl@aclweb.org

Additional copies of this publication are available from:

Curran Associates, Inc.
57 Morehouse Lane
Red Hook, NY 12571 USA
Phone: 845-758-0400
Fax: 845-758-2633
Email: curran@proceedings.com
Web: www.proceedings.com

ACL 2023

The Fourth Workshop on Insights from Negative Results in NLP

Proceedings of the Workshop

May 5, 2023

The ACL organizers gratefully acknowledge the support from the following sponsors.

Silver

Google

Introduction

Publication of negative results is difficult in most fields, and the current focus on benchmark-driven performance improvement exacerbates this situation and implicitly discourages hypothesis-driven research. As a result, the development of NLP models often devolves into a product of tinkering and tweaking, rather than science. Furthermore, it increases the time, effort, and carbon emissions spent on developing and tuning models, as the researchers have little opportunity to learn from what has already been tried and failed.

Historically, this tendency is hard to combat. ACL 2010 invited negative results as a special type of research paper submissions[1], but received too few submissions and did not continue with it. *The Journal for Interesting Negative Results in NLP and ML*[2] has only produced one issue in 2008.

However, the tide may be turning. The fourth iteration of the *Workshop on Insights from Negative Results* attracted 25 submissions and 10 from EACL 2023 Findings.

The workshop maintained roughly the same focus, welcoming many kinds of negative results with the hope that they could yield useful insights and provide a much-needed reality check on the successes of deep learning models in NLP. In particular, we solicited the following types of contributions:

- broadly applicable recommendations for training/fine-tuning, especially if X that didn't work is something that many practitioners would think reasonable to try, and if the demonstration of X's failure is accompanied by some explanation/hypothesis;
- ablation studies of components in previously proposed models, showing that their contributions are different from what was initially reported;
- datasets or probing tasks showing that previous approaches do not generalize to other domains or language phenomena;
- trivial baselines that work suspiciously well for a given task/dataset;
- cross-lingual studies showing that a technique X is only successful for a certain language or language family;
- experiments on (in)stability of the previously published results due to hardware, random initializations, preprocessing pipeline components, etc;
- theoretical arguments and/or proofs for why X should not be expected to work;
- demonstration of issues with data processing/collection/annotation pipelines, especially if they are widely used;
- demonstration of issues with evaluation metrics (e.g. accuracy, F1 or BLEU), which prevent their usage for fair comparison of methods.

In terms of topics/themes, 6 papers from our accepted proceedings discussed "Representation Learning / Pre-training"; 1 discussed "Entity Detection/Resolution"; 1 paper examined text classification; 1 dealt with issues of robustness, generalizability, error analysis; 2 on the topic of "text comprehension / VQA"; 2 papers focused on text generation such as summarization, machine translation; 1 on replication of human evaluations in NLP. Some submissions fit in more than one category.

We accepted 14 short papers (56.0% acceptance rate) and 10 papers from EACL 2023 Findings.

We hope the workshop will continue to contribute to the many reality-check discussions on progress in NLP. If we do not talk about things that do not work, it is harder to see what the biggest problems are and where the community effort is the most needed.

[1] `https://mirror.aclweb.org/acl2010/papers.html`

[2] `http://jinr.site.uottawa.ca/`

Organizing Committee

Organizers

Shabnam Tafreshi, University of Maryland: ARLIS, USA
Arjun Reddy Akula, Google, USA
João Sedoc, New York University, USA
Anna Rogers, University of Copenhagen, Denmark
Aleksandr Drozd, RIKEN, Japan
Anna Rumshisky, University of Massachusetts Lowell / Amazon Alexa, USA

Program Committee

Chairs

Arjun Akula, Google, USA
Aleksandr Drozd, RIKEN Center for Computational Science
Anna Rogers, University of Copenhagen
Anna Rumshisky, University of Massachusetts Lowell
João Sedoc, New York University
Shabnam Tafreshi, UMD:ARLIS

Program Committee

Amittai Axelrod, Apple
Ameya Godbole, University of Southern California
Andrey Kutuzov, University of Oslo
Anil Nelakanti, Amazon
Ali Seyfi, The George Washington University
Anuj Khare, Google LLC
Arijit Adhikari, Amazon
Ashutosh Modi, Indian Institute of Technology Kanpur
Chanjun Park, Upstage
Chung-chi Chen, National Institute of Advanced Industrial Science and Technology
Constantine Lignos, Brandeis University
David Samuel, University of Oslo, Language Technology Group
Edison Marrese-taylor, National Institute of Advanced Industrial Science and Technology (AIST)
Efsun Sarioglu Kayi, Johns Hopkins APL
Emil Vatai, Riken R-CCS
Gaurav Mishra, Google
Giovanni Puccetti, Scuola Normale Superiore di Pisa
Guenter Neumann, DFKI & Saarland University
Happy Buzaaba, RIKEN
John Ortega, Northeastern University
Joinal Ahmed, Google
Kaveri Anuranjana, Saarland University
Mahesh Goud Tandarpally, Amazon
Marzena Karpinska, University of Massachusetts Amherst
Maximilian Spliethöver, Leibniz University Hannover
Neha Nayak Kennard, University of Massachusetts Amherst
Salvatore Giorgi, University of Pennsylvania
Shubham Chatterjee, University of Glasgow
Tamás Ficsor, University of Szeged
Tristan Naumann, Microsoft Research
Wazir Ali, Institute of Business Management

Keynote Talk: My fruitless endeavours with neuro-symbolic NLP

Vered Shwartz
University of British Columbia, Canada

Bio: Vered Shwartz is an Assistant Professor of Computer Science at the University of British Columbia, and a CIFAR AI Chair at the Vector Institute. Her research interests include commonsense reasoning, computational semantics and pragmatics, and multiword expressions. Previously, Vered was a postdoctoral researcher at the Allen Institute for AI (AI2) and the University of Washington, and received her PhD in Computer Science from Bar-Ilan University. Vered's work has been recognized with several awards, including The Eric and Wendy Schmidt Postdoctoral Award for Women in Mathematical and Computing Sciences, the Clore Foundation Scholarship, and an ACL 2016 outstanding paper award.

Keynote Talk: Do not give up on projects with negative results!

Mohit Iyyer
UMass Amherst, USA

Bio: Mohit Iyyer is an assistant professor in computer science at the University of Massachusetts Amherst. His research focuses broadly on designing machine learning models for discourse-level language generation (e.g., for story generation and machine translation), and his group also works on tasks involving creative language understanding (e.g., modeling fictional narratives and characters). He is the recipient of best paper awards at NAACL (2016, 2018) and a best demo award at NeurIPS 2015, and he received the 2022 Samsung AI Researcher of the Year award. He received his PhD in computer science from the University of Maryland, College Park in 2017, advised by Jordan Boyd-Graber and Hal Daumé III, and spent the following year as a researcher at the Allen Institute for Artificial Intelligence.

Keynote Talk: How negative results fuel our research: insights from gender bias and multilinguality

Hila Gonen
University of Washington, USA

Bio: Hila is a postdoctoral Researcher at Meta AI and at the Paul G. Allen School of Computer Science & Engineering at the University of Washington. Hila's research lies in the intersection of Natural Language Processing, Machine Learning and AI. She is interested in analyzing and better understanding the cutting-edge technology used in the field, and focuses mainly on multilinguality and fairness in her research. Before joining UW and Meta AI, Hila was a postdoctoral researcher at Amazon. Prior to that she did her Ph.D in Computer Science at the NLP lab at Bar Ilan University. She obtained her Ms.C. in Computer Science from the Hebrew University. Hila is the recipient of several postdoc awards and an EECS rising stars award. Her work received the best paper awards at CoNLL 2019 and at the repL4nlp workshop 2022, and also an outstanding thesis award from IAAI.

Keynote Talk: Three lessons from negative results in NLP research

Rachel Rudinger
University of Maryland, USA

Bio: Rachel is an assistant professor at university of Maryland. Her research is focused on problems in natural language understanding, including knowledge acquisition, commonsense reasoning, an semantic representation.

Table of Contents

Program

Friday, May 5, 2023

09:00 - 09:15 *Opening Remarks*

09:15 - 10:00 *Thematic Session 1: Text Generation*

Hiding in Plain Sight: Insights into Abstractive Text Summarization
Vivek Srivastava, Savita Bhat and Niranjan Pedanekar

Encoding Sentence Position in Context-Aware Neural Machine Translation with Concatenation
Lorenzo Lupo, Marco Dinarelli and Laurent Besacier

Exploring the Reasons for Non-generalizability of KBQA systems
Sopan Khosla, Ritam Dutt, Vinayshekhar Bannihatti Kumar and Rashmi Gangadharaiah

10:00 - 10:45 *Invited Talk: Vered Shwartz*

10:45 - 11:15 *Coffee Break*

11:15 - 11:45 *Thematic Session 2: Text Classification & Comprehension*

A Data-centric Framework for Improving Domain-specific Machine Reading Comprehension Datasets
Iva Bojic, Josef Halim, Verena Suharman, Sreeja Tar, Qi Chwen Ong, Duy Phung, Mathieu Ravaut, Shafiq Joty and Josip Car

An Empirical Study on Active Learning for Multi-label Text Classification
Mengqi Wang and Ming Liu

11:45 - 12:15 *Thematic Session 3: Representation Learning & Pre-training*

SocBERT: A Pretrained Model for Social Media Text
Yuting Guo and Abeed Sarker

Edit Aware Representation Learning via Levenshtein Prediction
Edison Marrese-taylor, Machel Reid and Alfredo Solano

Friday, May 5, 2023 (continued)

	What changes when you randomly choose BPE merge operations? Not much. Jonne Saleva and Constantine Lignos
12:15 - 14:00	*Lunch*
14:00 - 14:30	*Invited Talk: Mohit Iyyer*
14:30 - 15:00	*Thematic Session 4: Robustness & Error Analysis*
	Annotating PubMed Abstracts with MeSH Headings using Graph Neural Network Faizan Mustafa, Rafika Boutalbi and Anastasiia Iurshina
15:00 - 15:30	*Invited Talk: Rachel Rudinger*
15:30 - 16:00	*Coffee Break*
16:00 - 16:30	*Invited Talk: Hila Gonen*
16:30 - 18:00	*Poster Session*
18:00 - 18:10	*Closing Remarks*

Missing Information, Unresponsive Authors, Experimental Flaws: The Impossibility of Assessing the Reproducibility of Previous Human Evaluations in NLP

Anya Belz[a,b] (anya.belz@adaptcentre.ie), **Craig Thomson**[b], **Ehud Reiter**[b], **Gavin Abercrombie**[8], **Jose M. Alonso-Moral**[17], **Mohammad Arvan**[16], **Jackie Cheung**[10], **Mark Cieliebak**[20], **Elizabeth Clark**[6], **Kees van Deemter**[19], **Tanvi Dinkar**[8], **Ondřej Dušek**[9], **Steffen Eger**[1], **Qixiang Fang**[19], **Albert Gatt**[19], **Dimitra Gkatzia**[4], **Javier González-Corbelle**[17], **Dirk Hovy**[2], **Manuela Hürlimann**[20], **Takumi Ito**[21], **John D. Kelleher**[12], **Filip Klubička**[12], **Huiyuan Lai**[7], **Chris van der Lee**[13], **Emiel van Miltenburg**[13], **Yiru Li**[7], **Saad Mahamood**[14], **Margot Mieskes**[15], **Malvina Nissim**[7], **Natalie Parde**[16], **Ondřej Plátek**[9], **Verena Rieser**[8], **Pablo Mosteiro Romero**[19], **Joel Tetreault**[3], **Antonio Toral**[7], **Xiaojun Wan**[11], **Leo Wanner**[18], **Lewis Watson**[4], **Diyi Yang**[5]

[a]ADAPT/DCU, Ireland; [b]University of Aberdeen, UK; [1]Bielefeld University, Germany; [2]Bocconi University, Italy; [3]Dataminr, US; [4]Edinburgh Napier University, UK; [5]Georgia Tech, US; [6]Google Research, US; [7]Groningen University, Netherlands; [8]Heriot-Watt University, UK; [9]Charles University Prague, Czechia; [10]McGill University, Canada; [11]Peking University, China; [12]Technological University Dublin, Ireland; [13]Tilburg University, Netherlands; [14]trivago, Germany; [15]University of Applied Sciences Darmstadt, Germany; [16]University of Illinois Chicago, US; [17]Universidade de Santiago de Compostela, Spain; [18]Universitat Pompeu Fabra, Spain; [19]Utrecht University, Netherlands; [20]Zurich University of Applied Sciences, Switzerland; [21]Tohoku University, Japan

Abstract

We report our efforts in identifying a set of previous human evaluations in NLP that would be suitable for a coordinated study examining what makes human evaluations in NLP more/less reproducible. We present our results and findings, which include that just 13% of papers had (i) sufficiently low barriers to reproduction, and (ii) enough obtainable information, to be considered for reproduction, and that all but one of the experiments we selected for reproduction was discovered to have flaws that made the meaningfulness of conducting a reproduction questionable. As a result, we had to change our coordinated study design from a reproduce approach to a standardise-then-reproduce-twice approach. Our overall (negative) finding that the great majority of human evaluations in NLP is not repeatable and/or not reproducible and/or too flawed to justify reproduction, paints a dire picture, but presents an opportunity for a rethink about how to design and report human evaluations in NLP.

1 Introduction

There is increasing awareness in Natural Language Processing (NLP) that reproducibility of results, most particularly of results from system evaluations, matters greatly, and that currently the field does not assess reproducibility of results rigorously enough, and lacks a common approach to it. Recent work has made progress particularly with respect to automatic evaluation (Pineau, 2020; Whitaker, 2017), but reproducibility of human evaluation, widely considered the litmus test of quality in NLP, has received less attention. It could be argued that if it is not known how reproducible human evaluations are, it is not known how reliable they are; and if it is not known how reliable they are, then it is not known how reliable automatic evaluations meta-evaluated against them are either.

The work reported in this paper forms part of the ReproHum project[1] in which our aim is to build on existing work on recording properties of human evaluations datasheet-style (Shimorina and Belz, 2022), and assessing how close results from a reproduction study are to the original study (Belz et al., 2022a), to investigate systematically what factors make a human evaluation more—or less—reproducible. In this paper, we present the findings from our work on the project so far which necessitated a rethink of our entire approach to designing such an investigation.

Section 2 outlines our motivation for carrying

[1]https://gow.epsrc.ukri.org/NGBOViewGrant.aspx?GrantRef=EP/V05645X/1

The Fourth Workshop on Insights from Negative Results in NLP, pages 1–10
May 5, 2023 ©2023 Association for Computational Linguistics

out a multi-lab multi-test (MLMT) study of factors affecting reproduciblity in NLP, and our original design for the study. Section 3 describes our paper selection, annotation and filtering process which yielded a surprisingly small number of candidate papers for reproduction. In Section 4 we describe the numerous further issues with original evaluation studies we encountered in the process of setting up reproductions of them with partner labs. Section 6 summarises our negative findings regarding the infeasibilty of assessing the reproducibility of previously conducted human evaluations in NLP as they are, and outlines the changes to our multi-lab multi-test study necessitated by the findings.

2 Motivation and Overall Study Design

Individual studies can tell us how close a reproduction study's results are to those in the original study. A large number of such studies can show general tendencies regarding what kinds of evaluations have better reproducibility. However, we do not currently have a large number of reproduction studies in NLP and because of their cost and lack of appeal, this is unlikely to change. Moreover, accumulations of individual studies do not provide the conditions in which the effect size and significance of specific factors on reproducibility, and interactions between them, can be measured.

To create such conditions, a controlled study of equal numbers of reproductions with and without factors of interest is needed. Moreover, we know from existing work (Belz et al., 2022b; Huidrom et al., 2022) that different reproductions of the *same* original work can produce very different results. Finally, while it is instructive to test for reproducibility under identical conditions, it is also of interest to test how far good reproducibility can stretch – e.g. is reproducibility affected by replacing, say, a 7-point quality scale with a 5-point one.

A study of factors that increase/decrease reproducibility therefore needs to (i) conduct more than one reproduction of each original study, (ii) carried out by a good mix of different teams, and to (iii) incorporate multiple rounds with decreasing similarity of conditions. The steps in setting up such a study would be as follows:

1. Identifying candidate evaluation experiments from which to select experiments with balanced factors to include in the MLMT study;
2. Recording properties of evaluation experiments to make it possible to select factors and control for them;
3. Selecting factors to control for and corresponding subsets of experiments; and
4. Carrying out reproductions for the selected evaluation studies and factors.

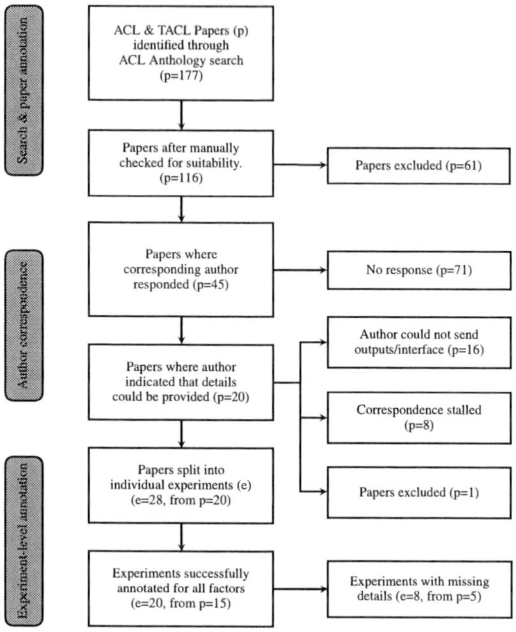

Figure 1: Flow diagram of the paper selection process, showing the decreasing number of papers that were suitable as more information was sought.

We describe Steps 1 and 2 in Sections 3.1 and 3.2, Step 3 in 3.3, and Step 4 up to the point where we aborted the original study design in Section 4.

3 Selection and Assessment of Candidate Evaluation Experiments

Figure 1 shows the selection and annotation process in the form of a flow diagram showing the decreasing number of remaining papers/experiments. The first step was to conduct a search on the ACL Anthology for papers published in ACL (main conference) or TACL in the 2018–2022 period[2] which included the phrases "human evaluation" and "participants;" we found 177 such papers.

3.1 High-level paper annotation

In a first round of annotating papers with properties of human evaluations, we used the following paper-level properties, annotated using only information from the paper or supplementary material:

[2]Search performed in July 2022, so some TACL papers from later that year are not included.

1. How many systems were evaluated;
2. How many datasets were used;
3. Type of participant (e.g. MTurk);
4. How many unique participants;
5. Rough estimate of how many judgments;
6. Type of NLP task implemented by the system(s) evaluated (e.g. summarisation);
7. Input/output language(s) used (e.g. English).

During this first annotation, we manually filtered out papers only discussing human evaluation rather than including one (e.g., surveys of human evaluation), longitudinal studies, any that used highly specialised participants such as medical doctors, and any that we roughly estimated to be too expensive for us to repeat (threshold $2,000 in evaluator payments). This left 116 papers. For these papers, Table 3 in the appendix shows the counts[3] of the most common values for each property annotated. English was dominant as system language, used in over 90% of papers. The second most common language was Chinese, which was used in just under 10% of experiments. Language generation tasks were most common, with summarisation the most frequent task, followed by dialogue and MT.

About a third of papers did not specify type of participant. Among papers that did specify this, 60% used crowd-sourcing, with the vast majority of these being run on Mechanical Turk. It was generally difficult to find information about participants, with about half of papers not reporting the total number of participants. Very few papers included a clear description of the relationship between systems, data sets, items, and participants; number of judgments is therefore an estimate.

It became clear during high-level annotation that fewer than 5% of the 116 papers remaining after filtering were repeatable from publicly available information alone. Fundamental details like number and type of evaluators, instructions and training, and data evaluated are often omitted. Our next step was therefore to contact authors in the hope of obtaining the missing information. Lack of information about human evaluations has been commented on a number of times recently (Van Der Lee et al., 2019; Howcroft et al., 2020; Belz et al., 2020).

[3]Because some papers include multiple properties, for example, multiple languages in machine translation systems, some rows will not sum to 116.

Training or expertise	neither	only one	both
	11	13	4
Number of participants	small		not small
	14		14
Complexity	low	medium	high
	9	11	8

Table 1: Frequency of control-factor annotations.

3.2 More detailed annotation of experiments

In the next stage we carried out detailed annotation of evaluation properties preparatory to selecting a subset of such properties to control in our multi-lab multi-test study. We emailed the corresponding author (defaulting to first author) for each of the 116 papers to ask if they would support reproduction studies and, if they could provide more detailed information about their experiments.

The requested information included the user interface from the evaluation and the set of outputs shown to the evaluators (complete list see Appendix A.2). We received replies for just 39% of papers, even after sending reminders. Many of those who did reply were unable to provide the information needed. In the end, only 20 authors (20 papers containing 28 experiments) gave us enough information to progress the paper to the detailed annotation stage.[4] The most common reason for authors responding but being unable to provide information was that they had moved on from their (usually graduate student) position and files had not been kept. In some cases, authors from commercial research groups who were unable to provide information for business reasons. There were also eight papers where the authors responded initially, but the correspondence stalled.

Using the author-provided information together with paper, supplementary material and online resources, we annotated the 20 papers that progressed to this stage for the detailed properties of evaluations shown in Section A.4, annotated at the level of individual experiments (28), because at this more fine-grained annotation level, properties can differ between different experiments in the same paper.

One of the first three authors of the present paper annotated the 28 experiments with the detailed properties; the other two each checked half of the annotations. Any differences were discussed and

[4]One further author did provide sufficient information, but upon further analysis of the paper and the resources they sent, we decided that the evaluation experiment reported in it was too different from the other 20 papers; the systems detected change in language use over time.

resolved. To complete these annotations, we had to ask authors additional questions (usually in multiple rounds of questions and responses) for all experiments except two. In the end, for 8 of the 28 experiments we did not succeed in obtaining all the information needed for the above properties.

Note that the last two properties in Section A.4 (evaluation task complexity, interface complexity) have a different status from the others, in that they are secondary properties, subjectively assessed during annotation, rather than deriving from author-provided information. We found we tended to either agree on what their value should be, and when there was disagreement, values were adjacent. We used discussion rather than attempting to formalise rules to resolve disagreement, as it would seem an impossible task to exhaustively capture the latter.

Table 1, and Table 4 in the Appendix, show the frequency of the most common property values across the 28 experiments (here including unclear values). We found that most of the annotated properties have one or two values that are the most frequent by large margins. For example, assessments were *intrinsic* in 26 out of 28 experiments, *subjective* in 26 out of 28, and *absolute* in 20 out of 28. Only two experiments were *extrinsic* and *objective* evaluations, the other 26 were *intrinsic* and *subjective*. There was large variation in the number of participants, with a low of 2 and a high of 233. None of the experiments provided explicit training sessions for participants, and only one included a practice session. About three quarters of experiments provided instructions and/or criterion definitions.[5] Around half of the experiments used subjects with specialist expertise, which was usually linguistics or NLP.

3.3 Choosing properties to control for

The issues discussed in previous sections posed serious problems for selecting papers for a controlled study: we had only 20 fully annotated experiments; and we were left with very skewed distributions for many of the properties we had annotated, with many property combinations not occurring at all, or only occurring in one or two cases. Given the above issues it was clear that we were only going to be able to select a small set of properties to control for. We therefore whittled down the set of properties we had annotated to three that were both feasible and had a reasonable likelihood, based on existing work, of affecting reproducibility. For these, we created between two and three bins from the original value ranges, as follows:

1. ***Number of evaluators (small, not small)***: Experiments with 1–5 evaluators were assigned the *small* value, those with more than 5 evaluators the *not small* value.
2. ***Cognitive complexity of assessment performed by evaluators (low, medium, high)***: Experiments were assigned to one of the three possible values on the basis of the task complexity and interface complexity properties listed in Section A.4.
3. ***Training and/or expertise of evaluators (both, one, neither)***: Experiments that had both trained, and required specific expertise from, evaluators were assigned *both*; those that either trained evaluators or required expertise (but not both) were assigned *one*; the remainder were assigned *neither*.

Even for this much reduced set of control factors, we did not have enough experiments to cover all $2\times3\times3$ combinations of values, so we settled for a final set of 6 experiments, where there was an equal quantity of the pairwise combinations of the *Number of evaluators* and *Training/expertise* properties, as well as equal pairwise combinations of the *Number of evaluators* and *Complexity* properties.

4 Setting up Reproductions

Beginning the process of reproduction of the six experiments finally selected for reproduction (for common agreed approach to reproduction see Appendix A.5) necessarily involved delving into full implementational details for each of them. One particularly troubling finding has been the number of experimental flaws, errors and bugs we unearthed in the process. The more we dug into the properties of evaluation experiments that we needed in order to repeat an evaluation experiment, the more we uncovered flaws which made us question whether it made sense to repeat the experiment at all, in some cases because any conclusions drawn on the basis of the flawed experiments would be unsafe. Six specific issues are listed in Section A.6.[6] Note

[5] We cannot be precise because this information was in some cases not provided even after we interacted with authors.

[6] Note that we report these in anonymised form, because of the reputational risks involved. See also the Responsible Research Checklist included in the appendix.

Task	Num. Evaluators		Cognitive Complexity			Training and/or Experise		
	small	not small	low	medium	high	neither	either	both
Dialogue	1	0	0	1	0	0	1	0
Generation	6	5	4	5	2	4	5	2
Summarisation	3	1	2	1	1	1	3	0
Other	2	2	1	0	3	2	0	2

Table 2: Counts of control property values per NLP task for the 20 experiments (from 15 papers) where all properties were clear.

that only one of our six selected experiments had none of these issues. We are still discovering more.

The structure we designed for our original study is shown in the Appendix Section A.1, Figure 2.

5 Discussion

The reasons why we decided to abandon our original study design were as follows. One, we struggled to find enough papers that did not have (i) prohibitive barriers to reproduction, and/or (ii) unavailable information that would be needed for repeating experiments, and/or (iii) experimental flaws and errors. Two, no matter how much effort we put into obtaining full experimental details from authors, there still remained questions, albeit increasingly fine-grained, that we did not have the answer to, such as if the presentation order of evaluated items was randomised, or what instructions/training participants were given. In some cases, information about additional things that had been done, but could not be guessed from previously provided information, transpired coincidentally, necessitating further changes to experimental design.

A potential solution to not having enough papers at the end is selecting more papers at the start (more years, more events). However, given the inordinate amount of work we put into obtaining enough information from authors, simply tripling or quadrupling our initial pool of papers was not a viable solution. Similarly, there was little we were able to do about the reproduction barriers of excessive cost and highly specialised evaluators.

On the other hand, accepting to work from less than complete experimental information would have been problematic because information for different papers is incomplete in different ways, and we would not have been comparing like with like.

Correcting flaws and errors would similarly have introduced differences between original and reproduction studies, moreover different ones in different cases. In this case we would strictly speaking no longer have been conducting reproductions.

We considered designing new evaluations from scratch with the properties we wanted for our MLMT study. However, it would have been very difficult to ensure that newly created studies were somehow representative of the kind of studies that are actually being conducted in NLP.

We have now opted for a solution incorporating elements from most of the above, where we select a somewhat larger set of existing studies in a process similar to before, reduce the number of different values of factors we control for, and then *standardise and where necessary correct studies before reproduction*. Reproducibility is then measured between two new studies, rather than between them and the original study.

6 Conclusion

The track record of NLP as a field in recording information about human evaluation experiments is currently dire (Howcroft et al., 2020). We saw in the paper-level annotations (Appendix Table 3) that in 37 out of 116 papers the type of participant was unclear, in 59 the number of participants was unclear, and in 15 the number of judgements was unclear. Even after prolonged exchanges with authors during the experiment-level detailed annotation stage, very fundamental details were in some cases not obtainable: number of participants, details of training, instruction and practice items, whether participants were required to be native speakers, and even the set of outputs evaluated.

Our overall conclusion is that, on the basis of the unobtainability of information about experiments, barriers to reproduction and/or experimental flaws in our sample of 177 papers, only a small fraction of previous human evaluations in NLP can be repeated under the same conditions, hence that their reproducibility cannot be tested by repeating them. The way forward would appear to be to accept the overhead of detailed recording of experimental details, e.g. with HEDS (Shimorina and Belz, 2022), in combination with substantially increased standardisation in all aspects of experimental design.

Acknowledgements

The ReproHum project is funded by EPSRC grant EP/V05645X/1. We would like to thank all authors who took the time to respond to our requests for information.

Limitations

The small subset of our findings that are based on information obtained from authors are necessarily limited in that they do not reflect information that might have been obtained from authors who did not respond.

Moreover, we selected our initial set of papers via search with key phrases "human evaluation" and "participants." While this phrase is very commonly used to refer to non-automatic forms of evaluation, there is a chance that we may have missed papers because they used a different term.

The small subset of conclusions based on our sample of experiments are limited by their sample size in terms of how representative they are of current human evaluations in NLP more generally.

Ethics Statement

As a paper that meta-reviews other academic publications, the present paper can be considered low-risk. Over and above collating information from publications, we annotated papers, analysed results and obtained descriptive statistics from annotations. In Section 5, we summarise the flaws, bugs and errors we found in experiments we were preparing for reproduction studies. We decided not to cite the papers where we found these, because the important information was that such issues occur, not which researchers were responsible for them.

See also the responsible NLP research checklist completed for this paper (Appendix A.7).

References

Anya Belz, Simon Mille, and David Howcroft. 2020. Disentangling the properties of human evaluation methods: A classification system to support comparability, meta-evaluation and reproducibility testing. In *Proceedings of the 13th International Conference on Natural Language Generation.*

Anya Belz, Maja Popovic, and Simon Mille. 2022a. Quantified reproducibility assessment of NLP results. In *Proceedings of the 60th Annual Meeting of the Association for Computational Linguistics (Volume 1: Long Papers)*, pages 16–28, Dublin, Ireland. Association for Computational Linguistics.

Anya Belz, Maja Popović, and Simon Mille. 2022b. Quantified reproducibility assessment of nlp results. In *Proceedings of the 60th Annual Meeting of the Association for Computational Linguistics (Volume 1: Long Papers)*, pages 16–28.

David M. Howcroft, Anya Belz, Miruna-Adriana Clinciu, Dimitra Gkatzia, Sadid A. Hasan, Saad Mahamood, Simon Mille, Emiel van Miltenburg, Sashank Santhanam, and Verena Rieser. 2020. Twenty years of confusion in human evaluation: NLG needs evaluation sheets and standardised definitions. In *Proceedings of the 13th International Conference on Natural Language Generation*, pages 169–182, Dublin, Ireland. Association for Computational Linguistics.

Rudali Huidrom, Ondřej Dušek, Zdeněk Kasner, Thiago Castro Ferreira, and Anya Belz. 2022. Two reproductions of a human-assessed comparative evaluation of a semantic error detection system. In *Proceedings of the 15th International Conference on Natural Language Generation: Generation Challenges*, Waterville, Maine, USA. Association for Computational Linguistics.

Joelle Pineau. 2020. The machine learning reproducibility checklist v2.0.

Anastasia Shimorina and Anya Belz. 2022. The human evaluation datasheet: A template for recording details of human evaluation experiments in NLP. In *Proceedings of the 2nd Workshop on Human Evaluation of NLP Systems (HumEval)*, pages 54–75, Dublin, Ireland. Association for Computational Linguistics.

Chris Van Der Lee, Albert Gatt, Emiel Van Miltenburg, Sander Wubben, and Emiel Krahmer. 2019. Best practices for the human evaluation of automatically generated text. In *Proceedings of the 12th International Conference on Natural Language Generation*, pages 355–368.

Kirstie Whitaker. 2017. The MT Reproducibility Checklist. `https://www.cs.mcgill.ca/~jpineau/ReproducibilityChecklist.pdf`.

A Appendix

A.1 Original study design

Figure 2 shows the original design of the multi-lab multi-test study.

A.2 Initial information requested from authors

Our initial email to authors asked if they would be able to provide the following information:

1. The system outputs that were shown to participants.
2. The interface, form, or document that participants completed; the exact document or form that was used would be ideal.
3. Details on the number and type of participants (students, researchers, Mechanical Turk, etc.) that took part in the study.
4. The total cost of the original study.

A.3 Counts for high-level annotations

Table 3 shows counts for the first round of annotating paper-level properties.

A.4 Details of experiment-level annotation

All of the property names and values from our detailed annotations are listed below, along with descriptions of what was recorded for each property:

1. Specific data sets used;
2. Specific evaluation criteria names used; the criterion names as stated in the paper if possible, otherwise a criterion name that represents what is being assessed.
3. System languages; the language(s) used by the system as either input or output.
4. System task; the NLP task that the system is tackling. Values from the 28 experiments were cross-lingual summarisation, data-to-text generation, definition generation with controllable complexity, dialogue summarisation, dialogue turn generation, explanation generation, fact-check justification generation, machine translation error prediction, prompted generation, question generation, question-answer generation, referring expression generation, simplification, summarisation, text to speech.
5. Evaluator type; the type of evaluator, values included colleagues, commercial in-house evaluators, crowd-sourced, mix of author and colleague, mix of colleague and students, professional, student.
6. Evaluation modes (Belz et al., 2020):
    (a) Intrinsic vs. extrinsic;
    (b) Absolute vs. relative;
    (c) Objective vs. subjective.
7. Number of participants; the total number of unique participants that took part in the study,
8. Number of items evaluated; in the case of an absolute evaluation this is one system output. In the case of a relative evaluation, it refers to the set of outputs, e.g., a pair, that is being compared.
9. How many participants evaluated each item; for some experiments, this varied.
10. How many items were evaluated by each participant; for some experiments, this varied. In particular, for the 13 of 28 experiments that were crowd-sourced, 5 were known integers, 4 varied, and 4 could not be determined (we suspect these also varied).
11. Were training and/or practice sessions provided for participants; see the discussion below.
12. Were participants given instructions? Were they given definitions of evaluation criteria; see the discussion below.
13. Were participants required to have a specific expertise? If so, what type, and was this self-reported or externally assessed?; see the discussion below.
14. Were participants required to be native speakers? If so, was this self-reported or externally assessed?; For the first part we used the options yes, no, crowd-source region filters, and in one case that the experiment was performed with students at a university where the language was native. The latter two are inherently self-reported, although with some limited control by the researchers. Only for one of the experiments with native speakers did the researchers indicate that they had confirmed this, all others were self-reports.

Structural design for a multi-lab, multi-test controlled study of experimental factors affecting reproducibility:

Round 1: Testing precision under repeatability conditions of measurement.

- Reproductions per experiment: 2 by two different labs;
- Conditions (experimental factors) to vary: evaluator cohort;
- If reproduction close enough, go to Round 2, else repeat Round 1 with improvements to experimental design, in terms of increased number of evaluators, and decreased cognitive complexity of evaluation task;
- For Round 1 repeats, if reproducibility is increased between reproduction studies (compared to each other, not the original study), proceed to Round 2, else stop.

Round 2: Testing reproducibility under varied conditions.

- Reproductions per experiment: 2 by two different labs;
- Conditions (experimental factors) to vary: evaluator cohort, and either number of evaluators *or* task complexity;
- If reproduction close enough, go to Round 3, else repeat Round 2 with improvements to experimental design, in terms of increased number of evaluators, and decreased cognitive complexity of evaluation task.
- For Round 2 repeats, if reproducibility is increased between reproduction studies (compared to each other, not the original study), proceed to Round 3, else stop.

Round 3: Testing reproducibility under increasingly varied conditions.

- Reproductions per experiment: 2 by two different labs;
- Conditions (experimental factors) to vary: evaluator cohort, number of evaluators *and* complexity.

Figure 2: Original design for the multi-lab, multi-test controlled study with a set of original human evaluation experiments with balanced experimental factors.

System language(s)	*English*	*Chinese*	*German*	*other*
	109	11	9	5
NLP Task	*summarisation*	*dialogue systems*	*machine translation*	*other*
	33	22	9	55
Number of systems	*1-5*	*6-7*	*> 7*	*unclear*
	89	14	13	0
Number of datasets	*1*	*2*	*> 3*	*unclear*
	83	25	8	0
Type of participant	*crowd (e.g., MTurk)*	*author/colleague/student*	*other*	*unclear*
	47	21	14	37
Number of unique participants	*< 5*	*5-20*	*> 20*	*unclear*
	27	19	11	59
Number of judgments	*< 100*	*100-1000*	*> 1000*	*unclear*
	1	34	66	15

Table 3: Frequency of the high-level experimental properties in the 116 papers, at the paper level. Some papers have multiple categorical properties therefore some rows will not sum to 116.

15. How complex was the evaluation task (low, medium, high); assessment by authors of this paper.
16. How complex was the interface (low, medium, high); assessment by authors of this paper.

Classifying the type of participant, training, instruction, and expertise was very difficult. Firstly, not all experiments necessarily require detailed instructions but setting a threshold beyond which instructions become non-perfunctory is difficult. The same is true for training. In the end, we decided to record whether there non-perfunctory training, instruction, practice, or criterion definition.

Expertise was also difficult to classify. Some papers would have originally reported 'expert annotators', but following our queries stated participants were graduate students or colleagues. Such participants were often called 'NLP experts'. In the end, we considered participants to be expert if the authors of the original study indicated that they were.

A.5 Common Approach to Reproduction

In order to ensure comparability between studies, we agreed the following common-ground approach to carrying out reproduction studies:

1. Plan for repeating the original experiment identically, then apply to research ethics committee for approval.
2. If participants were paid during the original

Property				
Quality criteria names	*fluency*	*coherence*	*informativeness*	*other*
	10	5	3	54
System language(s)	*English*	*Chinese*	*German*	*other*
	26	3	2	0
NLP Task	*summarisation*	*question answering*	*explanation*	*other*
	6	3	3	16
Type of participant	*crowd*	*student*	*colleague*	*other*
	13	8	7	4
Intrinsic or extrinsic	*intrinsic*		*extrinsic*	
	26		2	
Absolute or relative	*absolute*		*relative*	
	20		8	
Objective or subjective	*objective*		*subjective*	
	2		26	
Num. of unique participants	*< 5*	*5–20*	*> 20*	*unclear*
	11	4	8	5
Num. of items evaluated	*< 200*	*200–1000*	*> 1000*	*unclear*
	9	10	7	2
Num. of participants per item	*< 4*	*4–9*	*> 9*	*varies*
	17	3	3	5
Num. of items per participant	*< 50*	*50–200*	*> 200*	*varies/unclear*
	5	5	7	11
Training given	*no*		*unclear*	
	24		4	
Instructions given	*yes*	*no*	*unclear*	
	8	15	5	
Criterion definitions given	*yes*	*no*	*n/a*	*unclear/mixed*
	17	3	4	4
Practice session held	*yes*	*no*	*unclear*	
	1	23	4	
Participant expertise type	*none*	*researcher*	*linguist*	*domain*
	16	9	2	1
Participants native speakers	*yes*	*no*	*of region*	*unknown*
	2	12	10	4

Table 4: Frequency of detailed experimental properties in set of 28 experiments.

experiment, determine pay in accordance with the common procedure for calculating fair pay (see appendix).

3. Complete HEDS datasheet.
4. Identify the following types of results reported in the original paper for the experiment:
    (a) Type I results: single numerical scores, e.g. mean quality rating, error count, etc.
    (b) Type II results: sets of numerical scores, e.g. set of Type I results .
    (c) Type III results: categorical labels attached to text spans of any length.
    (d) Qualitative conclusions/findings stated explicitly in the original paper.
5. Carry out the allocated experiment exactly as described in the HEDS sheet.
6. Report quantified reproducibility assessments for 8a–c as follows:
    (a) Type I results: Coefficient of variation (debiased for small samples).
    (b) Type II results: Pearson's r, Spearman's ρ.
    (c) Type III results: Multi-rater: Fleiss's κ; Multi-rater, multi-label: Krippendorff's α.
    (d) Conclusions/findings: Side-by-side summary of conclusions/findings that are / are not confirmed in the repeat experiment.

A.6 Issues, flaws and errors found

1. Mistakes in the reported figures for the human evaluation in the published paper, with the result that systems were reported as being better or worse that they actually were.
2. Reporting a total number of items in the paper which did not match the files that were sent.

3. Failure to randomise the order of items to be evaluated (when the stated intention was to randomise) due to wrongly applied randomisation.
4. Reporting that evaluators did equal numbers of assessments but it's clear from the files that they did very different numbers.
5. Ad-hoc attention checks (exact nature of which authors were unable to provide) applied to some but not all participants who if they failed the check were excluded from further contributing to the experiment, but whose already completed work was kept.
6. Biased methods of aggregating judgments (choosing a preferred participant rather than using some form of average).

On a more general note, ambiguities in the reporting can be an issue. Even when checked against the HEDS sheet, authors could feel like they have mentioned all experimental details that are asked for in HEDS, but often these are described at such a high level that there is still room for misinterpretation, which means that authors still need to confirm that their paper has been interpreted correctly. One solution for NLP authors could be to let a third party fill in the HEDS sheet and see where they get stuck, but this does add a further overhead.

A.7 ARR Responsible Research Checklist

A. **For every submission:**

   A1. **Did you describe the limitations of your work?** Yes, e.g. we discuss the limitations from having a self-selecting subset of papers (where authors responded) available for analysis rather than a complete one.

   A2. **Did you discuss any potential risks of your work?** The work analyses previously peer-reviewed and published human evaluation experiments, and while conventional risk considerations don't apply, we do mention the potential harm to individual authors from non-anonymously reporting experimental flaws and/or low reproducibility in their work.

   A3. **Do the abstract and introduction summarise the paper's main claims?** Yes, abstract, introduction and conclusion summarise main aims and conclusions from the work.

B. **Did you use or create scientific artefacts?** No new data or computational resources were created.

C. **Did you run computational experiments?** No experiments were run.

D. **Did you use human annotators (e.g., crowdworkers) or research with human participants?** No human annotation or evaluations were carried out for this paper (other than by the authors).

ERATE: Efficient Retrieval Augmented Text Embeddings

Vatsal Raina* **Nora Kassner** **Kashyap Popat**
Patrick Lewis **Nicola Cancedda** **Louis Martin**
Meta AI
vr311@cam.ac.uk louismartin@meta.com

Abstract

Embedding representations of text are useful for downstream natural language processing tasks. Several universal sentence representation methods have been proposed with a particular focus on self-supervised pre-training approaches to leverage the vast quantities of unlabelled data. However, there are two challenges for generating rich embedding representations for a new document. 1) The latest rich embedding generators are based on very large costly transformer-based architectures. 2) The rich embedding representation of a new document is limited to only the information provided without access to any explicit contextual and temporal information that could potentially further enrich the representation. We propose efficient retrieval-augmented text embeddings (ERATE) that tackles the first issue and offers a method to tackle the second issue. To the best of our knowledge, we are the first to incorporate retrieval to general purpose embeddings as a new paradigm, which we apply to the semantic similarity tasks of SentEval. Despite not reaching state-of-the-art performance, ERATE offers key insights that encourages future work into investigating the potential of retrieval-based embeddings.

1 Introduction

State-of-the-art sentence embedding models (Raffel et al., 2020; Neelakantan et al., 2022) have competed against one another to approach human-like performance in several NLP tasks. Despite the gains observed in performance of sentence embeddings on public benchmarks such as SentEval (Conneau and Kiela, 2018a), the progress has come at a large computational expense. For example, the largest model amongst the Sentence-T5 series consists of up to billions of parameters while GPT-3 based sentence embedding model released by Neelakantan et al. (2022) has 175 billion parameters with marginal gains observed in performance when compared against older, smaller models. Models of these sizes are compute intensive and very difficult to host and use for most downstream use cases.

We propose a new paradigm that aims to maintain the benefits of high-complexity rich embedding models at reduced computational requirements. Our novel paradigm investigates whether retrieval can be used to bypass the compute intensive embedding model in a similar manner to the application of retrieval for generation (Lewis et al., 2020; Cai et al., 2022) tasks for real world large scale use cases with latency and compute constraints. We propose to use a lightweight retrieval model combined with rich pre-computed representations, in order to approximate the richer representations of a large embedding model.

We find retrieval-based embeddings struggle against standard text embedding models but their performance can be improved by aggregating neighbours from different light embedding representations and increasing the size of the datastore of precomputed embeddings.

To our knowledge, this is the first attempt to use retrieval approaches for developing general purpose sentence embeddings. Our main contributions can be summarised as follows:

- Introduction of a novel paradigm for generating sentence embeddings by exploiting retrieval-based approaches.
- Releasing efficient retrieval augmented text embeddings (ERATE) baseline systems with an exploration of methods that work well and don't work as well to assess the scope of retrieval to recover the performance of rich embedding models with low compute.

*Work done during internship.

The Fourth Workshop on Insights from Negative Results in NLP, pages 11–18
May 5, 2023 ©2023 Association for Computational Linguistics

We hope other researchers will engage in this novel setup to develop more efficient sentence embeddings that will allow high-performing representations to be accessible to a broader community.

Our work focuses on developing lightweight embeddings that out-compete existing lightweight embeddings but we believe ERATE can be used for a wider range of applications. Specifically, input documents often lack the full contextual information or temporal relevance to generate the necessary high-quality text embedding. ERATE offers the opportunity for the embedding of a given document to encapsulate information from other similar documents to increase the information content whilst also being more up-to-date with more recent documents added to a datastore.

2 Related Work

Reimers and Gurevych (2019) introduced Sentence-BERT as an improvement to the sentence representations from BERT (Devlin et al., 2019) by explicitly training Siamese BERT-networks using pairs of similar/dissimilar sentences. Yan et al. (2021) released ConSERT to learn sentence representations in an unsupervised manner by applying various forms of augmentations to a sentence to create its pair for contrastive learning. In a similar vain, SimCSE (Gao et al., 2021) relied on unsupervised contrastive learning by using dropout masks as the augmentation technique. DiffCSE (Chuang et al., 2022) further incorporated masked language modelling as an augmentation technique. Ni et al. (2022), released a family of sentence-T5 models that finetuned the T5 (Raffel et al., 2020) architecture in a supervised manner with pairs of naturally occurring similar sentences. Most recently, Neelakantan et al. (2022) developed a model finetuned using GPT-3 (Brown et al., 2020).

Several works have looked at approaches to make less expensive sentence embedding representations. For example, embedding recycling (Saad-Falcon et al., 2022) for language models is proposed as a reduced compute approach for downstream tasks. This involves caching activations from intermediate layers in large pre-trained models such that when similar inputs are seen during inference time, the cached output can be used in order to skip a part of the model structure. Embedding recycling has been demonstrated to out-compete distilled models, such as DistilBERT (Sanh et al., 2019). In contrast, we investigate whether fixed embedding representations can be generated more efficiently using retrieval without any additional training, relying only on pre-computed embeddings.

Other works have investigated efficient methods for retrieval from a large set of documents such as ColBERT (Khattab and Zaharia, 2020) and PLAID (Santhanam et al., 2022) interaction models that use offline encoding of documents. Rather than making the retrieval step more efficient, our work focuses on using retrieval as a tool for enhancing the development of general purpose embeddings.

Text generation and language modelling has seen several works involving performance boost with retrieval. Khandelwal et al. (2019) investigates extending a pre-trained language model by including the k-nearest neighbours, which Kassner and Schütze (2020) applies to question-answering. Similarly, Lewis et al. (2020) introduced retrieval-augmented generation (RAG) models where a pre-trained retriever and a pre-trained sequence-to-sequence model are fine-tuned end-to-end. Borgeaud et al. (2022) released RETRO as a successor of REALM (Guu et al., 2020) where an autoregressive language work is retrieval-enhanced by making the training documents explicitly available at inference time. Finally, Izacard et al. (2022) present ATLAS for retrieval-enhanced language modelling where the sequence-to-sequence model takes the retrieved documents and the query to generate the output text for knowledge-intensive tasks. We probe whether retrieval-incorporated approaches can bring similar benefits for the development of fixed embedding representations, not end-to-end sequence-to-sequence models.

3 Retrieval for text embeddings

This section explains how efficient retrieval augmented text embeddings are developed. The main idea is that a query document only needs to be embedded using a light embedder and by outlining the nearest neighbours in the light space, the corresponding pre-computed embeddings can be combined to generate the rich query embedding.

Let $\hat{d}$ denote a new document, for which we want to determine the rich embedding representation, $\hat{\mathbf{x}}$. Let $f_{\text{light}}(\cdot)$ and $f_{\text{rich}}(\cdot)$ be embedding generators that map a given document to the light and rich embedding spaces respectively:

$$\mathbf{h} = f_{\text{light}}(d) \qquad \mathbf{x} = f_{\text{rich}}(d) \tag{1}$$

Note, we assume that the operation $f_{\text{rich}}(d)$ is pro-

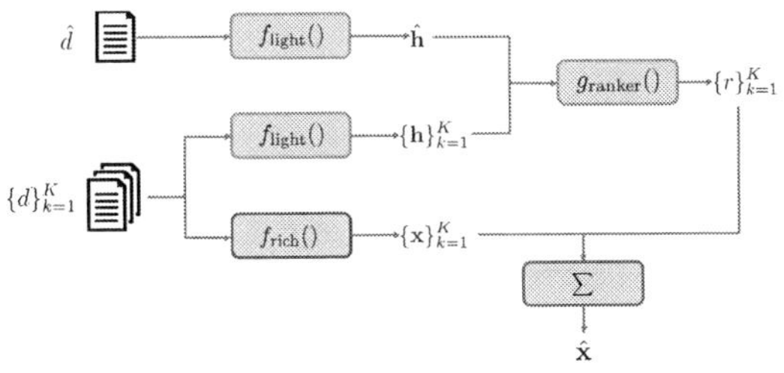

Figure 1: Schematic for ERATE embedding generation.

hibitively compute intensive while $\hat{\mathbf{h}} = f_{\text{light}}(\hat{d})$ is feasible. Instead, there exists a set of documents $\{d\}_{k=1}^K$ for which the rich embeddings, $\{\mathbf{x}\}_{k=1}^D$, have been pre-computed. Let $g_{\text{ranker}}(\cdot)$ denote a retrieval system that ranks all embeddings (with pairwise cosine distance) in a set based upon a query embedding. Hence, the ranks are:

$$\{r\}_{k=1}^K = g_{\text{ranker}}(\hat{\mathbf{h}}; \{\mathbf{h}\}_{k=1}^K) \tag{2}$$

The final rich embedding can then be calculated as a combination of the rich embedding representations of the top R documents:

$$\hat{\mathbf{x}} = \frac{1}{R}\sum_{k=1}^{K} \mathbf{1}_{r_k \le R} \cdot \mathbf{x}_k \tag{3}$$

The process is depicted in the pipeline of Figure 1. Alternative approaches can be considered for the combination process of Equation 3 [1].

3.1 Dropout masks

The proposed set-up for ERATE relies on identifying neighbours to the query document in the light space. However, the set of neighbours identified in the light space are correlated with the light embedding model that may not necessarily align with the desired neighbours in the rich space. Consequently, it is useful to create a neighbour set curated from multiple light embedding models which reduces the bias to a single light embedder (see Figure 2).

Dropout (Srivastava et al., 2014) is a common regularisation technique that has been extended to create diverse outputs at inference time such as Monte Carlo dropout (Gal and Ghahramani, 2016). Similarly, randomly *dropping* out embedding dimensions can be used to create a diverse set of light embedders that can expect to have different, potentially complementary, neighbour sets. Therefore dropout masks are applied to the light embeddings prior to performing retrieval in the ERATE process to create enchanced neighbour sets.

4 Experiments

4.1 Setup

SentEval (Conneau and Kiela, 2018b) is a popular benchmark dataset for assessing the quality of sentence embeddings, consisting of semantic text similarity (STS) tasks STS-12 to STS-16 and STS-B, SICK-R. These tasks evaluate how well the cosine distances of embeddings from pairs of sentences correlate with human annotated similarity scores using Spearman's rank correlation coefficient[2].

For ERATE to work effectively, a large datastore of documents/sentences must exist for which the sentence embeddings must be pre-calculated using both a light embedder and a rich embedder. We select the average GloVe word embeddings[3] (Pennington et al., 2014) as the light embedder as the model involves a simple lookup for each word in the sentence to determine its word embedding and hence low compute. State-of-the-art performance on the STS tasks of SentEval is achieved by Sentence-T5-xxl[4] (Ni et al., 2022). Hence, we adopt this Sentence-T5 model as our rich embedder. Additionally, we consider an *Oracle* ERATE model to breakdown the retrieval and combination stages of ERATE embeddings. Oracle embeddings are calculated by retrieving the closest neighbours in the rich space instead of the light space.

	Wiki	SNLI	MNLI	CC
# sentences	1M	629K	519K	100M
avg. words	$19_{\pm 12}$	$8_{\pm 4}$	$12_{\pm 9}$	$25_{\pm 19}$

Table 1: Statistics for unique datastore sentences.

The datastore of sentences with pre-computed embeddings is constructed from combining the 1 million Wikipedia (Wiki) sentences that acted as the unsupervised training data for SimCSE (Gao et al., 2021) and DiffCSE (Chuang et al., 2022) with the unique sentences of the *premise* and *hypothesis* from the SNLI (Bowman et al., 2015) and

[1]Empirical experiments indicated that weighing the importance of a retrieved embedding by its inverse distance to the query in the light space did not improve performance and hence the simplest approach of a linear average was adopted.

[2]Consistent with previous works, the 'all' setting that aggregates the subsets in a given STS task is used from `https://github.com/facebookresearch/SentEval`.

[3]Available at: `https://huggingface.co/sentence-transformers/average_word_embeddings_glove.840B.300d`

[4]Available at: `https://huggingface.co/sentence-transformers/sentence-t5-xxl`

MNLI (Williams et al., 2018) datasets. An additional 100 million sentences sampled from common crawl (CC)[5] are included in an expanded datastore to investigate the impact of increasing the datastore size. Table 1 details the statistics for each of these subsets. Sentences from STS on average have $13_{\pm 10}$ words, which is of a similar length to the sentences that are being used for the datastore as well as in terms of the diversity of topics.

4.2 Results

For a 512 token sentence the vanilla ERATE model (with a datastore size of 1 million) requires 3×10^9 floating point operations (FLOPs) while the Sentence-T5 model requires 8.7×10^{12} FLOPs.

Table 2 presents the performance of the baseline ERATE system against the existing state-of-the-art performance from Sentence-T5. Using the compute intensive rich embeddings directly achieves an average correlation coefficient of 84.8% across all the STS tasks while the light embedding model achieves a performance of 62.8% at a fraction of the compute. In contrast, the ERATE embeddings (100 closest neighbours are selected in the retrieval step), which have a similar compute to the light embedder, only achieve 55.3%. This low performance is underwhelming as let alone being close to state-of-the-art, it is not able to compete against the light embedding model.

	Avg.	sts12	sts13	sts14	sts15	sts16	stsB	sickR
Rich	84.8	78.9	88.9	84.9	89.3	84.7	86.7	80.4
Light	62.8	57.5	71.0	60.7	70.8	63.8	60.9	54.8
Oracle	72.3	66.8	76.9	70.9	73.6	73.7	75.2	69.1
ERATE	55.3	57.2	59.7	47.3	59.9	54.5	53.8	54.7
+drop.	57.4	60.8	62.0	52.8	59.8	54.4	56.5	55.4
+expand	57.9	55.4	60.0	52.9	64.1	60.0	58.8	53.8

Table 2: Performance with Sentence-T5 (Rich), GloVe (Light), oracle neighbours and vanilla ERATE with dropout and an expanded datastore.

The significant boost in performance to 72.3% from the Oracle suggests that the combination process by averaging is somewhat successful and the loss in performance comes from a mismatch in the surrounding neighbours for the light vs rich space. Further work would benefit from investigating alignment between the light and rich spaces.

Figure 2a further depicts an example PCA plot (using the two most dominant dimensions). Here, the rich embedding of an example query sentence is compared to the rich embeddings of the closest neighbours identified from the light space. On observation [6], the query lies on the periphery of the neighbours, which leads to the the centroid of the neighbours being afar from the desired query's position. We confirm the anisotropy hypothesis as the ratio of the distance between the query to the centroid and the averaged neighbour distance to the centroid (averaged across all test examples) is $1.1_{\pm 0.4}$ while the equivalent ratio using the Oracle neighbours is $0.5_{\pm 0.2}$ - about twice as close.

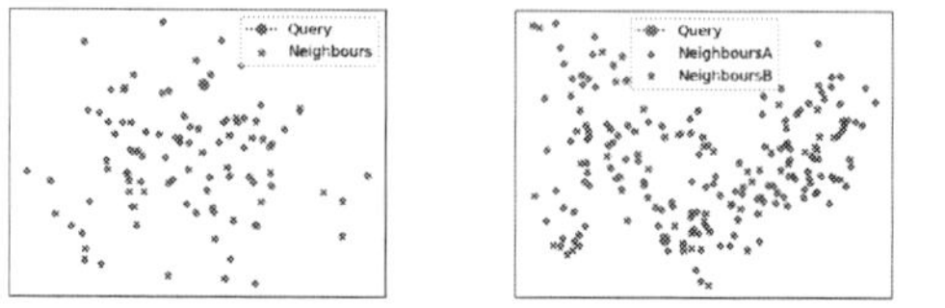

(a) Query vs neighbours. (b) Neighbours with dropout.

Figure 2: PCA on rich embeddings showing the query is closer to the centroid with multiple neighbour sets.

Consequently, as discussed in Section 3.1, an expanded neighbour set is considered by applying different dropout masks on 50% of the dimensions. Visually, Figure 2b suggests that the neighbour set from each dropout mask is somewhat different and hence the centroid of all the neighbours is more likely to approach the query's rich embedding. The hypothesis is supported by Table 2 where the performance increases to 57.4% by using 10 dropout masks simultaneously.

The performance can expect to be higher if the neighbours of the query are from a dense region as the combination of the embeddings will have less error. Therefore, Table 2 details the performance when using an expanded datastore size consisting of an additional 100 million sentences from Common Crawl (see Table 1). The baseline ERATE system performance is boosted by 2.5%.

5 Ablations

This section presents three ablations: (1) using an alternative light embedder; (2) an attempt to align the light and rich embedding spaces; (3) distillation of a rich embedder onto a light embedder.

Table 2 presents the results of ERATE where the average GloVe embeddings are used for the light embedder and the Sentence-T5-xxl model is used as the rich embedder. Here, an alternative light embedder is considered: the embedding associated

[5] https://commoncrawl.org/

[6] Observed on several examples.

with the [CLS] token of the DistilBERT (Sanh et al., 2019) model[7]. From Table 3, the ERATE approach successfully out-competes the DistilBERT light embedder by an encouraging 3.7% but it is still worse performing than the ERATE approach with the average GloVe embedder from Table 2.

	Avg.	sts12	sts13	sts14	sts15	sts16	stsB	sickR
Rich	84.8	78.9	88.9	84.9	89.3	84.7	86.7	80.4
Light*	39.6	32.1	38.0	31.3	44.1	52.8	31.0	47.7
ERATE*	45.0	37.6	34.3	51.1	47.0	43.1	50.1	44.0

Table 3: Performance with Sentence-T5 (Rich), DistilBERT (Light*), oracle neighbours and vanilla ERATE*.

ERATE relies on combining the rich embeddings of the neighbours identified from a light embedding space. Table 2 showed that the Oracle neighbours from the rich space substantially out-compete ERATE. Hence, it is expected that if the neighbour sets between the light and rich spaces have greater agreement, there will be improved performance for ERATE. A projection system is trained from the average GloVe embedding space to the ST5-xxl embedding space for better alignment.

Spaces	$P@1$	$P@10$	$P@100$
GloVe vs ST5	13.31	13.92	15.64
Projected[GloVe] vs ST5	12.51	13.10	14.33

Table 4: Impact of aligning light and rich spaces with a projection layer using Precision@K for $K \in \{1, 10, 100\}$.

The projection model consists of an input layer followed by a ReLU followed by a single hidden layer that predicts an embedding in the target embedding space with a cosine embedding loss. The vanilla datastore embeddings are used as the training data with 10% of the data cut-out for validation. Table 4 assesses the improved alignment by applying the projection layer. The averaged Precision@K is used as an assessment metric that measures the fraction of the closest K neighbours that match in each space for a given query. Despite that the model is trained to project the light space onto the rich space, there is degradation in the alignment of neighbours, possibly because the ordering of surrounding neighbours is not maintained in the training regime that impacts the retrieved neighbours.

A distillation inspired approach is considered where a light embedding model aims to mimic the embeddings of the rich Sentence-T5 model as an alternative strategy to ERATE. DistilBERT is selected as the light model[8]. For every datastore embedding, the light model is finetuned (all parameters) to predict the output embedding from the rich model. The distilled model achieves an average score on the STS tasks of 45.6% which is lower than the light model from Table 3. The lower performance may occur due to no emphasis on maintaining semantic similarity explicitly.

6 Conclusions

Retrieval-based embeddings are proposed as ERATE that bypass inference through an expensive embedding generation model but hope to leverage its richness. However, the current set-up for ERATE achieves subpar performance on text similarity tasks with some gains observed from combining neighbours of a unique dropout mask approach and extending the datastore size of pre-computed light and rich embeddings for retrieval. We highlight multiple areas of future work.

Future work should investigate ERATE-based approaches in a hybrid setting: ERATE embeddings are used for sentences where they are likely to work effectively (neighbours are in a dense space allowing accurate approximations) while the default expensive embedder can be used when ERATE is unlikely to be effective. ERATE can be increasingly effective when only partial information is available in a query for which an embedding is desired as combining the embeddings of neighbouring documents can enrich the information content. However, sentence-level embeddings offer little opportunity to explore the gains by additional information and hence future work should investigate the scope of ERATE at the document-level; MTEB (Muennighoff et al., 2022) potentially offers suitable tasks. We should also investigate alternative approaches for aligning the light and rich spaces and better combining neighbours' embeddings e.g. self-attention.

References

Sebastian Borgeaud, Arthur Mensch, Jordan Hoffmann, Trevor Cai, Eliza Rutherford, Katie Millican, George Bm Van Den Driessche, Jean-Baptiste Lespiau, Bogdan Damoc, Aidan Clark, et al. 2022.

[7]Available at: https://huggingface.co/distilbert-base-uncased

[8]The GloVe model is not used as there is no availability to finetune the model.

Improving language models by retrieving from trillions of tokens. In *International Conference on Machine Learning*, pages 2206–2240. PMLR.

Samuel Bowman, Gabor Angeli, Christopher Potts, and Christopher D Manning. 2015. A large annotated corpus for learning natural language inference. In *Proceedings of the 2015 Conference on Empirical Methods in Natural Language Processing*, pages 632–642.

Tom Brown, Benjamin Mann, Nick Ryder, Melanie Subbiah, Jared D Kaplan, Prafulla Dhariwal, Arvind Neelakantan, Pranav Shyam, Girish Sastry, Amanda Askell, et al. 2020. Language models are few-shot learners. *Advances in neural information processing systems*, 33:1877–1901.

Deng Cai, Yan Wang, Lemao Liu, and Shuming Shi. 2022. Recent advances in retrieval-augmented text generation. In *Proceedings of the 45th International ACM SIGIR Conference on Research and Development in Information Retrieval*, pages 3417–3419.

Yung-Sung Chuang, Rumen Dangovski, Hongyin Luo, Yang Zhang, Shiyu Chang, Marin Soljačić, Shang-Wen Li, Wen-tau Yih, Yoon Kim, and James Glass. 2022. Diffcse: Difference-based contrastive learning for sentence embeddings. *arXiv preprint arXiv:2204.10298*.

Alexis Conneau and Douwe Kiela. 2018a. SentEval: An evaluation toolkit for universal sentence representations. In *Proceedings of the Eleventh International Conference on Language Resources and Evaluation (LREC 2018)*, Miyazaki, Japan. European Language Resources Association (ELRA).

Alexis Conneau and Douwe Kiela. 2018b. Senteval: An evaluation toolkit for universal sentence representations. In *Proceedings of the Eleventh International Conference on Language Resources and Evaluation (LREC 2018)*.

Jacob Devlin, Ming-Wei Chang, Kenton Lee, and Kristina Toutanova. 2019. BERT: Pre-training of deep bidirectional transformers for language understanding. In *Proceedings of the 2019 Conference of the North American Chapter of the Association for Computational Linguistics: Human Language Technologies, Volume 1 (Long and Short Papers)*, pages 4171–4186, Minneapolis, Minnesota. Association for Computational Linguistics.

Yarin Gal and Zoubin Ghahramani. 2016. Dropout as a bayesian approximation: Representing model uncertainty in deep learning. In *international conference on machine learning*, pages 1050–1059. PMLR.

Tianyu Gao, Xingcheng Yao, and Danqi Chen. 2021. Simcse: Simple contrastive learning of sentence embeddings. In *Proceedings of the 2021 Conference on Empirical Methods in Natural Language Processing*, pages 6894–6910.

Kelvin Guu, Kenton Lee, Zora Tung, Panupong Pasupat, and Ming-wei Chang. 2020. Realm: Retrieval-augmented language model pre. *Training*.

Gautier Izacard, Patrick Lewis, Maria Lomeli, Lucas Hosseini, Fabio Petroni, Timo Schick, Jane Dwivedi-Yu, Armand Joulin, Sebastian Riedel, and Edouard Grave. 2022. Few-shot learning with retrieval augmented language models. *arXiv preprint arXiv:2208.03299*.

Nora Kassner and Hinrich Schütze. 2020. Bert-knn: Adding a knn search component to pretrained language models for better qa. In *Findings of the Association for Computational Linguistics: EMNLP 2020*, pages 3424–3430.

Urvashi Khandelwal, Omer Levy, Dan Jurafsky, Luke Zettlemoyer, and Mike Lewis. 2019. Generalization through memorization: Nearest neighbor language models. *arXiv preprint arXiv:1911.00172*.

Omar Khattab and Matei Zaharia. 2020. Colbert: Efficient and effective passage search via contextualized late interaction over bert. In *Proceedings of the 43rd International ACM SIGIR conference on research and development in Information Retrieval*, pages 39–48.

Patrick Lewis, Ethan Perez, Aleksandra Piktus, Fabio Petroni, Vladimir Karpukhin, Naman Goyal, Heinrich Küttler, Mike Lewis, Wen-tau Yih, Tim Rocktäschel, et al. 2020. Retrieval-augmented generation for knowledge-intensive nlp tasks. *Advances in Neural Information Processing Systems*, 33:9459–9474.

Niklas Muennighoff, Nouamane Tazi, Loïc Magne, and Nils Reimers. 2022. Mteb: Massive text embedding benchmark. *arXiv preprint arXiv:2210.07316*.

Arvind Neelakantan, Tao Xu, Raul Puri, Alec Radford, Jesse Michael Han, Jerry Tworek, Qiming Yuan, Nikolas Tezak, Jong Wook Kim, Chris Hallacy, Johannes Heidecke, Pranav Shyam, Boris Power, Tyna Eloundou Nekoul, Girish Sastry, Gretchen Krueger, David Schnurr, Felipe Petroski Such, Kenny Hsu, Madeleine Thompson, Tabarak Khan, Toki Sherbakov, Joanne Jang, Peter Welinder, and Lilian Weng. 2022. Text and code embeddings by contrastive pre-training.

Jianmo Ni, Gustavo Hernandez Abrego, Noah Constant, Ji Ma, Keith Hall, Daniel Cer, and Yinfei Yang. 2022. Sentence-t5: Scalable sentence encoders from pre-trained text-to-text models. In *Findings of the Association for Computational Linguistics: ACL 2022*, pages 1864–1874.

Jeffrey Pennington, Richard Socher, and Christopher D Manning. 2014. Glove: Global vectors for word representation. In *Proceedings of the 2014 conference on empirical methods in natural language processing (EMNLP)*, pages 1532–1543.

Colin Raffel, Noam Shazeer, Adam Roberts, Katherine Lee, Sharan Narang, Michael Matena, Yanqi Zhou, Wei Li, Peter J Liu, et al. 2020. Exploring the limits of transfer learning with a unified text-to-text transformer. *J. Mach. Learn. Res.*, 21(140):1–67.

Nils Reimers and Iryna Gurevych. 2019. Sentence-bert: Sentence embeddings using siamese bert-networks. In *Proceedings of the 2019 Conference on Empirical Methods in Natural Language Processing and the 9th International Joint Conference on Natural Language Processing (EMNLP-IJCNLP)*, pages 3982–3992.

Jon Saad-Falcon, Amanpreet Singh, Luca Soldaini, Mike D'Arcy, Arman Cohan, and Doug Downey. 2022. Embedding recycling for language models. *arXiv preprint arXiv:2207.04993*.

Victor Sanh, Lysandre Debut, Julien Chaumond, and Thomas Wolf. 2019. Distilbert, a distilled version of bert: smaller, faster, cheaper and lighter. *arXiv preprint arXiv:1910.01108*.

Keshav Santhanam, Omar Khattab, Christopher Potts, and Matei Zaharia. 2022. Plaid: an efficient engine for late interaction retrieval. In *Proceedings of the 31st ACM International Conference on Information & Knowledge Management*, pages 1747–1756.

Nitish Srivastava, Geoffrey Hinton, Alex Krizhevsky, Ilya Sutskever, and Ruslan Salakhutdinov. 2014. Dropout: a simple way to prevent neural networks from overfitting. *The journal of machine learning research*, 15(1):1929–1958.

Adina Williams, Nikita Nangia, and Samuel Bowman. 2018. A broad-coverage challenge corpus for sentence understanding through inference. In *Proceedings of the 2018 Conference of the North American Chapter of the Association for Computational Linguistics: Human Language Technologies, Volume 1 (Long Papers)*, pages 1112–1122.

Yuanmeng Yan, Rumei Li, Sirui Wang, Fuzheng Zhang, Wei Wu, and Weiran Xu. 2021. Consert: A contrastive framework for self-supervised sentence representation transfer. In *Proceedings of the 59th Annual Meeting of the Association for Computational Linguistics and the 11th International Joint Conference on Natural Language Processing (Volume 1: Long Papers)*, pages 5065–5075.

Appendix A Limitations

The experiments for ERATE are currently limited to the semantic text similarity tasks of SentEval. More comprehensive experiments should investigate the applicability of ERATE against benchmark text embedding representations for a wide range of downstream NLP tasks.

Appendix B Computational resources

All experiments were conducted using NVIDIA A100 graphical processing units.

Appendix C Reproducibility

The experiments conducted in this work has only relied on publicly available data and publicly available models. There was no additional training of models. Additional hyperparameters for ERATE embeddings (e.g. the size of the datastore, the number of neighbours, the dropout rate) is detailed in the relevant sections of the main paper.

Appendix D Licenses

This section details the license agreements of the scientific artifacts used in this work. The Stanford Natural Language Inference (SNLI) Corpus is licensed under a Creative Commons Attribution-ShareAlike 4.0 International License. For MNLI, the majority of the corpus is released under the OANC's license, which allows all content to be freely used, modified, and shared under permissive terms. The data in the FICTION section falls under several permissive licenses; Seven Swords is available under a Creative Commons Share-Alike 3.0 Unported License, and with the explicit permission of the author, Living History and Password Incorrect are available under Creative Commons Attribution 3.0 Unported Licenses; the remaining works of fiction are in the public domain in the United States (but may be licensed differently elsewhere). SentEval is released under the BSD License. Common Crawl is released under the MIT License.

Appendix E Additional experiments

In the main paper, ERATE relies on combining the rich embedding representations of the neighbours that have been identified using the light embedding representations. The number of neighbours was set to 100. In this section, the impact on the downstream STS tasks is investigated when a different number of neighbours are considered instead. Table Appendix E.1 details the performance when using a different number of neighbours from the datastore. The best averaged results are observed empirically when 100 neighbours are used from the datastore.

#neigh.	Avg.	sts12	sts13	sts14	sts15	sts16	stsB	sickR
1	40.9	30.2	40.7	35.1	50.8	43.7	39.8	46.0
10	52.4	51.6	52.9	43.5	61.9	49.1	53.8	54.0
100	**55.3**	57.2	59.7	47.3	59.9	54.5	53.8	54.7
1000	54.7	54.2	58.8	48.6	61.3	54.0	52.3	53.8
10,000	52.4	51.2	57.3	46.9	59.1	50.9	49.1	52.4

Table Appendix E.1: Varying the number of neighbours for ERATE.

A Data-centric Framework for Improving Domain-specific Machine Reading Comprehension Datasets

Iva Bojic[1] and **Josef Halim**[1] and **Verena Suharman**[1] and **Sreeja Tar**[1] and **Qi Chwen Ong**[1] and **Duy Phung**[1] and **Mathieu Ravaut**[1] and **Shafiq Joty**[1,2] and **Josip Car**[1,3]
[1]Nanyang Technological University, Singapore
[2]Salesforce Research, USA
[3]Imperial College London, United Kingdom

Abstract

Low-quality data can cause downstream problems in high-stakes applications. Data-centric approach emphasizes on improving dataset quality to enhance model performance. High-quality datasets are needed for general-purpose Large Language Models (LLMs) training, as well as for domain-specific models, which are usually small in size as it is costly to engage a large number of domain experts for their creation. Thus, it is vital to ensure high-quality domain-specific training data. In this paper, we propose a framework for enhancing the data quality of original datasets[1]. We applied the proposed framework to four biomedical datasets and showed relative improvement of up to 33%/40% for fine-tuning of retrieval/reader models on the *BioASQ* dataset when using back translation to enhance the original dataset quality.

1 Introduction

Data-centric approach emphasizes the collection of high-quality data as a centrally important step in the model development (Jarrahi et al., 2022). While model-centric approaches were more prominent in the past, recently data-centric approaches are also gaining importance (Xu et al., 2021; Liu et al., 2021). This trend was especially emphasized since 2021 when Andrew Ng launched his campaign for a more data-centric approach to AI by starting the data-centric competition[2], which encouraged participants to increase accuracy by solely improving the datasets while keeping the model fixed.

Large Language Models (LLMs), such as Generative Pre-trained Transformer 3 (GPT-3) (Floridi and Chiriatti, 2020), generate text that is grammatically correct, fluent, and informative. However, there is little to no control over the data that were used for model training. Consequently, LLMs are prone to hallucinating and providing untruthful outputs (Evans et al., 2021). Ironically, this reflects LLMs' ability to be better at learning the training distribution and consequently follow inverse scaling law (Lin et al., 2021). And while some of the recent research efforts are focused on providing explanations of where the LLM's outputs came from (Menick et al., 2022), such research is in its infancy.

In this work, we focus on language models with a Transformer encoder architecture such as *BERT* (Devlin et al., 2018), that extract relevant outputs from a domain-specific evidence-based text corpus. Deep neural networks trained on domain-specific datasets, including those used in Natural Language Processing (NLP), are most heavily dependent on the quality of the training dataset, which is usually small in size (Zarcone et al., 2021) as it is costly to engage a large number of domain experts for annotation. It is thus important to create high-quality training data for language models to perform better. In this paper, we propose a data-centric framework for Machine Reading Comprehension (MRC) datasets that increases the original dataset quality by both (i) keeping the size of the original dataset fixed, and (ii) augmenting the original dataset by adding new training samples.

MRC is a Natural Language Understanding (NLU) task. Its goal is to answer questions based on the information provided in a passage (Zhang et al., 2020). Training datasets for MRC models come in the form of triplets: passage (i.e., positive context), question, and answer. Typically, the MRC pipeline works in two phases, where a passage *retriever* is followed by a passage *reader* (Chen et al., 2017). For a given question, the retriever first extracts a set of relevant passages from a knowledge base (i.e., text corpus), and then the reader selects an answer (e.g., text span) from one of the retrieved passages (Zhu et al., 2021).

[1]Code and dataset are available at https://github.com/IvaBojic/framework

[2]https://https-deeplearning-ai.github.io/data-centric-comp

The Fourth Workshop on Insights from Negative Results in NLP, pages 19–32
May 5, 2023 ©2023 Association for Computational Linguistics

2 Related Work

Data-centric approaches can be divided into (i) *data quality enhancement methods* that keep the original size of the dataset fixed (e.g., data filtering or label consistency checking), and (ii) *data augmentation methods* that increase the original dataset size (i.e., adding more training samples). Results from the literature on using data-centric approaches to improve model performance in MRC are inconclusive.

Several studies have reported that data filtering can lead to significant model improvements (Dou et al., 2020; Sanyal et al., 2021; Mollá, 2022). However, this might not hold if data are filtered in a random way (Firsanova, 2021). Additionally, while increasing labelling consistency and excluding or cleaning noisy data points were shown to improve model performance on the *BioASQ* dataset (Yoon et al., 2022), shortening answers in *AASDQA* led to a decrease of F1-score by 4% (Firsanova, 2021).

Adaptation of data augmentation is still comparatively less explored in NLP (Feng et al., 2021), with a body of work presenting positive results (Kaushik et al., 2019; Khashabi et al., 2020; Qin et al., 2020; Pappas et al., 2022) as well as papers showing little or no improvements for the given task (Huang et al., 2020; Chopard et al., 2021; Okimura et al., 2022).

To the best of our knowledge, this paper is the first that proposes framework for data quality enhancement for improving domain-specific MRC datasets by (i) keeping the original dataset size of data the same and (ii) increasing the original dataset size using augmentation methods. Our framework includes methods for (i) a better selection of negative passages for retriever training, and (ii) reformulating questions using paraphrasing, word substitution, and back translation.

Paraphrasing, word substitution, and back translation were previously used as data augmentation methods in various NLP tasks (Liu and Hulden, 2021; Pappas et al., 2022; Ishii et al., 2022). However, those papers did not look at how each of these methods enhanced the original dataset without increasing its size. Keeping the size of the dataset fixed is necessary in resources-constrained scenarios, as the resources (e.g., time) needed for fine-tuning are proportional to the size of training sets. Moreover, previous studies did not present a cost-benefit analysis of the resources needed to generate extended training sets and perform fine-tuning processes in comparison with the performance increase.

3 A Data-centric Framework for MRC

In our framework, we first generate new training sets using four data quality enhancement methods. We then fine-tune retrieval and reader models on each new training set individually. Secondly, we fine-tune retrieval/reader models continually starting from the best individual checkpoint using enhanced training sets that showed improvements in the first step. Finally, we create new augmented datasets by concatenating all training sets if they show fine-tuning improvements in the first step.

Labels in MRC datasets are triplets which include a passage, a question, and an answer. In MRC datasets, an answer is part of a passage which is also called a *positive context*. To fine-tune a retrieval model as proposed in (Karpukhin et al., 2020), it is necessary to not only provide a positive context of passages that contains the answer to a given question, but also *negative contexts*. Some previous work employed a method of randomly selecting negative contexts from a text corpus (Bojic et al., 2022). Here we propose a method to improve the random selection of negative contexts.

One of the problems with manually collecting labels for MRC datasets is that questions are too similar to their answers (Rajpurkar et al., 2018). To solve this, we investigate the use of three different methods applied to the original set of questions: (i) *paraphrasing* - we use two different language models fine-tuned for paraphrasing; (ii) *word substitution* - we use two libraries: one to extract a keyword from a given question and another to obtain a list of synonyms for the chosen keyword; and (iii) *back translation* - we use 25 different machine translation language models to translate a source text into another language, and back into the original language.

3.1 Negative Contexts

To enhance the quality of the negative contexts for each passage, we implemented the following procedure. For each positive context, passages were sorted in ascending order of BERTScore (Zhang et al., 2019) similarity with the positive context, and the ones with the lowest score were kept to form negative contexts. A global counting dictionary was maintained to prevent the replication of negative contexts across different training examples. This ensured that each negative context did not exceed the *threshold* for number of occurrences in total in the whole dataset.

3.2 Questions

In this section, we describe the various techniques used to augment the questions from MRC datasets.

For *question paraphrasing*, we used two models: *T5*[3] and *Pegasus*[4]. To enhance the data quality of an original dataset, for each original question, we used the two aforementioned methods to generate up to five paraphrased questions. Subsequently, we created five different training sets in which we grouped the most, second most, up to the least similar paraphrases for each original question together. The word similarity was calculated using a word vector model from *spaCy*[5]. We also generated a sixth set comprising a randomly-selected question from the list of five unique paraphrases generated.

In *word substitution* process, we extracted a keyword from each question with the help of the *spaCy* library and obtained a list of synonyms for each keyword using Natural Language Tool Kit (NLTK)'s English dictionary, *WordNet*[6]. The top five synonyms were extracted from this list in descending order of word similarity calculated using the aforementioned word vector model from *spaCy*. We then generated five versions of the training data for each dataset such that in set 1, the keyword for each question was replaced by its most similar synonym; in set 2, the keyword for each question was replaced by its second most similar synonym and so forth, with set 5 containing the questions with the least similar synonyms as substitutes. For keywords with $n < 5$ synonyms, we kept the question unchanged in the first (5 - n) versions and used the synonyms as substitutes in the remaining n versions. We also created a sixth set in which we randomly selected one of the top five (or n) synonyms to substitute the keyword for each question.

We used *Hugging Face Helsinki* model[7] for *back translation*. In total, we generated 25 different training sets based on the number of downloads for translation from English to the respective languages, followed by the availability of translation models from the respective languages to English. We selected checkpoints based on the number of downloads, taking the top 25 most downloaded.

To understand how different the resulting questions obtained from each of the enhancement methods are, we performed pairwise comparisons between questions from each method using ROUGE-1. Results are shown in Appendix B.6. *Back-translation* overall yields the questions most different to the baseline and the other enhancement methods.

3.3 Answers

Since MRC relies on extracting the exact answer (i.e., text span) from a passage, we could not apply any of the automatic data quality enhancement methods that we applied to questions (as explained in the previous section). However, we created new training datasets in which we manually shortened the original answers wherever appropriate. We explained further in Appendix A.3.

4 Datasets

To test our framework, we made adjustments (see Appendix A) to four biomedical datasets: *BioASQ* (Lamurias et al., 2020), *COVID-QA* (Möller et al., 2020), *cpgQA* (Mahbub et al., 2023) and *SleepQA* (Bojic et al., 2022). We refer the reader to Table 1 for statistics on the final version of datasets that we used in all experiments: original/final size of text corpus, original/final number of labels and finally, train/dev/test split.

Original *BioASQ* dataset contained over 3k manually-annotated biomedical labels. Questions in these datasets came in four different flavours: factoid, list, yes/no, and summary. We extracted only factoid questions for which the exact answer can be found in the positive context. Original *COVID-QA* dataset was annotated by biomedical experts and contained 2k labels on COVID-19 pandemic-related topics. Original *cpgQA* dataset contained 1k manually annotated labels in the domain of clinical practice guidelines. Original *SleepQA* was a manually annotated dataset in the sleep domain with 5k labels.

Table 1: Dataset statistics, for original and final versions.

Dataset	Original corpus	Final corpus	Original labels	Final labels	Final train/dev/test
BioASQ	4265	957	5821	957	765/96/96
COVID-QA	2079	1121	1327	1102	896/112/113
cpgQA	190	235	1097	1097	877/110/110
SleepQA	7000	7000	5000	5000	4000/500/500

[3] https://huggingface.co/Vamsi/T5_Paraphrase_Paws

[4] https://huggingface.co/tuner007/pegasus_paraphrase

[5] https://spacy.io/models/en#en_core_web_lg

[6] https://www.nltk.org/howto/wordnet.html

[7] https://huggingface.co/Helsinki-NLP

5 Evaluation

We evaluated our framework by performing fine-tuning of retrieval and reader models using *BioLinkBERT* (Yasunaga et al., 2022) and *BioBERT BioASQ*[8] respectively. We used *BioLinkBERT* for retrieval model fine-tuning as it was recently shown to achieve state-of-the-art performance on low-resource bio-MRC tasks (Mahbub et al., 2023). *BioBERT BioASQ* was used for fine-tuning of reader model as proposed in (Bojic et al., 2022). Intrinsic evaluation of fine-tuned models was done using automatic metrics on test sets: recall@1 for retrieval and Exact Match (EM) for reader models.

5.1 Fine-tuning on Enhanced Training Sets

Table 2 and Table 3 show recall@1/EM scores respectively for fine-tuned retrieval/reader models after enhancing the method of selecting negative contexts (i.e., using *BertScore*) for the retrieval training datasets, as well as reformulation of questions using paraphrasing, word substitution, back translation and answer shortening for the training datasets of *both* models. More specifically:

- The first row (*baseline*) in each table shows the results of *BioLinkBERT*/*BioBERT BioASQ* models fine-tuned on the original datasets (i.e., baselines).
- Each subsequential row shows the best results for each dataset using the four aforementioned methods for negative contexts (only for the retrieval models) and questions (for both models) enhancement.
- The following row (*answer shortening*) shows recall@1/EM scores for fine-tuning of models on the training datasets in which the original answers were manually shortened if needed.
- The following row (*continual*) shows the results of *continual fine-tuning*: starting from the best individual checkpoint, we fine-tune on the second-best training set, and so on. For example, for reader fine-tuning on the *BioASQ* dataset, we first took the checkpoint of fine-tuning on the training set created using paraphrasing and then continued fine-tuning on training sets created using back translation. Finally, we took the newest checkpoint and continued fine-tuning on the training set created using word substitution.
- The last row (*augmentation*) shows recall@1/EM scores for fine-tuning of models on the training datasets created by concatenating all data enhanced training sets if they showed fine-tuning improvements when using individually (i.e., rows 2-6 for retrieval models and rows 2-5 for reader models).

For retrieval fine-tuning (Table 2), the most significant improvement of +8.3 (+33%) from baseline was achieved for *BioASQ* dataset when using back translation on the Catalan language. The enhanced methods of selecting negative contexts and word substitution improved all four datasets, while paraphrasing and back translation caused a decrease in recall@1 scores for *SleepQA* dataset. Continual retrieval fine-tuning showed improvements when compared to baselines for all datasets, however, only for the *COVID-QA* and *cpgQA* datasets it was better than the best results of individual fine-tuning.

Table 2: Evaluation of fine-tuned **retrieval** models.

Methods	*BioASQ*	*COVID-QA*	*cpgQA*	*SleepQA*
baseline	**25.0**	**42.5**	**66.4**	**46.8**
negatives	32.3	48.7	67.3	**48.4**
paraphrasing	31.2	54.0	66.4	46.6
word substitution	30.2	50.4	69.1	**48.4**
back translation	**33.3**	49.6	66.4	45.8
answer shortening	29.2	45.1	66.4	44.8
continual	29.2	**62.8**	**70.9**	47.2
augmentation	31.2	60.2	65.5	45.0

For fine-tuned reader models (Table 3), the most significant improvement of 2.1 (+40%) from baseline was achieved for *BioASQ* dataset when using back translation on the Dutch language, as well as paraphrasing. Continual reader fine-tuning increased the EM score only for *cpgQA* dataset compared with the corresponding baselines. Lastly, augmentation was better than the best results of individual fine-tuning only for the *SleepQA* dataset with the total increase of 2.6 (+4%).

Table 3: Evaluation of fine-tuned **reader** models.

Methods	*BioASQ*	*COVID-QA*	*cpgQA*	*SleepQA*
baseline	**5.2**	**22.1**	**50.9**	**58.6**
paraphrasing	**7.3**	**23.9**	**50.9**	59.0
word substitution	6.3	22.1	**50.9**	59.4
back translation	**7.3**	23.0	46.4	59.4
answer shortening	5.2	23.0	49.1	60.8
continual	5.2	**23.9**	N/A	**58.0**
augmentation	5.2	**23.9**	N/A	**61.2**

[8] https://huggingface.co/gdario/biobert_bioasq

Greater relative improvements with *back-translation* compared to other methods could be supported by this method creating more diverse questions (Appendix B.6). However, *back-translation* gains are inconsistent from a dataset to the other. Moreover, we noticed that translation and paraphrasing with *Pegasus* gave questions noticeably more difference than the other data enhancing techniques.

5.2 Cost-benefit Analysis

In total, the data-centric methods that we described previously enabled us to generate 28 and 24 enhanced training sets for retrieval fine-tuning and reader fine-tuning respectively. Subsequently, we fine-tuned all retrieval/reader models on a single NVIDIA-A40 GPU with 46GB of GPU RAM. Table 4 and Table 5 shows time spent on fine-tuning. For example, we used one GPU for five hours to fine-tune retriever model on *BioASQ* dataset to achieve 33% improvement in recall@1 score. Meanwhile, we used one GPU for 22 hours to fine-tune retriever model on *SleepQA* dataset only to achieve a decrease in recall@1 score of 2%.

The last two rows in tables show the time needed for continual/augmentation fine-tuning only. However, in order to determine the order in which to fine-tune for continual learning, or which datasets to use for concatenation, all individual checkpoints need to be created. Hence, to obtain the total time for continual learning/augmentation, one needs to add up times from all previous rows as well.

Table 4: Total time spent (in hours) vs. maximum improvements of retrieval fine-tuning.

Methods	*BioASQ*	*COVID-QA*	*cpgQA*	*SleepQA*
baseline	**0.2**	**0.2**	**0.2**	**0.9**
negatives	0.9 (29%)	1.1 (15%)	1.0 (1%)	9.9 (3%)
paraphrasing	4.3 (25%)	3.7 (27%)	3.6 (0%)	25.4 (1%)
substitution	2.5 (21%)	1.4 (19%)	1.8 (4%)	6.1 (3%)
translation	4.9 (33%)	6.3 (17%)	4.9 (0%)	22.0 (2%)
answer shortening	0.4 (17%)	0.4 (6%)	0.4 (0%)	1.6 (4%)
continual	1.6 (17%)	1.7 (48%)	0.7 (7%)	1.1 (1%)
augmentation	0.9 (25%)	1.0 (42%)	0.6 (1%)	2.6 (4%)

Table 5: Total time spent (in hours) vs. maximum improvements of reader fine-tuning.

Methods	*BioASQ*	*COVID-QA*	*cpgQA*	*SleepQA*
baseline	**0.1**	**0.1**	**0.1**	**0.3**
paraphrasing	1.0 (40%)	0.9 (8%)	0.9 (0%)	5.0 (1%)
substitution	0.3 (21%)	0.5 (0%)	0.3 (0%)	1.1 (1%)
translation	1.0 (40%)	1.2 (4%)	1.7 (9%)	4.0 (1%)
answer shortening	0.1 (0%)	0.1 (4%)	0.1 (4%)	0.2 (4%)
continual	0.2 (0%)	0.3 (8%)	N/A	1.4 (1%)
augmentation	0.1 (0%)	0.1 (8%)	N/A	0.5 (4%)

6 Discussion and Conclusions

It is estimated that over 92% of data scientists who work in the Artificial Intelligence field encountered the "data cascades" phenomenon, which denotes downstream problems resulting from low-quality data (Sambasivan et al., 2021). One way to improve the original dataset quality is data-centric approach. In this paper, we showed that by enhancing the quality of original datasets, one can achieve model fine-tuning performance improvements for small datasets (e.g., biomedical datasets). However, the results suggest that the effects of data quality enhancement methods on performance improvements are small, and the performance of the test data deteriorates in many cases.

Despite the inconsistency of data-centric methods used in this paper in yielding improvement, two positive conclusions can be drawn. First, when taking into consideration the time needed to create data enhanced training sets as well as performance improvements in fine-tuning, word substitution method is the best, supporting previous findings (Feng et al., 2019; Pappas et al., 2022). Unlike other methods, word substitution is not model-based and thus is run for a few minutes, rather than a few hours like back translation and paraphrasing. Second, the best relative improvements were achieved for the *BioASQ* dataset with the smallest number of labels, a similar finding presented in (Okimura et al., 2022).

In addition to the data-centric methods discussed in this work, there are other techniques such as pseudo-labelling (Abney, 2007; Ruder and Plank, 2018; Cui and Bollegala, 2019; Zhu and Goldberg, 2022), data selection (Axelrod et al., 2011; Plank and Van Noord, 2011; Ruder and Plank, 2017), and pre-training methods (Han and Eisenstein, 2019; Guo et al., 2020). In future work, we will investigate whether those techniques would produce more reliable and consistent results across different datasets. Moreover, we will also consider approaches that incorporate aspects of multiple techniques, resulting in hybrid data-centric techniques as proposed in (Ramponi and Plank, 2020).

Acknowledgements

The authors would like to acknowledge the funding support from Nanyang Technological University, Singapore. Josip Car's post at Imperial College London is supported by the NIHR NW London Applied Research Collaboration.

References

Steven Abney. 2007. *Semisupervised learning for computational linguistics*. CRC Press.

Amittai Axelrod, Xiaodong He, and Jianfeng Gao. 2011. Domain adaptation via pseudo in-domain data selection. In *Proceedings of the 2011 conference on empirical methods in natural language processing*, pages 355–362.

Iva Bojic, Qi Chwen Ong, Megh Thakkar, Esha Kamran, Irving Yu Le Shua, Jaime Rei Ern Pang, Jessica Chen, Vaaruni Nayak, Shafiq Joty, and Josip Car. 2022. Sleepqa: A health coaching dataset on sleep for extractive question answering. In *Machine Learning for Health*, pages 199–217. PMLR.

Danqi Chen, Adam Fisch, Jason Weston, and Antoine Bordes. 2017. Reading Wikipedia to answer open-domain questions. *arXiv preprint arXiv:1704.00051*.

Daphné Chopard, Matthias S Treder, and Irena Spasić. 2021. Learning data augmentation schedules for natural language processing. In *Proceedings of the Second Workshop on Insights from Negative Results in NLP*, pages 89–102.

Xia Cui and Danushka Bollegala. 2019. Self-adaptation for unsupervised domain adaptation. *Proceedings-Natural Language Processing in a Deep Learning World*.

Jacob Devlin, Ming-Wei Chang, Kenton Lee, and Kristina Toutanova. 2018. Bert: Pre-training of deep bidirectional transformers for language understanding. *arXiv preprint arXiv:1810.04805*.

Zi-Yi Dou, Antonios Anastasopoulos, and Graham Neubig. 2020. Dynamic data selection and weighting for iterative back-translation. *arXiv preprint arXiv:2004.03672*.

Owain Evans, Owen Cotton-Barratt, Lukas Finnveden, Adam Bales, Avital Balwit, Peter Wills, Luca Righetti, and William Saunders. 2021. Truthful ai: Developing and governing ai that does not lie. *arXiv preprint arXiv:2110.06674*.

Steven Y Feng, Varun Gangal, Jason Wei, Sarath Chandar, Soroush Vosoughi, Teruko Mitamura, and Eduard Hovy. 2021. A survey of data augmentation approaches for nlp. *arXiv preprint arXiv:2105.03075*.

Steven Y Feng, Aaron W Li, and Jesse Hoey. 2019. Keep calm and switch on! preserving sentiment and fluency in semantic text exchange. *arXiv preprint arXiv:1909.00088*.

Victoria Firsanova. 2021. The advantages of human evaluation of sociomedical question answering systems. *International Journal of Open Information Technologies*, 9(12):53–59.

Luciano Floridi and Massimo Chiriatti. 2020. Gpt-3: Its nature, scope, limits, and consequences. *Minds and Machines*, 30(4):681–694.

Han Guo, Ramakanth Pasunuru, and Mohit Bansal. 2020. Multi-source domain adaptation for text classification via distancenet-bandits. In *Proceedings of the AAAI conference on artificial intelligence*, volume 34, pages 7830–7838.

Xiaochuang Han and Jacob Eisenstein. 2019. Unsupervised domain adaptation of contextualized embeddings for sequence labeling. *arXiv preprint arXiv:1904.02817*.

William Huang, Haokun Liu, and Samuel R Bowman. 2020. Counterfactually-augmented snli training data does not yield better generalization than unaugmented data. *arXiv preprint arXiv:2010.04762*.

Etsuko Ishii, Yan Xu, Samuel Cahyawijaya, and Bryan Wilie. 2022. Can question rewriting help conversational question answering? *arXiv preprint arXiv:2204.06239*.

Mohammad Hossein Jarrahi, Ali Memariani, and Shion Guha. 2022. The principles of data-centric ai (dcai). *arXiv preprint arXiv:2211.14611*.

Vladimir Karpukhin, Barlas Oguz, Sewon Min, Patrick Lewis, Ledell Wu, Sergey Edunov, Danqi Chen, and Wen-tau Yih. 2020. Dense passage retrieval for open-domain question answering. In *Proceedings of the 2020 Conference on Empirical Methods in Natural Language Processing (EMNLP)*, pages 6769–6781, Online. Association for Computational Linguistics.

Divyansh Kaushik, Eduard Hovy, and Zachary C Lipton. 2019. Learning the difference that makes a difference with counterfactually-augmented data. *arXiv preprint arXiv:1909.12434*.

Daniel Khashabi, Tushar Khot, and Ashish Sabharwal. 2020. More bang for your buck: Natural perturbation for robust question answering. *arXiv preprint arXiv:2004.04849*.

Andre Lamurias, Diana Sousa, and Francisco M Couto. 2020. Generating biomedical question answering corpora from q&a forums. *IEEE Access*, 8:161042–161051.

Stephanie Lin, Jacob Hilton, and Owain Evans. 2021. Truthfulqa: Measuring how models mimic human falsehoods. *arXiv preprint arXiv:2109.07958*.

Ling Liu and Mans Hulden. 2021. Backtranslation in neural morphological inflection. In *Proceedings of the Second Workshop on Insights from Negative Results in NLP*, pages 81–88.

Zhengzhong Liu, Guanxiong Ding, Avinash Bukkittu, Mansi Gupta, Pengzhi Gao, Atif Ahmed, Shikun Zhang, Xin Gao, Swapnil Singhavi, Linwei Li, et al. 2021. A data-centric framework for composable nlp workflows. *arXiv preprint arXiv:2103.01834*.

Maria Mahbub, Edmon Begoli, Susana Martins, Alina Peluso, Suzanne Tamang, and Gregory Peterson. 2023. cpgqa: A benchmark dataset for machine reading comprehension tasks on clinical practice guidelines and a case study using transfer learning. *IEEE Access*.

Laura Martín Galván, Enrique Fernández-Rodicio, Javier Sevilla Salcedo, Álvaro Castro-González, and Miguel A Salichs. 2023. Using deep learning for implementing paraphrasing in a social robot. In *Ambient Intelligence—Software and Applications—13th International Symposium on Ambient Intelligence*, pages 219–228. Springer.

Jacob Menick, Maja Trebacz, Vladimir Mikulik, John Aslanides, Francis Song, Martin Chadwick, Mia Glaese, Susannah Young, Lucy Campbell-Gillingham, Geoffrey Irving, et al. 2022. Teaching language models to support answers with verified quotes. *arXiv preprint arXiv:2203.11147*.

Diego Mollá. 2022. Query-focused extractive summarisation for biomedical and covid-19 complex question answering. *arXiv preprint arXiv:2209.01815*.

Timo Möller, Anthony Reina, Raghavan Jayakumar, and Malte Pietsch. 2020. Covid-qa: A question answering dataset for covid-19. In *Proceedings of the 1st Workshop on NLP for COVID-19 at ACL 2020*.

Itsuki Okimura, Machel Reid, Makoto Kawano, and Yutaka Matsuo. 2022. On the impact of data augmentation on downstream performance in natural language processing. In *Proceedings of the Third Workshop on Insights from Negative Results in NLP*, pages 88–93.

Dimitris Pappas, Prodromos Malakasiotis, and Ion Androutsopoulos. 2022. Data augmentation for biomedical factoid question answering. *arXiv preprint arXiv:2204.04711*.

Barbara Plank and Gertjan Van Noord. 2011. Effective measures of domain similarity for parsing. In *Proceedings of the 49th Annual Meeting of the Association for Computational Linguistics: Human Language Technologies*, pages 1566–1576.

Libo Qin, Minheng Ni, Yue Zhang, and Wanxiang Che. 2020. Cosda-ml: Multi-lingual code-switching data augmentation for zero-shot cross-lingual nlp. *arXiv preprint arXiv:2006.06402*.

Pranav Rajpurkar, Robin Jia, and Percy Liang. 2018. Know what you don't know: Unanswerable questions for SQuAD. *arXiv preprint arXiv:1806.03822*.

Alan Ramponi and Barbara Plank. 2020. Neural unsupervised domain adaptation in nlp—a survey. *arXiv preprint arXiv:2006.00632*.

Sebastian Ruder and Barbara Plank. 2017. Learning to select data for transfer learning with bayesian optimization. *arXiv preprint arXiv:1707.05246*.

Sebastian Ruder and Barbara Plank. 2018. Strong baselines for neural semi-supervised learning under domain shift. *arXiv preprint arXiv:1804.09530*.

Nithya Sambasivan, Shivani Kapania, Hannah Highfill, Diana Akrong, Praveen Paritosh, and Lora M Aroyo. 2021. "everyone wants to do the model work, not the data work": Data cascades in high-stakes ai. In *proceedings of the 2021 CHI Conference on Human Factors in Computing Systems*, pages 1–15.

Atindriyo Sanyal, Vikram Chatterji, Nidhi Vyas, Ben Epstein, Nikita Demir, and Anthony Corletti. 2021. Fix your models by fixing your datasets. *arXiv preprint arXiv:2112.07844*.

Connor Shorten, Taghi M Khoshgoftaar, and Borko Furht. 2021. Text data augmentation for deep learning. *Journal of big Data*, 8(1):1–34.

Liang Xu, Jiacheng Liu, Xiang Pan, Xiaojing Lu, and Xiaofeng Hou. 2021. Dataclue: A benchmark suite for data-centric nlp. *arXiv preprint arXiv:2111.08647*.

Michihiro Yasunaga, Jure Leskovec, and Percy Liang. 2022. Linkbert: Pretraining language models with document links. *arXiv preprint arXiv:2203.15827*.

Wonjin Yoon, Jaehyo Yoo, Sumin Seo, Mujeen Sung, Minbyul Jeong, Gangwoo Kim, and Jaewoo Kang. 2022. Data-centric and model-centric approaches for biomedical question answering. In *Experimental IR Meets Multilinguality, Multimodality, and Interaction: 13th International Conference of the CLEF Association, CLEF 2022, Bologna, Italy, September 5–8, 2022, Proceedings*, pages 204–216. Springer.

Jianfei Yu, Minghui Qiu, Jing Jiang, Jun Huang, Shuangyong Song, Wei Chu, and Haiqing Chen. 2018. Modelling domain relationships for transfer learning on retrieval-based question answering systems in e-commerce. In *Proceedings of the Eleventh ACM International Conference on Web Search and Data Mining*, pages 682–690.

Alessandra Zarcone, Jens Lehmann, and Emanuël AP Habets. 2021. Small data in nlu: Proposals towards a data-centric approach. In *35th Conference on Neural Information Processing Systems (NeurIPS 2021)*.

Tianyi Zhang, Varsha Kishore, Felix Wu, Kilian Q Weinberger, and Yoav Artzi. 2019. Bertscore: Evaluating text generation with bert. *arXiv preprint arXiv:1904.09675*.

Zhuosheng Zhang, Hai Zhao, and Rui Wang. 2020. Machine reading comprehension: The role of contextualized language models and beyond. *arXiv preprint arXiv:2005.06249*.

Fengbin Zhu, Wenqiang Lei, Chao Wang, Jianming Zheng, Soujanya Poria, and Tat-Seng Chua. 2021. Retrieving and reading: A comprehensive survey on open-domain question answering. *arXiv preprint arXiv:2101.00774*.

Xiaojin Zhu and Andrew B Goldberg. 2022. *Introduction to Semi-Supervised Learning*. Springer Nature.

A Datasets

A.1 Dataset Construction

In this subsection, we describe how we built the final version of datasets from Table 1. Where necessary, we divided passages from the original text corpus into one or more parts, so their length was less than 300 words. This step was done so that all passages were of a similar length across different datasets and that the same model hyperparameters can be used for fine-tuning retrieval and reader models. We then removed those labels for which the answer could not be found in the corresponding positive context. Finally, we divided each original dataset into three parts (in the ratio of 80:10:10) to create training, development, and test sets. Table 1 shows the original number of passages in each text corpora, the original number of labels, and the final numbers after the aforementioned adjustments were done.

A.2 Data Cleaning

BioASQ: The original dataset did not include positive passages, but instead contained links to the journal articles where the answers can be found. To obtain positive passages, we first retrieved them from the individual links provided in the dataset, and then divided them into passages of no longer than 300 words. Only triplets that contain the exact answers in the retrieved passages were included in the final dataset. We encountered a challenge that, of the 5,821 triplets of the factoid type identified, only 16% had the exact answers that could be found in the provided passages.

COVID-QA: We first divided the original corpus into passages containing no more than 300 words. We also removed redundant keywords, such as 'introduction:', 'introductions:', 'objective:', 'objectives:', 'conclusion:', 'conclusions:', 'method:', 'methods:', 'background:', 'backgrounds:', 'result:', 'results:', 'result(s):', and 'aim:'. Additionally, we eliminated leading and trailing spaces and changed all letters to lowercase. To ensure dataset accuracy, further manual cleaning was carried out. This includes filling in incomplete words, removing medical abbreviations, and correcting missing brackets such as "()" and "[]".

cpgQA: To prepare the text corpus, we partitioned passages into segments of no more than 300 words, resulting in a corpus of 235 passages. Unfortunately, this division caused some answers to be separated from their corresponding positive contexts due to issues such as inaccurate sentence tokenization and answer fragmentation between two adjacent passages. These discrepancies were addressed through manual intervention. It should be noted that no labels were excluded from the original dataset as a result of this cleaning procedure.

SleepQA The original dataset already contained passages shorter than 300 words, and all answers were found in their provided passages. We eliminated leading and trailing spaces and changed all letters to lowercase.

A.3 Shortening Answers

BioASQ: The original answers varied from two to more than 120 words in length. Our focus was on shortening the answers which were excessively long, and thus all answers longer than 30 words were manually reviewed. The primary adjustments made to the answers involved isolating the main response to the corresponding question, thereby truncating lengthy sentences into shorter phrases. This approach effectively reduced answer length for both the test and training sets by a significant degree. The mean answer length for the training set decreased from **30.9** to **17.6** words (Figure 1), while the mean answer length for the test set decreased from **26.1** to **18.4** words (Figure 2).

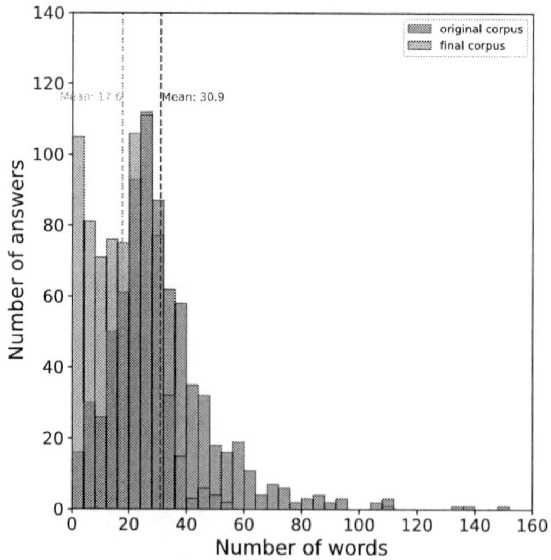

Figure 1: Answer length (in number of words) before and after shortening answers for BioASQ training set.

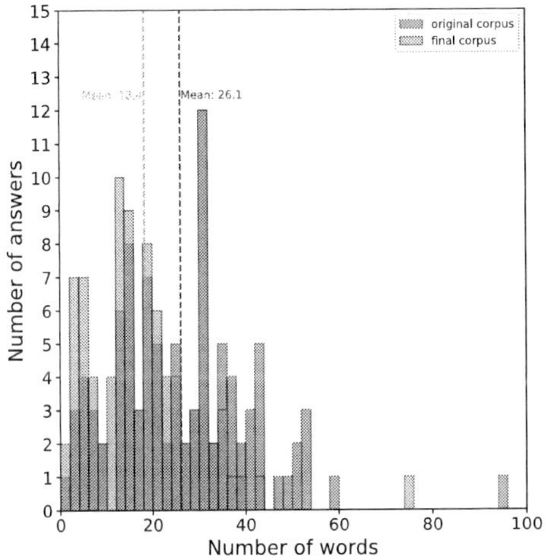

Figure 2: Answer length (number of words) before and after shortening answers for the BioASQ test set.

COVID-QA: In the original dataset, the length of the answers was not more than 120 words. However, some answers contained incomplete words at the beginning and/or end of sentences. To improve the dataset's accuracy, these words were either manually removed or completed. Moreover, scientific abbreviations were eliminated manually to improve the accuracy of exact matches. Unfortunately, this had no significant effect on the mean length of answers for both the training and test sets. This result can be attributed to the training set's prevalence of sentences with only one or two abbreviations. In other cases, completing the incomplete words also had no effect on the mean word count.

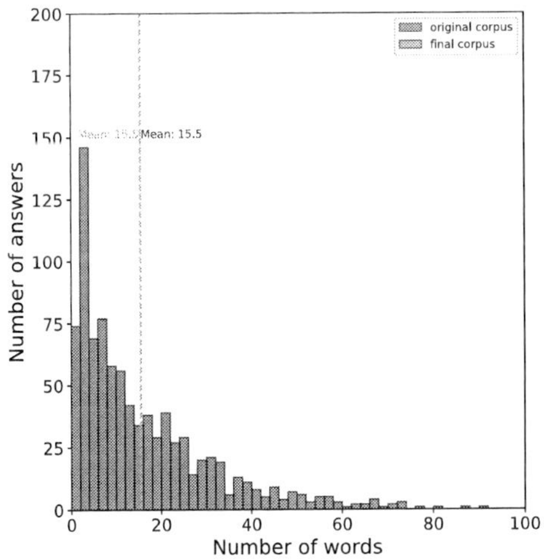

Figure 3: Answer length (in number of words) before and after shortening answers for COVID-QA training set.

cpgQA: In both the training and test sets, answers were shortened manually by removing extraneous phrases and articles (such as "a/an/the") from the beginning of the responses. After shortening, the mean answer length in the training set reduced from **12.7** words to **12.4** words, whereas for the test set, the mean answer length reduced from **12.1** words to **11.6** words. The minimal difference in the mean number of words is due to the fact that most answers in the original dataset were clear and concise.

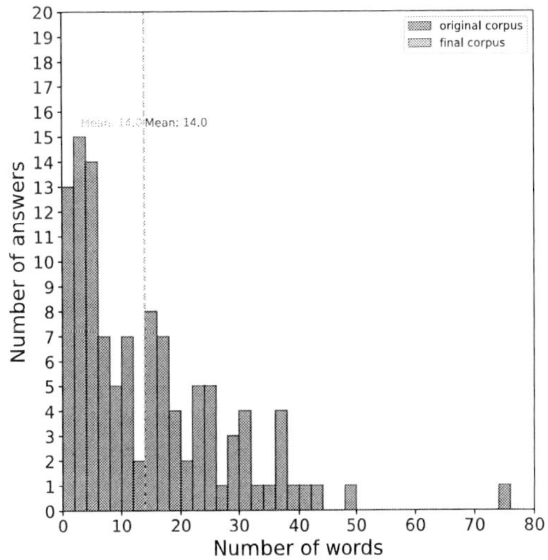

Figure 4: Answer length (in number of words) before and after shortening answers for COVID-QA test set.

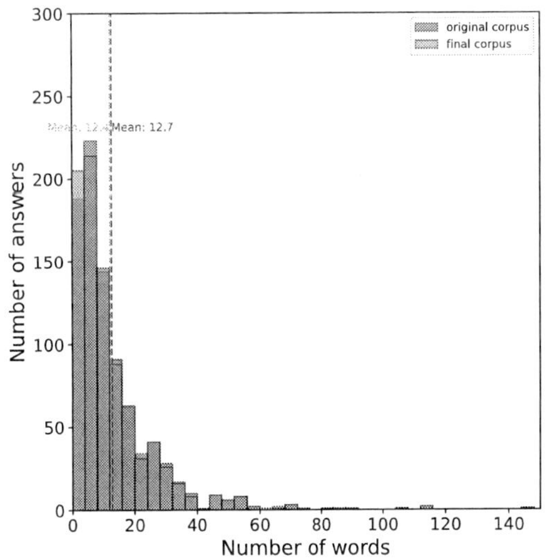

Figure 5: Answer length (in number of words) before and after shortening answers for cpgQA training set.

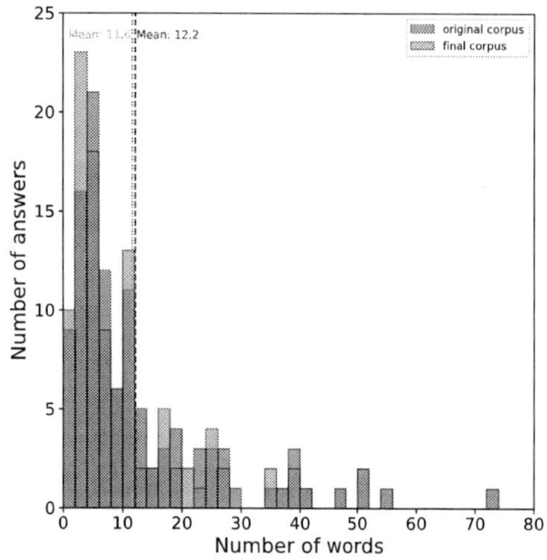

Figure 6: Answer length (in number of words) before and after shortening answers for cpgQA test set.

sleepQA: The initial average answer lengths for the sleepQA dataset are **10.15** and **9.13** for the train and test set respectively, making it the dataset with the shortest average answer length among all datasets studied. We focused on cutting down answers more than 15 words long, which range up to 40 words long. The was done by extracting the main phrases of the answers that directly respond to the associated questions. The resulting cleaned answers are in the form of shorter, more concise phrases instead of wordy full sentences. The final average answer lengths after the cleaning process are **9.11** and **8.01** for the train and test set respectively.

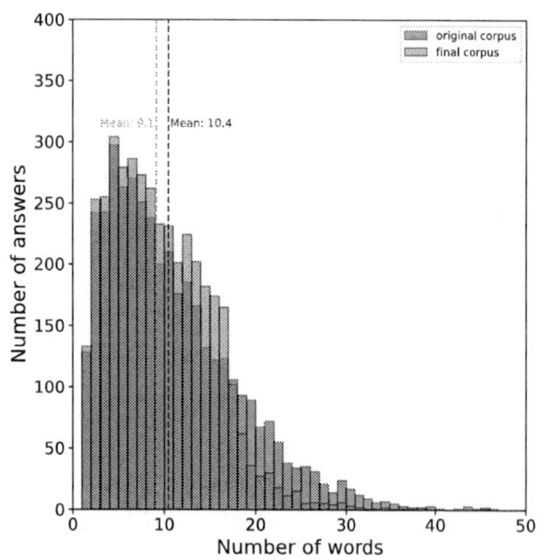

Figure 7: Answer length (in number of words) before and after shortening answers for SleepQA training set.

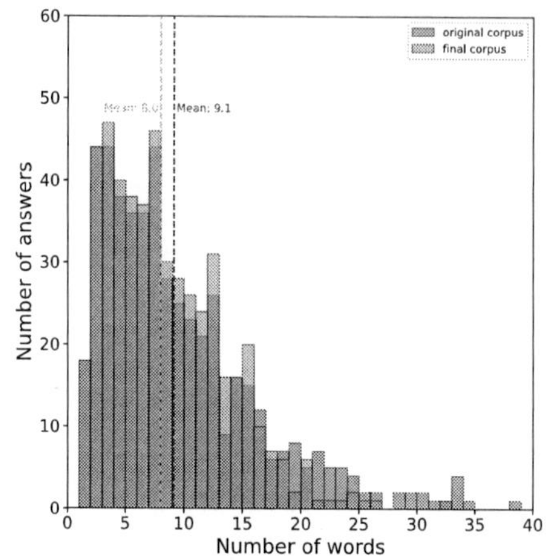

Figure 8: Answer length (in number of words) before and after shortening answers for SleepQA test set.

B Evaluation

B.1 Model Hyperparameters

Hyperparameters of retrieval models fine-tuning are shown in Table 6, and of reader models in Table 7. When fine-tuning retrieval models on training sets in which method of selecting the negative contexts for each passage was enhanced, we changed *other negatives* hyperparameters to reflect the number of negative contexts in the corresponding training set (e.g., 1 to 5). Additionally, when fine-tuning reader models on different datasets, we set *eval step* to 50 for *BioASQ*, *COVID-QA* and *cpgQA* datasets and 500 for the *SleepQA* dataset. The reason behind this is because the *SleepQA* dataset has 4,000 labels in the train set, while the other datasets have less than 1,000 labels. For continual retrieval fine-tuning, we set the *num train epochs* to 60, and for reader to 30. Other parameters were left the same.

B.2 Negative Contexts

Using the enhanced method of selecting negative contexts, we produced five different training sets for each dataset (see Table 8). Although generally, this method produced enhanced training sets for each dataset, it is not possible to conclude which number of negatives improved the fine-tuning process the best, as this is very much dataset-specific. The last row in Table 8 shows the time (in hours) needed to generate all five training sets for each dataset using A100 GPU 40GB. While for most of the datasets, the generation process took around one hour, for *SleepQA* it took more than one day.

Table 6: Hyperparameters of retrieval model fine-tuning.

Hyperparameter	**Value**
batch size	32
dev batch size	32
adam eps	$1e-8$
adam betas	(0.9, 0.999)
max grad norm	1.0
log batch step	100
train rolling loss step	100
weight decay	0.0
learning rate	$1e-5$
warmup steps	100
gradient accumulation steps	1
num train epochs	30/60*
eval per epoch	1
hard negatives	0
other negatives	1(2,3,4,5)*
val av rank hard neg	0
val av rank other neg	10
val av rank bsz	128
val av rank max qs	10000

Table 7: Hyperparameters of reader model fine-tuning.

Hyperparameter	**Value**
eval step	50/500*
batch size	32
dev batch size	32
adam eps	$1e-8$
adam betas	(0.9, 0.999)
max grad norm	1.0
log batch step	100
train rolling loss step	100
weight decay	0.0
learning rate	$1e-5$
warmup steps	0
gradient accumulation steps	1
num train epochs	10/30*

Table 8: Automatic evaluation of fine-tuned retrieval models using recall@1 scores when using the enhanced method of selecting negative contexts.

Methods	*BioASQ*	*COVID-QA*	*cpgQA*	*SleepQA*
baseline	**25.0**	**42.5**	**66.4**	**46.8**
BertScore **(1 neg)**	31.2	41.6	66.4	47.2
BertScore **(2 neg)**	28.1	**48.7**	**67.3**	45.8
BertScore **(3 neg)**	**32.3**	45.1	**67.3**	47.4
BertScore **(4 neg)**	29.2	45.1	63.6	46.6
BertScore **(5 neg)**	30.2	**48.7**	61.8	**48.4**
generation time	1.3	1.3	0.7	28.3

B.3 Paraphrasing

For question paraphrasing, we used *T5* and *Pegasus* as they are based on Transformer architecture and utilize transfer learning, in which resource-rich sources can be efficiently adapted for resource-poor target fields, such as the domain-specific datasets (Yu et al., 2018).

Table 9: Average similarity index of each training set for each dataset, calculated using a word vector model from spaCy for paraphrasing.

Methods	set 1	set 2	set 3	set 4	set 5	set 6
BioASQ (T5)	0.997	0.991	0.979	0.962	0.927	0.970
BioASQ (Pegasus)	0.953	0.932	0.917	0.886	0.846	0.903
COVID-QA (T5)	0.996	0.987	0.970	0.949	0.904	0.959
COVID-QA (Pegasus)	0.959	0.940	0.918	0.890	0.849	0.909
cpgQA (T5)	0.995	0.987	0.973	0.954	0.920	0.967
cpgQA (Pegasus)	0.960	0.946	0.930	0.910	0.883	0.925
SleepQA (T5)	0.996	0.985	0.969	0.947	0.906	0.960
SleepQA (Pegasus)	0.974	0.957	0.938	0.915	0.880	0.933

Previous research showed that the *Pegasus* method produces paraphrases that are semantically more different, while the *T5* method is found to keep more of the original meaning (Martín Galván et al., 2023). We found that the *Pegasus* consistently produces the same set of paraphrased questions, regardless of the number generated. For *T5*, we generated paraphrased questions up to 50 times, after which we took the first five unique paraphrases. For several questions (between 3% for *cpgQA* dataset and 12% for *COVID-QA* dataset), *T5* failed to produce the required number of unique paraphrases, for which cases we added the original question to the set of five paraphrased questions. Although we used two different libraries, question paraphrasing failed to enhance training set quality for *cpgQA* dataset altogether. Generating training sets took around 15 hours for *SleepQA* dataset and 3 hours for other datasets on one NVIDIA TESLA P100 GPU 16GB (Kaggle).

Table 10: Automatic evaluation of fine-tuned retrieval models using recall@1 scores for paraphrasing. Baseline recall@1 scores for *BioASQ*, *COVID-QA*, *cpgQA* and *SleepQA* datasets are: **25.0**, **42.5**, **66.4**, and **46.8**.

Methods	set 1	set 2	set 3	set 4	set 5	set 6
BioASQ (T5)	25.0	**29.2**	26.0	26.0	24.0	24.0
BioASQ (Pegasus)	28.1	**31.2**	**31.2**	29.2	**31.2**	30.2
COVID-QA (T5)	49.6	45.7	44.2	47.8	46.0	**54.0**
COVID-QA (Pegasus)	45.1	44.2	43.4	43.4	**46.9**	46.9
cpgQA (T5)	65.5	65.5	65.5	**66.4**	65.5	**66.4**
cpgQA (Pegasus)	63.6	62.7	60.0	62.7	**65.5**	69.0
SleepQA (T5)	43.6	**46.6**	42.4	46.4	44.2	43.6
SleepQA (Pegasus)	43.2	39.8	**45.0**	39.0	38.0	41.0

Table 11: Automatic evaluation of fine-tuned reader models using EM scores for paraphrasing. Baseline EM scores for *BioASQ*, *COVID-QA*, *cpgQA* and *SleepQA* datasets are: **5.2**, **22.1**, **50.9**, and **58.6**.

Methods	set 1	set 2	set 3	set 4	set 5	set 6
BioASQ (T5)	4.2	**6.2**	4.2	3.1	6.2	4.2
BioASQ (Pegasus)	6.2	**7.3**	**7.3**	6.2	6.2	6.2
COVID-QA (T5)	21.2	19.5	20.4	**23.9**	20.4	19.5
COVID-QA (Pegasus)	22.1	18.6	18.6	20.4	**23.0**	19.5
cpgQA (T5)	**50.9**	49.1	48.2	**50.9**	48.2	50.0
cpgQA (Pegasus)	46.4	46.4	47.3	44.5	46.4	**49.1**
SleepQA (T5)	57.4	57.6	58.2	58.4	**58.8**	58.2
SleepQA (Pegasus)	58.2	57.8	58.0	58.2	57.2	**59.0**

B.4 Word Substitution

Word substitution is the process of substituting similar words (such as synonyms or words with similar embeddings) from the original data (Pappas et al., 2022). This method for enhancing the original training sets increased almost all recall@1/EM scores for all datasets for both retrieval/reader fine-tuning, except for the reader models for *cpgQA* and *COVID-QA* datasets. In cases where applying word substitution on the original dataset did not increase the EM scores for the reader fine-tuning, the scores stayed the same as the corresponding baselines (i.e., this method did not worsen them). Moreover, the generation of training sets took only 11 minutes for *SleepQA* dataset and around two minutes for other datasets on one NVIDIA TESLA P100 GPU 16GB (Kaggle).

Table 12: Average similarity index of each training set for each dataset, calculated using a word vector model from spaCy for word substitution.

Datasets	set 1	set 2	set 3	set 4	set 5	set 6
BioASQ	0.999	0.998	0.997	0.996	0.994	0.997
COVID-QA	0.997	0.996	0.995	0.993	0.988	0.993
cpgQA	0.998	0.997	0.996	0.994	0.989	0.995
SleepQA	0.996	0.993	0.992	0.990	0.986	0.991

Table 13: Automatic evaluation of fine-tuned retrieval models using recall@1 for word substitution. Baseline recall@1 scores for *BioASQ*, *COVID-QA*, *cpgQA* and *SleepQA* datasets are: **25.0**, **42.5**, **66.4**, and **46.8**.

Datasets	set 1	set 2	set 3	set 4	set 5	set 6
BioASQ	28.1	24.0	28.1	27.1	**30.2**	21.9
COVID-QA	49.6	49.6	**50.4**	46.9	48.7	48.7
cpgQA	63.6	68.2	67.3	**69.1**	67.3	66.4
SleepQA	45.8	**48.4**	46.4	46.8	43.0	46.0

B.5 Back Translation

The main idea behind back translation method is to use machine translation from a source to a pivot language and back, obtaining paraphrases. In total, we generated 25 different training sets for Spanish (es), French (fr), German (de), Russian (ru), Chinese (zh), Arabic (ar), Dutch (nl), Finnish (fi), Hungarian (hu), Multiple Languages (mul), Ukrainian (uk), Hindi (hi), Danish (da), Czech (cs), Romance Languages (roa), Bulgarian (bg), Catalan (ca), Afrikaans (af), Estonian (et), Turkic Languages (trk), Slavik Languages (sla), Indonesian (id), Slovak (sk), Tagalog (tl), and Kinyarwanda (rw) pivot languages. Back translation has been used as a data augmentation method for several different NLP tasks (Feng et al., 2021; Shorten et al., 2021). Generally, it produced the best results for *BioASQ* dataset. The generation of training sets took 10 hours for *SleepQA* dataset and around two hours for other datasets on one NVIDIA TESLA P100 GPU 16GB (Kaggle). Results are in Table 15 and Table 16.

Table 14: Automatic evaluation of fine-tuned reader models using EM scores for word substitution. Baseline EM for *BioASQ*, *COVID-QA*, *cpgQA* and *SleepQA* datasets are: **5.2**, **22.1**, **50.9**, and **58.6**.

Datasets	set 1	set 2	set 3	set 4	set 5	set 6
BioASQ	5.2	**6.2**	5.2	5.2	**6.2**	**6.2**
COVID-QA	21.2	21.2	21.2	**22.1**	21.2	19.5
cpgQA	50.0	50.0	**50.9**	50.0	**50.9**	**50.9**
SleepQA	57.8	58.6	58.8	**59.4**	58.0	58.0

Table 15: Automatic evaluation of fine-tuned retrieval models using recall@1 for back translation. Baseline recall@1 scores for *BioASQ*, *COVID-QA*, *cpgQA* and *SleepQA* datasets are: **25.0**, **42.5**, **66.4**, and **46.8**.

Methods	*BioASQ*	*COVID-QA*	*cpgQA*	*SleepQA*
en-es-en	31.2	48.7	62.7	45.4
en-fr-en	29.2	47.8	60.9	44.8
en-de-en	27.1	45.1	61.8	41.6
en-ru-en	31.2	40.7	54.5	39.8
en-zh-en	30.2	46.9	61.8	42.2
en-ar-en	30.2	49.6	56.4	41.2
en-nl-en	31.2	40.7	64.5	44.8
en-fi-en	27.1	48.7	61.8	40.6
en-hu-en	29.2	**49.6**	**66.4**	41.6
en-mul-en	25.0	43.4	57.3	39.4
en-uk-en	28.1	45.1	64.5	40.8
en-hi-en	27.1	44.2	59.1	38.4
en-da-en	29.2	44.2	60.0	43.8
en-cs-en	27.1	43.4	63.6	**45.8**
en-roa-en	29.2	47.8	60.9	42.0
en-bg-en	29.2	43.4	58.2	40.0
en-ca-en	**33.3**	41.6	60.0	41.2
en-af-en	30.2	46.9	61.8	37.2
en-et-en	29.2	46.0	58.2	40.2
en-trk-en	18.8	23.9	35.5	19.6
en-sla-en	25.0	45.1	63.6	43.6
en-id-en	30.2	47.8	63.6	40.4
en-sk-en	30.2	48.7	57.3	44.2
en-tl-en	30.2	41.6	64.5	40.8
en-rw-en	28.1	29.2	50.0	34.4

Table 16: Automatic evaluation of fine-tuned reader models using EM scores for back translation. Baseline EM scores for *BioASQ*, *COVID-QA*, *cpgQA* and *SleepQA* datasets are: **5.2**, **22.1**, **50.9**, and **58.6**.

Methods	*BioASQ*	*COVID-QA*	*cpgQA*	*SleepQA*
en-es-en	4.2	21.2	40.0	58.2
en-fr-en	6.2	20.4	45.5	58.4
en-de-en	**7.3**	21.2	**46.4**	57.4
en-ru-en	3.1	18.6	45.5	58.4
en-zh-en	6.2	21.2	43.6	58.8
en-ar-en	5.2	**23.0**	44.5	58.2
en-nl-en	**7.3**	21.2	45.5	57.6
en-fi-en	6.2	20.4	44.5	58.0
en-hu-en	6.2	19.5	43.6	58.2
en-mul-en	3.1	19.5	43.6	57.0
en-uk-en	6.2	18.6	40.9	**59.4**
en-hi-en	5.2	20.4	40.9	57.4
en-da-en	6.2	**23.0**	43.6	**59.4**
en-cs-en	4.2	19.5	43.6	58.0
en-roa-en	6.2	18.6	43.6	57.6
en-bg-en	6.2	21.2	43.6	59.2
en-ca-en	5.2	18.6	43.6	58.2
en-af-en	**7.3**	20.4	44.5	59.0
en-et-en	6.2	20.4	43.6	58.0
en-trk-en	4.2	15.9	39.1	56.4
en-sla-en	6.2	18.6	44.5	57.6
en-id-en	3.1	17.7	44.5	57.2
en-sk-en	5.2	21.2	44.5	58.6
en-tl-en	4.2	22.1	46.4	58.4
en-rw-en	5.2	17.7	40.0	56.2

B.6 Mean and Standard Deviation

Table 17 shows the mean and standard deviation for different data quality enhancement methods for retrieval fine-tuning. Table 18 shows the mean and standard deviation for different data quality enhancement methods for reader fine-tuning.

Table 17: Mean and standard deviation of different data quality enhancement methods for retrieval fine-tuning.

Methods	*BioASQ*	*COVID-QA*	*cpgQA*	*SleepQA*
negatives	30.2 ± 1.7	45.8 ± 3.0	66.0 ± 2.4	47.1 ± 1.0
paraphrasing (T5)	25.7 ± 1.9	48.4 ± 3.4	65.8 ± 0.5	44.5 ± 1.7
paraphrasing (Pegasus)	30.2 ± 1.3	45.0 ± 1.6	64.0 ± 3.1	41.0 ± 2.7
substitution	26.6 ± 3.1	49.0 ± 1.2	67.0 ± 1.9	46.1 ± 1.8
translation	28.7 ± 2.8	44.0 ± 6.0	59.6 ± 6.2	40.6 ± 5.1

Table 18: Mean and standard deviation of different data quality enhancement methods for reader fine-tuning.

Methods	*BioASQ*	*COVID-QA*	*cpgQA*	*SleepQA*
paraphrasing (T5)	4.7 ± 1.3	20.8 ± 1.6	49.6 ± 1.2	58.1 ± 0.6
paraphrasing (Pegasus)	6.6 ± 0.5	20.4 ± 1.8	46.7 ± 1.5	58.1 ± 0.6
substitution	5.7 ± 0.5	21.1 ± 0.8	50.5 ± 0.5	58.4 ± 0.6
translation	5.4 ± 1.3	20.0 ± 1.7	43.6 ± 2.0	58.0 ± 0.8

B.7 Similarity Between Enhancement Methods

In the following tables, we show the average similarity computed with ROUGE-1 metric between questions generated through each of the enhancement techniques, over all four datasets {*BioASQ*,*CovidQA*,*cpgQA*,*SleepQA*}, with Retrieval (first four tables) then Reader (next four).

Table 19: **Average ROUGE-1 score** between pairs of questions from different enhancement methods on **BioASQ retrieval datasets**. **Base.** stands for baseline, **Para/PG** for paraphrasing with PEGASUS, **Para/T5** for paraphrasing with T5, **Subst.** for substitution and **Transl.** for translation.

	Base.	**Para/PG**	**Para/T5**	**Subst.**	**Transl.**
Base.	100.0				
Para/PG	80.44	100.0			
Para/T5	91.49	76.73	100.0		
Subst.	95.11	76.25	86.98	100.0	
Transl.	57.68	51.10	56.98	55.01	100.0

Table 20: **Average ROUGE-1 score** between pairs of questions from different enhancement methods on **CovidQA retrieval datasets**.

	Base.	Para/PG	Para/T5	Subst.	Transl.
Base.	100.0				
Para/PG	74.63	100.0			
Para/T5	83.33	66.06	100.0		
Subst.	95.33	70.89	79.73	100.0	
Transl.	76.44	62.60	69.50	72.97	100.0

Table 21: **Average ROUGE-1 score** between pairs of questions from different enhancement methods on **cpgQA retrieval datasets**.

	Base.	Para/PG	Para/T5	Subst.	Transl.
Base.	100.0				
Para/PG	71.08	100.0			
Para/T5	80.96	62.79	100.0		
Subst.	94.62	67.01	76.93	100.0	
Transl.	71.06	58.85	64.82	67.36	100.0

Table 22: **Average ROUGE-1 score** between pairs of questions from different enhancement methods on **SleepQA retrieval datasets**.

	Base.	Para/PG	Para/T5	Subst.	Transl.
Base.	100.0				
Para/PG	77.43	100.0			
Para/T5	86.30	70.98	100.0		
Subst.	92.95	71.09	79.79	100.0	
Transl.	79.05	65.98	73.53	73.20	100.0

Table 23: **Average ROUGE-1 score** between pairs of questions from different enhancement methods on **BioASQ reader datasets**.

	Base.	Para/PG	Para/T5	Subst.	Transl.
Base.	100.0				
Para/PG	80.44	100.0			
Para/T5	91.49	76.73	100.0		
Subst.	97.71	78.51	89.46	100.0	
Transl.	86.72	72.32	82.66	84.86	100.0

Table 24: **Average ROUGE-1 score** between pairs of questions from different enhancement methods on **CovidQA reader datasets**.

	Base.	Para/PG	Para/T5	Subst.	Transl.
Base.	100.0				
Para/PG	72.11	100.0			
Para/T5	83.33	64.65	100.0		
Subst.	93.84	67.50	78.59	100.0	
Transl.	66.01	54.99	60.87	61.55	100.0

Table 25: **Average ROUGE-1 score** between pairs of questions from different enhancement methods on **cpgQA reader datasets**.

	Base.	Para/PG	Para/T5	Subst.	Transl.
Base.	100.0				
Para/PG	79.46	100.0			
Para/T5	86.09	72.62	100.0		
Subst.	95.58	75.34	82.15	100.0	
Transl.	80.67	68.91	75.40	77.41	100.0

Table 26: **Average ROUGE-1 score** between pairs of questions from different enhancement methods on **SleepQA reader datasets**.

	Base.	Para/PG	Para/T5	Subst.	Transl.
Base.	100.0				
Para/PG	68.15	100.0			
Para/T5	85.57	62.76	100.0		
Subst.	90.92	61.59	77.38	100.0	
Transl.	63.06	51.40	59.00	57.15	100.0

Encoding Sentence Position in Context-Aware Neural Machine Translation with Concatenation

Lorenzo Lupo[1] **Marco Dinarelli**[1] **Laurent Besacier**[2]
[1]Université Grenoble Alpes, France
[2]Naver Labs Europe, France
lorenzo.lupo@univ-grenoble-alpes.fr
marco.dinarelli@univ-grenoble-alpes.fr
laurent.besacier@naverlabs.com

Abstract

Context-aware translation can be achieved by processing a concatenation of consecutive sentences with the standard Transformer architecture. This paper investigates the intuitive idea of providing the model with explicit information about the position of the sentences contained in the concatenation window. We compare various methods to encode sentence positions into token representations, including novel methods. Our results show that the Transformer benefits from certain sentence position encodings methods on En→Ru, if trained with a context-discounted loss (Lupo et al., 2022b). However, the same benefits are not observed on En→De. Further empirical efforts are necessary to define the conditions under which the proposed approach is beneficial.

1 Introduction

Current neural machine translation (NMT) systems have reached human-like quality in translating standalone sentences, but there is still room for improvement when it comes to translating entire documents (Läubli et al., 2018; Castilho et al., 2020). Researchers have attempted to close this gap by developing various context-aware NMT (CANMT) approaches, where *context* refers to the sentences preceding or following the *current* sentence to be translated. A common approach to CANMT is sentence concatenation (Tiedemann and Scherrer, 2017; Agrawal et al., 2018; Junczys-Dowmunt, 2019). The current sentence and its context are concatenated into a unique sequence that is fed to the standard Transformer architecture (Vaswani et al., 2017). Despite its simplicity, the concatenation approach has been shown to achieve competitive or superior performance to more sophisticated, multi-encoding systems (Lopes et al., 2020; Lupo et al., 2022a). However, learning with long concatenation sequences has been proven challenging for the Transformer architecture, because the self-attention can be "distracted" by long context (Zhang et al., 2020; Bao et al., 2021).

Recently, Lupo et al. (2022b) introduced the *segment-shifted position embeddings* as a way to help concatenation approaches discerning the sentences concatenated in the processed sequence and improve attention's local focus. Explicitly telling the model which tokens belong to each sentence is not a new idea, but an intuitive one that was already tested successfully in other tasks and approaches (Devlin et al., 2019; Voita et al., 2018; Zheng et al., 2020). We believe that encoding into token representations explicit information about the position of the sentences in the concatenation sequence can improve translation quality. The temporal structure of the document constitutes essential information for its understanding and for the correct disambiguation of inter-sentential discourse phenomena. This work investigates this intuitive idea by comparing various approaches to encoding sentence position in concatenation approaches.

Our contributions are the following: (i) we compare segment-shifted position embeddings with three kinds of segment embeddings, evaluating their impact on the performance of the concatenation approach; (ii) we propose and evaluate making sentence position encodings persistent over layers, adding them to the input of every layer in addition to the first; (iii) we propose and evaluate fusing position embeddings and segment embeddings into a single vector where token and sentence positions are encoded in two orthogonal sets of dimensions, allowing a clearer distinction between them, along with memory savings.

To the best of our knowledge, this is the first comparative study on the employment of sentence position encodings for CANMT. The sentence position encoding variants proposed are not found to improve the performance of the concatenation approach except for one specific setting where a context-discounted training loss is employed (Lupo

The Fourth Workshop on Insights from Negative Results in NLP, pages 33–44
May 5, 2023 ©2023 Association for Computational Linguistics

et al., 2022b). More empirical studies are needed to clearly define the conditions under which the proposed approaches are beneficial to CANMT with concatenation. Nonetheless, we find it useful to share these preliminary results with the scientific community. In fact, the proposed approaches are intuitive and easy to implement, hence something that many practitioners would presumably try. We hope that our findings can guide future research on sentence position encodings, by avoiding redundant experiments on failing settings.

2 Proposed approach

A common method for training a concatenation model and translating is by sliding windows (Tiedemann and Scherrer, 2017). The sliding concatenation approach sKtoK translates a window $\boldsymbol{x}_K^j = \boldsymbol{x}^{j-K+1}\boldsymbol{x}^{j-K+2}\cdots\boldsymbol{x}^{j-1}\boldsymbol{x}^j$, of K consecutive sentences belonging to the source document, including the current (jth) sentence and $K-1$ context sentences, into $\boldsymbol{y}_K^j$. In this work we only consider past context, although future context can also be present in the concatenation window. At training time, the standard NMT loss is calculated over the whole output $\boldsymbol{y}_K^j$. At inference time, only the translation $\boldsymbol{y}^j$ of the current sentence is kept, while the context translation is discarded. Then, the window is slid by one sentence forward to repeat the process for the $(j+1)$th sentence and its context.

2.1 Sentence position encodings

To improve the discernability of the sentences concatenated in the window, we propose to equip the sKtoK approach with sentence position encodings. In particular, we experiment with segment-shifted position embeddings and three segment embedding methods. **Segment-shifted position embeddings** (Lupo et al., 2022b) consist in a slight modification of the Transformer's token position scheme, where the original token positions are shifted by a constant factor every time a new sentence is encountered in the concatenation window. The resulting positions are encoded with sinusoidal embeddings as for Vaswani et al. (2017).

We also experiment with **one-hot**, **sinusoidal**, and **learned segment embeddings**, like BERT's segment embeddings (Devlin et al., 2019). Segment embeddings encode the position k of each sentence within the window of K concatenated sentences into a vector of size d. We attribute sentence positions $k = 1, 2, ..., K$ starting from right to left. The underlying rationale is always to attribute the position $k = 1$ to the current sentence, no matter how many sentences are concatenated as context. The simplest strategy to integrate segment embeddings (SE) with position embeddings (PE) and token embeddings (TE) is by adding them (Devlin et al., 2019). This operation requires that all three embeddings have same dimensionality d_{model}:

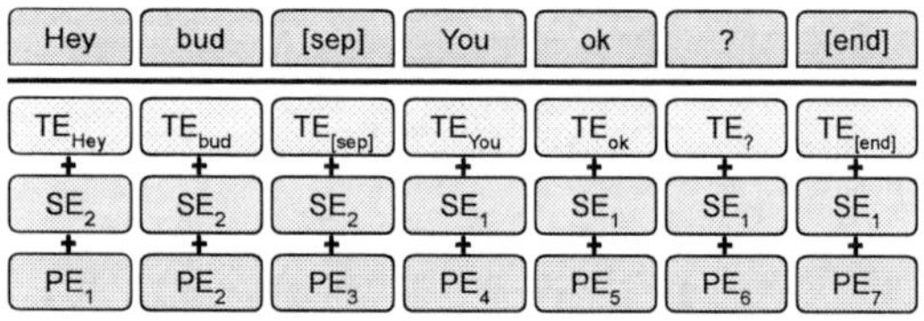

2.2 Persistent encodings

We propose to make sentence position encodings persistent across Transformer's blocks, as Liu et al. (2020) did for position embeddings. In other words, we propose adding segment-shifted position embeddings or segment embeddings to each block's input instead of limiting to the first one.

2.3 Position-segment embeddings (PSE)

In the Transformer, position embeddings are sinusoidal. Their sum with the learnable token embeddings is based on the premise that the model can still distinguish both signals after being added up. This distinction is accomplished by learning token embeddings in a way that guarantees them to be distinguishable. Adding non-learnable segment embedding to this sum, however, rises the question whether they can be distinguished from the sinusoidal position embeddings. In some cases, learning to distinguish these two sources of information after their sum might be impossible. For instance, if segment embeddings are sinusoidal too, their sum with sinusoidal position embeddings is not bijective.[1]

Instead, concatenating PE and SE would make them perfectly distinguishable because they would belong to orthogonal spaces. Unfortunately, concatenating two d_{model}-dimensional embeddings would then oblige to project the resulting vector back to a d_{model}-dimensional space. To avoid this expensive operation, we propose to reduce the dimensionality of PE and SE from $d_{PE} = d_{SE} = d_{model}$ to values that sum up to the model dimension, i.e., $d_{PE} + d_{SE} = d_{model}$. Thus, each

[1]Consider, for example, the equivalence between, $PE_t + SE_k$ and $PE_k + SE_t$.

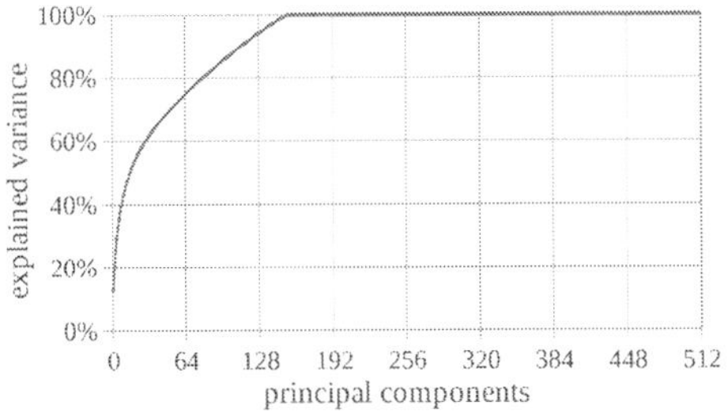

Figure 1: Cumulative ratio of the variance explained by the principal components of the of the sinusoidal position embedding matrix $PE \in \mathcal{R}^{1024\times512}$, representing 1024 positions with 512 dimensions. Less than half of the principal components can explain the entirety of the variance represented in the sinusoidal embeddings. In other words, 1024 positions can be represented with the same resolution using less than half the dimensions.

PE-SE pair can be concatenated into a unique vector named *position-segment embedding* (PSE): $PSE_{t,k} = [PE_t, SE_k]$, of size d_{model}.
Reducing the dimensionality of PE and SE can be made without loss of information up to a certain degree, as it can be shown with a Principal Component Analysis (Jolliffe and Cadima, 2016) of the sinusoidal position embedding matrix (Figure 1).

In the experimental section, we will empirically evaluate the impact of representing token and sentence positions with PSE, where the former are encoded with sinusoids and the latter with either one-hot, sinusoidal, or learned representations.

3 Experiments

We experiment with two models: ***base***, a context-agnostic *Transformer-base* (Vaswani et al., 2017), and **s4to4**, a context-sensitive concatenation approach with the same architecture as *base*. s4to4 process sliding windows of 4 concatenated sentences in input and decodes the whole window into the target language. We equip s4to4 with the sentence position encoding options presented in the previous Section, and we evaluate their impact on performance. When experimenting with PSE, we allocate 4 dimensions to segment embeddings ($d_{SE} = 4$), which is enough to encode the position of each of the 4 sentences in the concatenation window, with both one-hot and sinusoidal encodings. Since $d_{model} = 512$, this leaves $d_{PE} = 508$ dimensions available to the sinusoidal representation of token positions.

The models are trained and evaluated on two language pairs covering different domains: En→Ru movie subtitles prepared by Voita et al. (2019), and En→De TED talk subtitles released by IWSLT17 (Cettolo et al. (2012), see Table 6 for statistics). In addition to evaluating the average translation quality with BLEU[2], we employ two contrastive sets to evaluate the translation of context-dependent anaphoric pronouns. For En→Ru, we adopt Voita et al. (2019)'s set for the evaluation of inter-sentential deixis, lexical cohesion, verb-phrase ellipsis, and inflectional ellipsis. For En→De, we evaluate the models on the translation of context-dependent ambiguous pronouns with ContraPro (Müller et al., 2018), a large set of contrastive translations of inter-sentential pronominal anaphora. Appendix B includes more setup details. The implementation of our experiments is open-sourced on GitHub.[3]

3.1 Results

First, we study the impact of sentence position encodings in the En→Ru setting. In Table 1, we compare models equipped with different combinations of encodings (Enc.) and integration methods: persistency (Pers.) and fusion with position encodings (PSE). We primarily focus on the contrastive evaluation of discourse translation since average translation quality metrics like BLEU have been repeatedly shown to be ill-equipped to detect improvements in CANMT (Hardmeier, 2012). Indeed, BLEU displays negligible fluctuations throughout the whole table. However, the performance on the contrastive sets is not encouraging either: most of the encoding variants degrade s4to4'sperformance. The one-hot encoding helps, but only by a thin margin. Making encoding persistent or concatenating them into PSE does not help either. The only exception is s4to4+lrn+pers+PSE (last line), which gains more than two accuracy points over baseline. However, this result is solely driven by the net improvement on deixis disambiguation (almost +5 points, see Table 10), while the performance is degraded on the other three discourse phenomena. In conclusion, sentence position encodings do not seem to benefit the vanilla s4to4 approach.

3.1.1 Training with context-discounted loss

Following Lupo et al. (2022b), we hypothesize that sentence position encodings can be leveraged

[2]Moses' *multi-bleu-detok* (Koehn et al., 2007) for De, *multi-bleu* for lowercased Ru as Voita et al. (2019).

[3]https://github.com/lorelupo/focused-concat

System	Enc.	Pers.	PSE	Voita	BLEU
base				46.64	31.98
s4to4				72.02	32.45
s4to4	shift			71.28	32.27
s4to4	shift	✓		71.80	31.93
s4to4	1hot			**72.52**	32.61
s4to4	1hot	✓		71.44	32.42
s4to4	1hot		✓	71.24	32.33
s4to4	1hot	✓	✓	71.16	32.41
s4to4	sin			71.92	32.39
s4to4	sin	✓		71.20	32.38
s4to4	sin		✓	71.26	32.56
s4to4	sin	✓	✓	71.68	32.38
s4to4	lrn			71.80	32.56
s4to4	lrn	✓		71.40	32.50
s4to4	lrn		✓	70.36	32.37
s4to4	lrn	✓	✓	**73.20**	32.38

Table 1: En→Ru models' accuracy on Voita's contrastive set and BLEU on the test set. s4to4 models are equipped with sentence position encodings (Enc.) of four kinds: segment-shifted position embeddings, one-hot segment embeddings, sinusoidal segment embeddings, or learned segment embeddings. Persistent encodings (Pers.) are added to the input of each Transformer's block. Alternatively to being added, segment embeddings can be concatenated with position embeddings (PSE). Values in bold are the best within their block of rows and outperform the baselines (base, s4to4).

System	Enc.	Pers.	PSE	Voita	BLEU
base				46.64	31.98
s4to4				72.02	32.45
s4to4+CD				73.42	32.37
s4to4+CD	shift			73.56	32.45
s4to4+CD	shift	✓		**75.94**	31.98
s4to4+CD	1hot			73.06	32.35
s4to4+CD	1hot	✓		73.90	32.56
s4to4+CD	1hot	✓	✓	**74.50**	32.33
s4to4+CD	sin			73.48	32.53
s4to4+CD	sin	✓		73.40	32.52
s4to4+CD	sin	✓	✓	**74.68**	32.27
s4to4+CD	lrn			73.68	32.45
s4to4+CD	lrn	✓		**75.56**	32.43
s4to4+CD	lrn	✓	✓	74.48	32.35

Table 2: En→Ru context-discounted s4to4's accuracy on Voita's contrastive set and BLEU. Values in bold are the best within their block of rows and outperform the baselines (base, s4to4, s4to4+CD).

more effectively by training the concatenation approach with a context-discounted objective (see Appendix A for details). Indeed, the context-discounted objective function incentivizes distinguishing among different sentences. Table 2 displays the results of the s4to4+CD model equipped with the various combinations of encodings tested before, except the *non-persistent* PSE.[4] In this case, too, vanilla sentence encoding methods do not significantly help the s4to4+CD model. However, making the encodings persistent boosts performance in the case of segment-shifted positions (+2.52 accuracy points over s4to4+CD) and learned embeddings (+2.14). One-hot segment embeddings benefit only slightly (+0.48) from being persistent, while no improvement is measured in the case of sinusoidal segment embeddings. As discussed in Section 2.3, this was expected since one-hot or sinusoidal segment embeddings might not be distinguishable from sinusoidal position embeddings once they are added together. Instead, when one-hot and sinusoidal segment embeddings are concatenated to position embeddings into a unique PSE and made persistent, they boost s4to4+CD by +1.08 and +1.26 accuracy points, respectively.

With the aim of evaluating the generalizability of these results to another language pair and domain, we train the context-discounted approach on the En→De IWSLT17 dataset and evaluate it on ContraPro (Müller et al., 2018).[5] Table 3 summarizes the results. Unfortunately, the improvements achieved on En→Ru do not transfer to this setting. The s4to4+CD slightly benefits from segment-shifted position embeddings, but the other approaches degrade its performance. We hypothesize that the model does not undergo sufficient training in this setting to reap the benefits of sentence position encodings. In En→De IWSLT17, the training data volume is smaller than in the En→Ru setting by an order of magnitude: 0.2 million sentences versus 6 million (see Table 6). Therefore, we extended the experiments on En→De by training models on millions of sentences. The details and results are presented in Appendix C and Table 7. Unfortunately, even in this case, the En→De s4to4+*CD* does not benefit from the proposed sentence position encoding options.

[4] Since preliminary experiments where not encouraging, we do not provide results for the non-persistent PSE combination in order to economize experiments.

[5] We don't experiment again with one-hot encodings since it was the less promising approach on the En→Ru setting.

System	Enc.	Pers.	PSE	ContraPro	BLEU
base				43.57	29.63
s4to4				72.12	29.48
s4to4+CD				74.78	29.32
s4to4+CD	shift			74.56	29.20
s4to4+CD	shift	✓		71.46	27.50
s4to4+CD	sin			74.46	29.23
s4to4+CD	sin	✓		74.35	29.26
s4to4+CD	sin	✓	✓	74.02	28.73
s4to4+CD	lrn			72.49	28.35
s4to4+CD	lrn	✓		71.07	27.87
s4to4+CD	lrn	✓	✓	71.89	28.63

Table 3: Accuracy on ContraPro of models trained on En→De IWSLT17, and BLEU on the test set.

System[6]	Voita
Chen et al. (2021)	55.61
Sun et al. (2022)	58.13
Zheng et al. (2020)	63.30
Kang et al. (2020)	73.46
Lupo et al. (2022b)	73.56
Zhang et al. (2020)	75.61
s4to4 + shift_{pers} + CD	**75.94**

Table 4: Benchmarking on En→Ru (accuracy).

4 Benchmarking

In Tables 4 and 5, we compare our best performing systems with other CANMT systems from the literature. For En→Ru (Table 4), we compare with works that adopted the same experimental conditions as ours. Our s4to4 concatenation approach trained with context discounting and persistent segment-shifted positions achieves the best accuracy on Voita's contrastive set. For En→De (Table 5), we compare to the works adopting Müller et al. (2018)'s contrastive set for evaluation, even if the training conditions are not comparable. Our s4to4+CD trained on the high resource setting (see Appendix C) is second of the list, by a negligible margin. Notably, Huo et al. (2020)'s system is also a concatenation approach, but trained on x10 parallel sentences with respect to our system. This comparison indicates that context discounting (Lupo et al., 2022b) makes training efficient.

[6]Whenever the cited works present and evaluate multiple systems, we compare to the best performing one. For the majority of these works, BLEU scores are not available for comparison on the same test set.

[7]Reported in Müller et al. (2018).

System[6]	ContraPro
Maruf et al. (2019)	45.04
Voita et al. (2018)[7]	49.04
Stojanovski and Fraser (2019)	57.64
Müller et al. (2018)	59.51
Lupo et al. (2022a)	61.09
Lopes et al. (2020)	70.8
Lupo et al. (2022b)	74.56
Majumder et al. (2022)	78.00
Fernandes et al. (2021)	80.35
Huo et al. (2020)	**82.60**
s4to4 + CD	**82.54**

Table 5: Benchmarking on En→De (accuracy).

5 Conclusions

Intending to improve concatenation approaches to context-aware NMT (CANMT), we investigated an intuitive idea: encoding into token representations the position of their sentence within the processed sequence. Besides adopting existing encoding methods (segment-shifted position embeddings and segment embeddings), we proposed a novel approach to integrate token and sentence position embeddings in a unique vector called position-segment embedding (PSE). We also propose to make sentence position encodings persistent throughout the model's layers.

We compared these encoding approaches on the En→Ru/De language pairs. Consistent improvements were observed on En→Ru when persistent sentence position encoding methods were used in conjunction with the context-discounted training objective proposed by Lupo et al. (2022b). However, results on En→De were negative.

Further research is needed to clearly define the conditions under which the proposed approaches are beneficial to CANMT with concatenation. We encourage practitioners to test the most promising sentence-position encodings - **persistent segment-shifted positions** - should they want to get the most out of their CANMT systems, but only in conjunction with **context discounting**.

Acknowledgements

We thank the anonymous reviewers for their insightful comments. This work has been partially supported by the Multidisciplinary Institute in Artificial Intelligence MIAI@Grenoble Alpes (ANR-19-P3IA-0003).

References

Ruchit Rajeshkumar Agrawal, Marco Turchi, and Matteo Negri. 2018. Contextual Handling in Neural Machine Translation: Look Behind, Ahead and on Both Sides. In *Proceedings of the 21st Annual Conference of the European Association for Machine Translation*, pages 11–20, Alacant, Spain.

Guangsheng Bao, Yue Zhang, Zhiyang Teng, Boxing Chen, and Weihua Luo. 2021. G-transformer for document-level machine translation. In *Proceedings of the 59th Annual Meeting of the Association for Computational Linguistics and the 11th International Joint Conference on Natural Language Processing (Volume 1: Long Papers)*, pages 3442–3455, Online. Association for Computational Linguistics.

Sheila Castilho, Maja Popović, and Andy Way. 2020. On context span needed for machine translation evaluation. In *Proceedings of the Twelfth Language Resources and Evaluation Conference*, pages 3735–3742, Marseille, France. European Language Resources Association.

Mauro Cettolo, Christian Girardi, and Marcello Federico. 2012. WIT3: Web inventory of transcribed and translated talks. In *Proceedings of the 16th Annual conference of the European Association for Machine Translation*, pages 261–268, Trento, Italy. European Association for Machine Translation.

Linqing Chen, Junhui Li, Zhengxian Gong, Boxing Chen, Weihua Luo, Min Zhang, and Guodong Zhou. 2021. Breaking the corpus bottleneck for context-aware neural machine translation with cross-task pre-training. In *Proceedings of the 59th Annual Meeting of the Association for Computational Linguistics and the 11th International Joint Conference on Natural Language Processing (Volume 1: Long Papers)*, pages 2851–2861, Online. Association for Computational Linguistics.

Jacob Devlin, Ming-Wei Chang, Kenton Lee, and Kristina Toutanova. 2019. BERT: Pre-training of deep bidirectional transformers for language understanding. In *Proceedings of the 2019 Conference of the North American Chapter of the Association for Computational Linguistics: Human Language Technologies, Volume 1 (Long and Short Papers)*, pages 4171–4186, Minneapolis, Minnesota. Association for Computational Linguistics.

Patrick Fernandes, Kayo Yin, Graham Neubig, and André F. T. Martins. 2021. Measuring and increasing context usage in context-aware machine translation. In *Proceedings of the 59th Annual Meeting of the Association for Computational Linguistics and the 11th International Joint Conference on Natural Language Processing (Volume 1: Long Papers)*, pages 6467–6478, Online. Association for Computational Linguistics.

Christian Hardmeier. 2012. Discourse in Statistical Machine Translation. A Survey and a Case Study. *Discours. Revue de linguistique, psycholinguistique et informatique. A journal of linguistics, psycholinguistics and computational linguistics*, 1(11).

Jingjing Huo, Christian Herold, Yingbo Gao, Leonard Dahlmann, Shahram Khadivi, and Hermann Ney. 2020. Diving deep into context-aware neural machine translation. In *Proceedings of the Fifth Conference on Machine Translation*, pages 604–616, Online. Association for Computational Linguistics.

Ian T. Jolliffe and Jorge Cadima. 2016. Principal component analysis: a review and recent developments. *Philosophical Transactions of the Royal Society A: Mathematical, Physical and Engineering Sciences*, 374(2065):20150202. Publisher: Royal Society.

Marcin Junczys-Dowmunt. 2019. Microsoft translator at WMT 2019: Towards large-scale document-level neural machine translation. In *Proceedings of the Fourth Conference on Machine Translation (Volume 2: Shared Task Papers, Day 1)*, pages 225–233, Florence, Italy. Association for Computational Linguistics.

Xiaomian Kang, Yang Zhao, Jiajun Zhang, and Chengqing Zong. 2020. Dynamic context selection for document-level neural machine translation via reinforcement learning. In *Proceedings of the 2020 Conference on Empirical Methods in Natural Language Processing (EMNLP)*, pages 2242–2254, Online. Association for Computational Linguistics.

Yunsu Kim, Duc Thanh Tran, and Hermann Ney. 2019. When and why is document-level context useful in neural machine translation? In *Proceedings of the Fourth Workshop on Discourse in Machine Translation (DiscoMT 2019)*, pages 24–34, Hong Kong, China. Association for Computational Linguistics.

Philipp Koehn, Hieu Hoang, Alexandra Birch, Chris Callison-Burch, Marcello Federico, Nicola Bertoldi, Brooke Cowan, Wade Shen, Christine Moran, Richard Zens, Chris Dyer, Ondřej Bojar, Alexandra Constantin, and Evan Herbst. 2007. Moses: Open source toolkit for statistical machine translation. In *Proceedings of the 45th Annual Meeting of the Association for Computational Linguistics Companion Volume Proceedings of the Demo and Poster Sessions*, pages 177–180, Prague, Czech Republic. Association for Computational Linguistics.

Samuel Läubli, Rico Sennrich, and Martin Volk. 2018. Has machine translation achieved human parity? a case for document-level evaluation. In *Proceedings of the 2018 Conference on Empirical Methods in Natural Language Processing*, pages 4791–4796, Brussels, Belgium. Association for Computational Linguistics.

Xuanqing Liu, Hsiang-Fu Yu, Inderjit S. Dhillon, and Cho-Jui Hsieh. 2020. Learning to encode position for transformer with continuous dynamical model. In *Proceedings of the 37th International Conference on Machine Learning, ICML 2020, 13-18 July 2020,*

Virtual Event, volume 119 of *Proceedings of Machine Learning Research*, pages 6327–6335. PMLR.

António Lopes, M. Amin Farajian, Rachel Bawden, Michael Zhang, and André F. T. Martins. 2020. Document-level neural MT: A systematic comparison. In *Proceedings of the 22nd Annual Conference of the European Association for Machine Translation*, pages 225–234, Lisboa, Portugal. European Association for Machine Translation.

Lorenzo Lupo, Marco Dinarelli, and Laurent Besacier. 2022a. Divide and rule: Effective pre-training for context-aware multi-encoder translation models. In *Proceedings of the 60th Annual Meeting of the Association for Computational Linguistics (Volume 1: Long Papers)*, pages 4557–4572, Dublin, Ireland. Association for Computational Linguistics.

Lorenzo Lupo, Marco Dinarelli, and Laurent Besacier. 2022b. Focused Concatenation for Context-Aware Neural Machine Translation. In *Proceedings of the Seventh Conference on Machine Translation (WMT)*, pages 830–842, Abu Dhabi, United Arab Emirates (Hybrid). Association for Computational Linguistics.

Zhiyi Ma, Sergey Edunov, and Michael Auli. 2021. A Comparison of Approaches to Document-level Machine Translation. *ArXiv preprint*, abs/2101.11040.

Suvodeep Majumder, Stanislas Lauly, Maria Nadejde, Marcello Federico, and Georgiana Dinu. 2022. A baseline revisited: Pushing the limits of multi-segment models for context-aware translation.

Sameen Maruf, André F. T. Martins, and Gholamreza Haffari. 2019. Selective attention for context-aware neural machine translation. In *Proceedings of the 2019 Conference of the North American Chapter of the Association for Computational Linguistics: Human Language Technologies, Volume 1 (Long and Short Papers)*, pages 3092–3102, Minneapolis, Minnesota. Association for Computational Linguistics.

Mathias Müller, Annette Rios, Elena Voita, and Rico Sennrich. 2018. A large-scale test set for the evaluation of context-aware pronoun translation in neural machine translation. In *Proceedings of the Third Conference on Machine Translation: Research Papers*, pages 61–72, Brussels, Belgium. Association for Computational Linguistics.

Myle Ott, Sergey Edunov, Alexei Baevski, Angela Fan, Sam Gross, Nathan Ng, David Grangier, and Michael Auli. 2019. fairseq: A fast, extensible toolkit for sequence modeling. In *Proceedings of the 2019 Conference of the North American Chapter of the Association for Computational Linguistics (Demonstrations)*, pages 48–53, Minneapolis, Minnesota. Association for Computational Linguistics.

Gabriel Pereyra, George Tucker, Jan Chorowski, Lukasz Kaiser, and Geoffrey Hinton. 2017. Regularizing Neural Networks by Penalizing Confident Output Distributions. *ArXiv preprint*, abs/1701.06548.

Martin Popel and Ondřej Bojar. 2018. Training Tips for the Transformer Model. *ArXiv preprint*, abs/1804.00247.

Rico Sennrich, Barry Haddow, and Alexandra Birch. 2016. Neural machine translation of rare words with subword units. In *Proceedings of the 54th Annual Meeting of the Association for Computational Linguistics (Volume 1: Long Papers)*, pages 1715–1725, Berlin, Germany. Association for Computational Linguistics.

Dario Stojanovski and Alexander Fraser. 2019. Improving anaphora resolution in neural machine translation using curriculum learning. In *Proceedings of Machine Translation Summit XVII: Research Track*, pages 140–150, Dublin, Ireland. European Association for Machine Translation.

Zewei Sun, Mingxuan Wang, Hao Zhou, Chengqi Zhao, Shujian Huang, Jiajun Chen, and Lei Li. 2022. Rethinking document-level neural machine translation. In *Findings of the Association for Computational Linguistics: ACL 2022*, pages 3537–3548, Dublin, Ireland. Association for Computational Linguistics.

Jörg Tiedemann and Yves Scherrer. 2017. Neural machine translation with extended context. In *Proceedings of the Third Workshop on Discourse in Machine Translation*, pages 82–92, Copenhagen, Denmark. Association for Computational Linguistics.

Ashish Vaswani, Noam Shazeer, Niki Parmar, Jakob Uszkoreit, Llion Jones, Aidan N. Gomez, Lukasz Kaiser, and Illia Polosukhin. 2017. Attention is all you need. In *Advances in Neural Information Processing Systems 30: Annual Conference on Neural Information Processing Systems 2017, December 4-9, 2017, Long Beach, CA, USA*, pages 5998–6008.

Elena Voita, Rico Sennrich, and Ivan Titov. 2019. When a good translation is wrong in context: Context-aware machine translation improves on deixis, ellipsis, and lexical cohesion. In *Proceedings of the 57th Annual Meeting of the Association for Computational Linguistics*, pages 1198–1212, Florence, Italy. Association for Computational Linguistics.

Elena Voita, Pavel Serdyukov, Rico Sennrich, and Ivan Titov. 2018. Context-aware neural machine translation learns anaphora resolution. In *Proceedings of the 56th Annual Meeting of the Association for Computational Linguistics (Volume 1: Long Papers)*, pages 1264–1274, Melbourne, Australia. Association for Computational Linguistics.

Pei Zhang, Boxing Chen, Niyu Ge, and Kai Fan. 2020. Long-short term masking transformer: A simple but effective baseline for document-level neural machine translation. In *Proceedings of the 2020 Conference on Empirical Methods in Natural Language Processing (EMNLP)*, pages 1081–1087, Online. Association for Computational Linguistics.

Zaixiang Zheng, Xiang Yue, Shujian Huang, Jiajun Chen, and Alexandra Birch. 2020. Towards making the most of context in neural machine translation. In *Proceedings of the Twenty-Ninth International Joint Conference on Artificial Intelligence, IJCAI 2020*, pages 3983–3989. ijcai.org.

A Context-discounted loss

In CANMT with sliding concatenation windows we should prioritize the quality of the translation of the current sentence because the context translation will be discarded during inference. Therefore, the standard NMT objective function is not suitable in this case. Lupo et al. (2022b) propose to encourage the concatenation approach to focus on the translation of the current sentence $\boldsymbol{x}^j$ by applying a discount $0 \leq \text{CD} < 1$ to the loss generated by context tokens:

$$\begin{aligned}\mathcal{L}_{\text{CD}}(\boldsymbol{x}_K^j, \boldsymbol{y}_K^j) &= \text{CD}\cdot\mathcal{L}_{context} + \mathcal{L}_{current} \\ &= \text{CD}\cdot\mathcal{L}(\boldsymbol{x}_K^j, \boldsymbol{y}_{K-1}^{j-1}) + \mathcal{L}(\boldsymbol{x}_K^j, \boldsymbol{y}^j).\end{aligned} \tag{1}$$

with $\mathcal{L}(\boldsymbol{x}, \boldsymbol{y})$ being the standard NMT objective function:

$$\mathcal{L}(\boldsymbol{x}, \boldsymbol{y}) = \sum_{t=1}^{|\boldsymbol{y}|} \log P(y_t|\boldsymbol{y}_{<t}, \boldsymbol{x}), \tag{2}$$

The authors demonstrate the efficacy of this loss function, that leads to a self-attentive mechanism that is less influenced by noisy contextual information. As a result, they show a marked improvement in the translation of inter-sentential discourse phenomena.

B Details on experimental setup

All experiments are implemented in *fairseq* (Ott et al., 2019). All models follow the *Transformer-base* architecture (Vaswani et al., 2017): hidden size of 512, feed forward size of 2048, 6 layers, 8 attention heads. They are trained on 4 Tesla V100, with a fixed batch size of approximately 32k tokens for En→Ru and 16k for En→De, as it has been shown that Transformers need a large batch size to optimize performance (Popel and Bojar, 2018). We stop training after 12 consecutive non-improving validation steps (in terms of loss on dev), and we average the weights of the best-performing checkpoint and the 4 checkpoints that follow it. We train models with the optimizer configuration and learning rate (LR) schedule described in Vaswani et al. (2017). The maximum LR is optimized for each model over the search space $\{7e-4, 9e-4, 1e-3, 3e-3\}$. The LR achieving the best loss on the validation set after convergence was selected. We use label smoothing with an epsilon value of 0.1 (Pereyra et al., 2017) for all settings. We adopt strong model regularization (dropout=0.3) following Kim et al. (2019) and Ma et al. (2021). At inference time, we use beam search with a beam of 4 for all models. We adopt a length penalty of 0.6 for all models. The other hyperparameters were set according to the relevant literature (Vaswani et al., 2017; Popel and Bojar, 2018; Voita et al., 2019; Ma et al., 2021; Lopes et al., 2020). When experimenting with segment-shifted position embeddings, the shift is equal to the average sentence length calculated over the training data, following (Lupo et al., 2022b). In particular, we set shift= 8 for En→Ru, shift= 21 for En→De.

B.1 Data pre-processing

Since Voita's data have already been pre-processed (Voita et al., 2019), we only apply byte pair encoding (Sennrich et al., 2016) with 32k merge operations jointly for English and Russian. For IWSLT17, instead, we tokenize data with the Moses toolkit (Koehn et al., 2007), clean them by removing long sentences, and encode them with byte pair encoding. The byte pair encoding is learned on the En→De training data released by WMT17 for the news translation task using 32k merge operations jointly for source and target languages, to be compatible with the experiments presented in the next section of the Appendix (C).

C Increasing training data for the English to German pair

We hypothesize that the model does not undergo sufficient training in the En→De setting to reap the benefits of segment embeddings. Indeed, the training data volume is smaller than in the En→Ru setting: 0.2 million sentences versus 6 million (see Table 6). Therefore, we choose to experiment with more En→De training data, employing the same high-resource setting of Lupo et al. (2022a). This setting expands the IWSLT17 training data (Cettolo et al., 2012) by adding the News-Commentary-v12 and Europarl-v7 sets released

Corpus	Tgt	Docs	Sents	Doc Length			Sent Length			Sent Length (BPE)		
				mean	std	max	mean	std	max	mean	std	max
Voita	Ru	1.5M	6.0M	4.0	0.0	4	8.3	4.7	64	8.6	4.9	69
IWSLT17	De	1.7k	0.2M	117.0	58.4	386	20.8	14.3	153	23.3	16.3	195
High	De	12.2k	2.3M	188.4	36.2	386	27.3	16.1	249	29.1	17.4	408
Voita	Ru	10k	40k	4.0	0.0	4	8.2	4.8	50	8.5	5.0	58
Both	De	62	5.4k	87.6	53.5	296	19.0	12.5	114	21.1	14.0	132
Voita	Ru	10k	40k	4.0	0.0	4	8.2	4.8	42	8.5	5.0	50
Both	De	12	1.1k	90.0	29.2	151	19.3	12.7	102	21.6	14.3	116

Table 6: Statistics for the training (1st block), validation (2nd block) and test set (3rd block) after pre-processing, and after BPE tokenization. All figures refer to the English text (source side).

System	Enc.	Pers.	PSE	CP	BLEU
s4to4+CD				**82.24**	31.69
s4to4+CD	shift	✓		80.45	30.71
s4to4+CD	sin	✓	✓	80.85	31.40
s4to4+CD	lrn	✓		79.82	31.58

Table 7: Context-discounted s4to4 trained on the En→De high-resource setting, evaluated with the accuracy on ContraPro (CP) and BLEU on the test set.

by WMT17[8]. The resulting training set comprises 2.3M sentences (see statistics in Table 6). Training on this data is more expensive than training on the En→Ru setting, considering that the average sentence length is 27.3 tokens versus 8.3 tokens, respectively. Therefore, we only train the most promising approaches.[9] Their performances are compared in Table 7. As expected, the s4to4+CD model drastically improves its performance compared to training on IWSLT17 alone: +7.93 accuracy points on ContraPro and +2.37 BLEU points on the test set (c.f. Table 3). However, even with larger training volumes, segment position encodings do not seem to help s4to4+CD on the En→De language pair.

D Allocating more space to segments in PSE

For the En→Ru language pair, we have found that one-hot and sinusoidal segment embeddings need to be integrated into PSE for being leveraged by s4to4+CD (Section 3.1.1). Instead, learned embeddings worked best when added to position embeddings.

Here, we evaluate whether PSE with learned segment embeddings would perform better if more dimensions were allocated to segments. In particular, we let the model learn to represent sentence positions in $d_{SE} = 128$ dimensions, which leaves $d_{PE} = d_{model} - d_{SE} = 384$ dimensions to position embeddings, largely enough as shown in Section 2.3.

As shown in Table 8, increasing the number of dimensions allocated to segment embeddings deteriorates the performance on Voita's contrastive set. The reason could simply be that adding more learnable parameters makes the task harder.

E Persistent positions

Making sentence position encodings persistent across the layers have been found beneficial for context-discounted models on the En→Ru setting (Table 2). The best-performing model, s4to4+CD+shift+pers, shifts token positions by a constant factor every time we pass from one sentence to the next and makes the resulting position embeddings persistent throughout Transformer's blocks. In Table 9, we benchmark this model against models employing persistent token position embeddings but without segment-shifting. Both vanilla and context-discounted s4to4 perform better when positions are persistent across Transformer's blocks, as suggested by Liu et al. (2020) and Chen et al. (2021). Segment-shifting further enhances performance, which confirms that the model benefits from a sharper distinction between sentences.

[8]http://www.statmt.org/wmt17/translation-task.html

[9]We set shift= 27 for segment-shifted position embeddings, consistently with the average sentence length of the training data.

System	Enc.	Pers.	PSE	Deixis	Lex co.	Ell. inf	Ell. vp	Voita	BLEU
s4to4+CD	lrn	✓	4	93.20	47.40	72.20	64.40	74.48	32.35
s4to4+CD	lrn		128	83.88	46.33	65.20	50.20	67.38	32.43
s4to4+CD	lrn	✓	128	78.20	46.40	40.60	30.60	60.14	32.35

Table 8: s4to4 trained on En→Ru OpenSubtitles. Accuracy on Voita's En→Ru contrastive set and BLEU on the test set. The accuracy on the contrastive set is detailed on the left, with the accuracy on each subset corresponding to a specific discourse phenomenon. Result: allocating more dimensions to segments in PSE deteriorates performance.

System	Enc.	Pers.	PSE	Voita	BLEU
s4to4				72.02	32.45
s4to4		✓		**72.44**	32.29
s4to4+CD				73.42	32.37
s4to4+CD		✓		74.10	32.12
s4to4+CD	shift	✓		**75.94**	31.98

Table 9: En→Ru: making positions persistent across Transformer's blocks improve discourse disambiguation performance both for vanilla and context-discounted s4to4. Segment-shifting positions further improves performance.

F Details of the evaluation on discourse phenomena

In Tables 10 and 11, we provide more details on the evaluation of the models presented in the tables of the paper, documenting their accuracy on the different subsets of the contrastive sets employed. For Voita's En→Ru contrastive set (Voita et al., 2019), we report the accuracy on each of the 4 discourse phenomena included in it; for the En→De ContraPro (CP, Müller et al. (2018)), the accuracy on anaphoric pronouns with antecedents at different distances $d = 1, 2, ...$ (in number of sentences). We complement Voita/CP with two other metrics, Voita/CP$_{\text{avg}}$ and CP$_{d>0}$. Metrics are calculated as follow:

$$\text{Voita} = \frac{2500{*}\text{Deixis}+1500{*}\text{Lex co.}+500{*}\text{Ell. inf}+500{*}\text{Ell. vp}}{5000} \tag{3}$$

$$\text{CP}_{alld} = \frac{2400{*}(\text{d=0})+7075{*}(\text{d=1})+1510{*}(\text{d=2})+573{*}(\text{d=3})+442{*}(\text{d>3})}{12000} \tag{4}$$

$$\text{CP}_{d>0} = \frac{7075{*}(\text{d=1})+1510{*}(\text{d=2})+573{*}(\text{d=3})+442{*}(\text{d>3})}{9600} \tag{5}$$

$$\text{Voita}_{\text{avg}}/\text{CP}_{\text{avg}} = \frac{(\text{d=1}) + (\text{d=2}) + (\text{d=3}) + (\text{d=4})}{4} \tag{6}$$

System	Enc.	Pers.	PSE	Deixis	Lex co.	Ell. inf	Ell. vp	Voita	Voita_{avg}
base				50.00	45.87	51.80	27.00	46.64	43.67
s4to4				85.80	46.13	79.60	73.20	72.02	71.18
s4to4	shift			85.24	46.07	77.20	71.20	71.28	69.93
s4to4	shift	✓		**85.96**	**46.33**	75.20	**74.00**	71.80	70.37
s4to4	sin			**86.36**	45.80	76.40	73.60	71.92	70.54
s4to4	sin	✓		84.96	46.13	74.80	74.00	71.20	69.97
s4to4	sin		✓	84.64	**46.40**	76.60	73.60	71.26	70.31
s4to4	sin	✓	✓	85.24	46.33	76.40	**75.20**	71.68	70.79
s4to4	lrn			85.48	46.27	76.20	**75.60**	71.80	70.89
s4to4	lrn	✓		84.84	45.93	77.60	74.40	71.40	70.69
s4to4	lrn		✓	83.60	**46.67**	74.80	70.80	70.36	68.97
s4to4	lrn	✓	✓	**90.52**	46.00	74.80	66.60	**73.20**	69.48
s4to4	1hot			**86.08**	47.07	78.00	**75.60**	**72.52**	**71.69**
s4to4	1hot	✓		83.76	**47.53**	78.00	75.00	71.44	71.07
s4to4	1hot		✓	84.56	46.13	78.20	73.00	71.24	70.47
s4to4	1hot	✓	✓	84.56	46.47	76.00	73.40	71.16	70.11
s4to4+CD				87.16	46.40	81.00	78.20	73.42	73.19
s4to4+CD	shift			85.76	48.33	81.40	80.40	73.56	73.97
s4to4+CD	shift	✓		**88.76**	**52.13**	**83.00**	76.20	**75.94**	**75.02**
s4to4+CD	sin			87.96	46.80	78.00	76.60	73.48	72.34
s4to4+CD	sin	✓		86.80	**47.00**	80.80	78.20	73.40	73.20
s4to4+CD	sin	✓	✓	**89.28**	46.67	**83.20**	77.20	**74.68**	**74.09**
s4to4+CD	lrn			88.12	46.47	81.20	75.60	73.68	72.85
s4to4+CD	lrn	✓		86.84	**52.27**	**84.60**	**80.00**	**75.56**	**75.93**
s4to4+CD	lrn	✓	✓	**93.20**	47.40	72.20	64.40	74.48	69.30
s4to4+CD	1hot			86.40	46.73	82.00	76.40	73.06	72.88
s4to4+CD	1hot	✓		87.68	46.80	81.60	**78.60**	73.90	73.67
s4to4+CD	1hot	✓	✓	**88.88**	**47.67**	**82.20**	75.40	**74.50**	73.54
Sample size				2500	1500	500	500	5000	5000

Table 10: Accuracy on the En→Ru contrastive set for the evaluation of discourse phenomena (Voita, %), and on its 4 subsets: deixis, lexical cohesion, inflection ellipsis, and verb phrase ellipsis. Voita_{avg} denotes the average on the 4 discourse phenomena, while Voita represents the average weighted by the frequency of each phenomenon in the test set (see row "Sample size").

System	Enc.	Pers.	PSE	d=0	d=1	d=2	d=3	d>3	$CP_{d>0}$	CP_{avg}	CP
base				68.75	32.89	43.97	47.99	70.58	37.27	48.86	43.57
s4to4				75.20	68.89	74.96	79.58	87.78	71.35	77.80	72.12
s4to4+CD				76.66	72.86	75.96	80.10	84.38	74.31	78.33	74.78
s4to4+CD	shift			75.25	72.56	77.15	80.27	86.65	74.39	79.16	74.56
s4to4+CD	shift	✓		72.41	69.15	74.23	77.13	86.42	71.22	76.73	71.46
s4to4+CD	sin			76.75	71.83	76.82	80.97	87.55	73.88	79.29	74.46
s4to4+CD	sin	✓		76.50	72.08	76.35	79.23	85.97	73.82	78.41	74.35
s4to4+CD	sin	✓	✓	77.25	71.22	76.42	78.88	86.87	73.22	78.35	74.02
s4to4+CD	lrn			73.91	70.21	75.29	77.66	85.06	72.14	77.06	72.49
s4to4+CD	lrn	✓		73.66	68.53	72.51	75.74	86.65	70.42	75.86	71.07
s4to4+CD	lrn	✓	✓	73.54	68.40	79.07	80.27	83.48	71.48	77.81	71.89
					High Resource Setting						
base				82.83	35.18	44.90	51.13	66.28	39.09	49.37	47.84
s4to4				82.41	80.66	81.72	84.29	88.00	81.38	83.67	81.59
s4to4+CD				83.70	81.79	82.11	82.19	90.04	82.24	84.03	82.54
s4to4+CD	shift	✓		81.70	79.61	81.45	83.42	86.65	80.45	82.78	80.70
s4to4+CD	sin	✓	✓	84.12	79.85	82.38	84.46	86.87	80.85	83.39	81.50
s4to4+CD	lrn	✓		83.12	79.13	79.73	82.19	88.00	79.82	82.26	80.48
Sample size				2400	7075	1510	573	442	9600	9600	12000

Table 11: Accuracy on the En→De contrastive set for the evaluation of anaphoric pronouns (CP = ContraPro, %). The columns titled d=* represent the accuracy for each subset of pronouns with antecedents at a specific distance $d \in [0, 1, 2, 3, > 3]$ (in number of sentences). CP_{avg} denotes the average on the 4 subsets of pronouns with extra-sentential antecedents ($d > 0$) while $CP_{d>0}$ represents the average weighted by the size of each of the 4 subsets (see row "Sample size"). CP is equivalent to $CP_{d>0}$, but it includes the accuracy on $d = 0$.

SocBERT: A Pretrained Model for Social Media Text

Yuting Guo and Abeed Sarker
Department of Biomedical Informatics, School of Medicine
Emory University, Atlanta GA 30322, USA
yuting.guo@emory.edu
abeed@dbmi.emory.edu

Abstract

Pretrained language models (PLMs) on domain-specific data have been proven to be effective for in-domain natural language processing (NLP) tasks. Our work aimed to develop a language model which can be effective for the NLP tasks with the data from diverse social media platforms. We pretrained a language model on Twitter and Reddit posts in English consisting of 929M sequence blocks for 112K steps. We benchmarked our model and 3 transformer-based models—BERT, BERTweet, and RoBERTa on 40 social media text classification tasks. The results showed that although our model did not perform the best on all of the tasks, it outperformed the baseline model—BERT on most of the tasks, which illustrates the effectiveness of our model. Also, our work provides some insights of how to improve the efficiency of training PLMs.

1 Introduction

In recent years, pretraining language models (PLMs) such as BERT (Devlin et al., 2019) and RoBERTa (Liu et al., 2019) have proven to be effective for a wide range of natural language processing (NLP) tasks. Domain adaptive pretraining (DAPT), also known as pretraining on domain-specific data, has been a commonly employed approach to enhancing model performance on tasks that are specific to a particular domain (Gururangan et al., 2020). Numerous efforts have been made to achieve this goal. For example, Lee et al. (2019) proposed BioBERT by pretraining BERT on a large biomedical corpus of PubMed abstracts, and demonstrated that it outperformed BERT on three representative biomedical text mining tasks. Alsentzer et al. (2019) attempted to adapt pretrained models for clinical text by training BioBERT on clinical notes, resulting in the creation of BioClinical_BERT (Leroy et al., 2017). Encouraged by the success of pretraining models in different domains, recent studies have developed pretrained models for social media NLP tasks. For example, Dai et al. (2020) built a model by further pretraining the model developed by Devlin et al. (2019) by further training the model on English tweets. Nguyen et al. (2020a) pretrained a transformer model named BERTweet by training the model on a large scale of English tweets from scratch. However, these models only involve Twitter data and may not be effective enough for social media data from other platforms such as Reddit and Facebook. To fill this gap, we trained a language model using both Twitter and Reddit data. We used 92GB text data including 20GB English tweets and 72GB Reddit comments. Our model was trained from scratch for 112K steps following the model architecture of RoBERTa-base. For evaluation, We benchmarked our model and 3 transformer-based models—BERT, BERTweet, and RoBERTa on 40 social media text classification tasks covering diverse health-related and non-health-related topics and from 6 social media platforms. The results showed that although our model did not perform the best on all of the tasks, it outperformed the baseline model—BERT on most of the tasks. It showed that pretraining on the in-domain data can benefit the model on the downstream tasks. To sum up, our contributions are as follows:

- We pretrained and released a transformer-based language model on Twitter and Reddit data which outperformed BERT on most of the benchmarking tasks.
- We benchmarked our model and 3 PLMs on 40 social media text classification tasks.
- We analyzed the influence of training time, data source, and task domains to different PLMs, which.
- Our work provided some insights of how to improve the efficiency of training PLMs.

The Fourth Workshop on Insights from Negative Results in NLP, pages 45–52
May 5, 2023

We call our final pretrained model SocBERT—an abbreviation of Social Media BERT.

2 Method

2.1 Data collection and preprocessing

We collected 92GB pre-training data including 20GB English tweets and 72GB English Reddit comments. The Twitter data were collected via Twitter streaming API and downloaded from the Achive team [1], and the Reddit comments were downloaded from Pushshift[2]. Because Reddit comments are usually longer than the maximum sequence limitation of the language model, we chunked the comments into sequence blocks, and each sequence block is limited to the maximum sequence length. In addition, we used the open source tool named preprocess-twitter (Paulus and Pennington) to preprocessing the data. The preprocessing includes lowercasing, normalization of numbers, usernames, urls, hashtags and text smileys, and adding extra marks for capital words, hashtags and repeated letters. We applied fastBPE (Sennrich et al., 2016) to tokenize the data and obtained a dictionary including 74K subwords which was used for the model pretraining.

2.2 Model architecture

We developed a masked language model (MLM) for pretraining and a classification model for benchmarking. MLM is an unsupervised task in which some of the tokens in a text sequence are randomly masked in the input and the objective of the model is to predict the masked text segments. The model architectures for the masked language model (MLM) and classification are the same as the work of Liu et al. (2019). Specifically, MLM consists of an encoder layer that embeds the text sequence as an embedding matrix consisting of token embeddings and an output layer with Softmax activation that predict the masked token based on the embeddings of the masked tokens. The classification model consists of the same encoder layer and an output layer with Softmax activation to predict classes based on the embedding of the [CLS] token.

[1]https://archive.org/details/twitterstream

[2]https://files.pushshift.io/reddit/comments/

3 Benchmarking Tasks

We utilized a total of 40 social media text classification tasks to establish a benchmark, which represents the most extensive collection of social media text classification tasks currently available to us. Manually annotated data for all these tasks were either publicly available or had been made available through shared tasks. The tasks covered diverse health-related and non-health-related topics including, but not limited to, adverse drug reactions (ADRs) (Sarker and Gonzalez, 2015a; Sarker et al., 2018b), cohort identification for breast cancer (Al-Garadi et al., 2020), non-medical prescription medication use (NPMU) (Al-Garadi et al., 2021), informative COVID-19 content detection (Nguyen et al., 2020b), medication consumption (Sarker et al., 2018a), pregnancy outcome detection (Klein and Gonzalez-Hernandez, 2020), symptom classification (Magge et al., 2021), suicidal ideation detection (Gaur et al., 2021), identification of drug addiction and recovery intervention (Ghosh et al., 2020b), signs of pathological gambling and self-harm detection (Parapar et al., 2021), sentiment analysis and factuality classification in e-health forums (Carrillo-de Albornoz et al., 2018), offensive language identification (Zampieri et al., 2019), cyberbullying detection (Kumar et al., 2018; Bhattacharya et al., 2020), sentiment analysis (Mohammad et al., 2018; Preoţiuc-Pietro et al., 2016), and sarcasm language detection (Ghosh et al., 2020a).

The full details including the source, evaluation metric, training and test set sizes, the number of classes, and the inter-annotator agreement (IAA) for each task, if available, are shown in Appendix A. Seventeen tasks involved binary classification, 13 involved three-class classification, and 10 involved four-, five-, six- or nine-class classification each. The datasets combined included a total of 252,655 manually-annotated instances, with 204,989 (80%) instances for training and 47,666 (20%) for evaluation. The datasets involved data from multiple social media platforms—22 from Twitter, 6 from MedHelp[3], 6 from Reddit, 3 from Facebook, 2 from Youtube, and 1 from WebMD[4]. For evaluation, we used the F_1-score of the positive class for binary classification and the micro-averaged F_1-score for other multi-class classification.

[3]https://www.medhelp.org/

[4]https://www.webmd.com/

4 Experiments

4.1 Language model settings

The language model training consists of two phases. At the first phase, we initialized the language model with random initialization and trained the model on 20GB English tweets and 54GB Reddit comments for 100K steps from scratch. However, During this process, we observed that it would be extremely time-consuming to train the model on the whole dataset using our computation resources, and we could not inspect the model during this process. Therefore, at the second phase, we changed our training strategy into splitting the data and sequentially training the model on a each split so that we could check the model after each round. [5] Specifically, we split the Reddit data into small datasets with 10M sequence blocks and then trained the model on each dataset for 10 epochs. At the time of publication of this work, we finished the training of 11 small datasets involving another 18GB Reddit data. The maximum sequence limitation of our model is 128, and the batch size is 8192. Other hyper-parameters were the same for the two phases, which followed the settings of RoBERTa-base (Liu et al., 2019). We refer to the checkpoint at the end of first phase as SocBERT-base and the checkpoint at the end of second phase as SocBERT-final. In summary, SocBERT-base was pretrained on 819M sequence blocks for 100K steps. SocBERT-final was pretrained on 929M (819M+110M) sequence blocks for 112K (100K+12K) steps.

4.2 Classification model settings

For classification, we performed a limited parameter search with the learning rate $\in \{2 \times 10^{-5}, 3 \times 10^{-5}\}$ and fine-tuned each model for 10 epochs. The rest of hyper-parameters were the same as Liu et al. (2019). Because initialization can have a significant impact on convergence in training deep neural networks, we ran each experiment three times with different random initializations. The model that achieved the median performance over the test set is reported. In addition, we experimented with BERT-base, BERTweet, and RoBERTa-base to better evaluate the effectiveness of our model.

[5] The first phase training took about two and half a month. At the second phase, each round of training took about one week. The GPU model we used was 32GB Tesla V100. We used 8 GPUs at the first phase and 1 GPU at the second phase because of the limited budget.

5 Results

5.1 Classification results

The full classification results are listed in 1. We treated BERT as the baseline model and compared other models with BERT. BERTweet achieved better results on 33 (83%) tasks, RoBERTa on 35 (88%) tasks, SocBERT-base on 30 (75%) tasks, and SocBERT-final on 31 (78%) tasks. Although slightly underperforming RoBERTa and BERTweet, both of SocBERT-base and SocBERT-final outperformed BERT. It showed that our pretraining model is effective on the classification tasks with social media data. The gap between our model and RoBERTa was predictable because RoBERTa was pretrained on a much larger data set (160GB), for longer time (500K steps) than our model, and the pretraining data of RoBERTa also covered the Reddit data in our dataset. Compared to BERTweet, which was pretrained on 160M sequence blocks for 950K steps, our model was pretrained on a larger set of data for shorter time. This suggests that the training time may have a higher impact than the training data size on large language model pretraining. In addition, we observed that SocBERT-final outperformed SocBERT-base on 20 tasks. Considering that the second phase contained only 12K steps, it is reasonable that the influence of the second phase of training was small. Although the strategy we used for the second phase of training allowed us to check the model without waiting for several months, future studies are required to assess whether the strategy of the second phase of training is as efficient as training the model on the whole dataset. Since SocBERT-base and SocBERT-final performed similarly, we performed analysis only on SocBERT-base later in this section.

5.2 Model Comparison

In order to explore the influence of the data source and task domain, we compared the model performance of SocBERT-base, BERTweet, and RoBERTa over the tasks from different social media platforms or focusing on different topics shown in Table 2. The results showed that SocBERT-base outperformed BERTweet on 13 tasks and outperformed RoBERTa on 9 tasks. Although SocBERT-base and RoBERTa underperformed BERTweet on most of the tasks from Twitter, SocBERT-base and RoBERTa performed better on most of the tasks from Reddit and MedHelp. This suggests classification performance is likely to improve if the

ID	Task	Source	BERT	BT	RB	Soc-b	Soc-f
1	ADR Detection (Sarker and Gonzalez, 2015b)	Twitter	59.6	64.7	62.2	60.1	**66.0**
2	Breast Cancer (Sarker et al., 2020)	Twitter	85.6	88.1	**88.6**	86.1	86.6
3	NPMU characterization (Ali Al-Garadi et al., 2020)	Twitter	57.2	**66.1**	61.3	64.2	61.2
4	WNUT-20-task2 (COVID-19 tweet detection) (Nguyen et al., 2020c)	Twitter	86.6	88.5	**88.8**	87.9	87.8
5	SMM4H-17-task1 (ADR detection) (Sarker et al., 2018b)	Twitter	45.4	51.4	**53.8**	51.0	50.2
6	SMM4H-17-task2 (medication consumption) (Sarker et al., 2018b)	Twitter	76.5	**79.8**	78.6	77.4	78.1
7	SMM4H-21-task1 (ADR detection) (Magge et al., 2021)	Twitter	**70.5**	65.6	69.2	63.1	63.1
8	SMM4H-21-task3a (regimen change on Twitter) (Magge et al., 2021)	Twitter	55.6	55.9	**57.9**	57.4	55.5
9	SMM4H-21-task3b (regimen change on WebMD) (Magge et al., 2021)	WebMD	86.8	**88.4**	88.2	87.9	87.8
10	SMM4H-21-task4 (adverse pregnancy outcomes) (Magge et al., 2021)	Twitter	86.8	88.9	**89.7**	86.8	88.2
11	SMM4H-21-task5 (COVID-19 potential case) (Magge et al., 2021)	Twitter	69.6	72.3	**76.5**	71.8	74.3
12	SMM4H-21-task6 (COVID-19 symptom) (Magge et al., 2021)	Twitter	97.6	98.4	**98.2**	97.8	97.8
13	SMM4H-22-task9 (self-reporting exact age) (Weissenbacher et al., 2022)	Reddit	94.0	93.4	**94.2**	91.5	93.3
14	Suicidal Ideation Detection (Gaur et al., 2021)	Reddit	71.7	73.0	78.0	76.7	**78.6**
15	Drug Addiction and Recovery Intervention (Ghosh et al., 2020b)	Reddit	73.3	75.4	77.0	75.9	**77.5**
16	eRisk-21-task1 (Signs of Pathological Gambling) (Parapar et al., 2021)	Reddit	82.7	85.1	85.4	86.1	**87.6**
17	eRisk-21-task2 (Signs of Self-Harm) (Parapar et al., 2021)	Reddit	76.7	78.5	78.9	77.3	78.9
18	Sentiment Analysis (Food Allergy) (Carrillo-de Albornoz et al., 2018)	MedHelp	77.0	**75.8**	**75.8**	73.9	73.9
19	Sentiment Analysis (Crohn'S Disease) (Carrillo-de Albornoz et al., 2018)	MedHelp	70.8	73.9	**78.3**	76.4	73.9
20	Sentiment Analysis (Breast Cancer) (Carrillo-de Albornoz et al., 2018)	MedHelp	63.5	63.3	64.2	61.8	**64.6**
21	Factuality Classification (Food Allergy) (Carrillo-de Albornoz et al., 2018)	MedHelp	69.9	72.0	73.7	72.7	**74.0**
22	Factuality Classification (Crohn'S Disease) (Carrillo-de Albornoz et al., 2018)	MedHelp	**77.6**	71.7	71.4	74.5	75.9
23	Factuality Classification(Breast Cancer) (Carrillo-de Albornoz et al., 2018)	MedHelp	43.8	45.5	**50.0**	46.9	49.2
24	OLID-1 (Zampieri et al., 2019)	Twitter	83.1	84.9	84.9	**85.5**	85.3
25	OLID-2 (Zampieri et al., 2019)	Twitter	56.7	**90.8**	89.2	90.0	89.6
26	OLID-3 (Zampieri et al., 2019)	Twitter	36.6	70.0	69.0	**70.9**	66.7
27	TRAC-1-1 (Kumar et al., 2018)	Facebook	58.1	**60.3**	56.8	59.6	56.9
28	TRAC-1-2 (Kumar et al., 2018)	Twitter	56.6	**65.4**	59.8	59.3	58.6
29	TRAC2-1 (Bhattacharya et al., 2020)	Youtube	73.6	74.7	**75.6**	73.3	75.1
30	TRAC2-2 (Bhattacharya et al., 2020)	Youtube	**86.6**	85.8	85.6	86.3	85.3
31	SemEval-2018 Task 1-4 (Mohammad et al., 2018)	Twitter	67.8	69.1	68.6	66.5	**74.8**
32	SemEval-2018 Task 1-2-1 (Mohammad et al., 2018)	Twitter	70.1	**76.3**	73.3	75.4	76.1
33	SemEval-2018 Task 1-2-2 (Mohammad et al., 2018)	Twitter	86.6	86.4	**87.1**	86.4	85.4
34	SemEval-2018 Task 1-2-3 (Mohammad et al., 2018)	Twitter	72.8	**79.0**	77.8	77.5	73.0
35	SemEval-2018 Task 1-2-4 (Mohammad et al., 2018)	Twitter	62.9	**70.3**	67.6	67.1	64.7
36	Valence CLS (Preoţiuc-Pietro et al., 2016)	Facebook	63.3	**71.1**	**71.1**	64.7	65.3
37	Arousal CLS (Preoţiuc-Pietro et al., 2016)	Facebook	65.6	**71.5**	69.6	65.8	69.9
38	Sarcasm-FigLang-Reddit (Ghosh et al., 2020a)	Reddit	62.3	**67.5**	66.1	63.6	65.6
39	Sarcasm-FigLang-Twitter (Ghosh et al., 2020a)	Twitter	76.2	77.6	**80.9**	79.8	75.4
40	Airline (sentiment analysis) (Crowdflower, 2016)	Twitter	85.1	**86.3**	85.8	85.4	85.3

Table 1: The results of BERT, BERTweet (BT), RoBERTa (RB), SocBERT-base (Soc-b), and SocBERT-final (Soc-f) on 40 classification tasks. The task details can be found in Appendix. The best result for each task is in bold.

pretraining of a model includes data from the same social media source as the downstream tasks.

	Total	Soc >BT	Soc >RB	RB >BT
All tasks	40	13	9	19
Social media platform				
Twitter	22	5	5	9
Reddit	6	3	1	5
MedHelp	6	4	1	4
Facebook	3	0	1	0
Youtube	2	1	1	1
WebMD	1	0	0	0
Task domain				
Health	23	8	3	16
Non-health	17	5	6	3

Table 2: The comparison of model performance of SocBERT-base (Soc), BERTweet (BT), and RoBERTa (RB) over the tasks from different social media platforms or focusing on different topics. The symbol $A > B$ denotes that the model A outperforms the model B.

Another interesting observation is that on the health-related tasks, RoBERTa largely outperformed SocBERT-base and BERTweet, and SocBERT-Tweet slightly outperformed BERTweet. The possible explanation is that the linguistic characteristics of the pretraining data of RoBERTa and SocBERT-base can be more diverse than BERTweet because BERTWeet used a single-source corpus for pretraining.

6 Discussion

Our work initially aimed to develop a PLM which can efficiently work for the data from different social media platforms. However, the results showed that our model could not perform the best on all of the tasks compared to BERTweet and RoBERTa. The possible reason was that the training time of our model was not sufficient because of the limited computing resources. It revealed the dilemma for small labs in academia to develop large language models which has been studied since large language models became popular in the NLP field (Xu, 2022). However, our work can provide some insights for the NLP studies about developing and applying PLMs. First, training the model on a relatively small dataset for longer time might be more efficient than training the model on a large set of data for shorter time. Second, pretraining the model on in-domain data may more efficiently improve the performance on downstream tasks than pretraining on out-of-domain data. Also, the language models pretrained on sufficiently large open-domain data can be effective on domain-specific tasks. We released our model SocBERT-base [6] and SocBERT-final [7] via Huggingface to help the NLP community conduct further studies in this field.

7 Conclusion

In this work, we pre-trained a transformer-based model from scratch on social media data and benchmarked the model on 40 text classification tasks with social media data. Although our model did not perform the best on all of the tasks, it outperformed the baseline model—BERT on most of the benchmarking tasks. It showed that our model can be efficient for the text classification tasks with social media data. It may be possible to further improve the model performance if we continue training the model more efficiently. Further work is required to improve the efficiency and reduce the cost of large language model training.

References

M.A. Al-Garadi, Y.-C. Yang, S. Lakamana, J. Lin, S. Li, A. Xie, W. Hogg-Bremer, M. Torres, I. Banerjee, and A. Sarker. 2020. *Automatic Breast Cancer Cohort Detection from Social Media for Studying Factors Affecting Patient-Centered Outcomes*, volume 12299 LNAI.

Mohammed Ali Al-Garadi, Yuan Chi Yang, Haitao Cai, Yucheng Ruan, Karen O'Connor, Gonzalez Hernandez Graciela, Jeanmarie Perrone, and Abeed Sarker. 2021. Text Classification Models for the Automatic Detection of Nonmedical Prescription Medication Use From Social Media. *BMC Medical Informatics and Decision Making*, 21(1):1–13.

Mohammed Ali Al-Garadi, Yuan-Chi Yang, Haitao Cai, Yucheng Ruan, Karen O'Connor, Graciela Gonzalez-Hernandez, Jeanmarie Perrone, and Abeed Sarker. 2020. Text Classification Models for the Automatic Detection of Nonmedical Prescription Medication Use from Social Media. *medRxiv*.

Emily Alsentzer, John Murphy, William Boag, Wei-Hung Weng, Di Jindi, Tristan Naumann, and Matthew McDermott. 2019. Publicly Available Clinical BERT Embeddings. In *Proceedings of the 2nd Clinical Natural Language Processing Workshop*, pages 72–78, Minneapolis, Minnesota, USA. Association for Computational Linguistics.

Shiladitya Bhattacharya, Siddharth Singh, Ritesh Kumar, Akanksha Bansal, Akash Bhagat, Yogesh

[6]https://huggingface.co/sarkerlab/SocBERT-base

[7]https://huggingface.co/sarkerlab/SocBERT-final

Dawer, Bornini Lahiri, and Atul Kr. Ojha. 2020. Developing a Multilingual Annotated Corpus of Misogyny and Aggression. In *Proceedings of the Second Workshop on Trolling, Aggression and Cyberbullying*, pages 158–168, Marseille, France. European Language Resources Association (ELRA).

Jorge Carrillo-de Albornoz, Javier Rodriguez Vidal, and Laura Plaza. 2018. Feature Engineering for Sentiment Analysis in E-health Forums. *PLoS ONE*, 13(11):e0207996.

Crowdflower. 2016. Twitter US Airline Sentiment.

Xiang Dai, Sarvnaz Karimi, Ben Hachey, and Cecile Paris. 2020. Cost-effective Selection of Pretraining Data: A Case Study of Pretraining BERT on Social Media. pages 1675–1681. Association for Computational Linguistics (ACL).

Jacob Devlin, Ming-Wei Chang, Kenton Lee, and Kristina Toutanova. 2019. BERT: Pre-training of Deep Bidirectional Transformers for Language Understanding. In *Proceedings of the 2019 North American Chapter of the Association for Computational Linguistics: Human Language Technologies*.

Manas Gaur, Vamsi Aribandi, Amanuel Alambo, Ugur Kursuncu, Krishnaprasad Thirunarayan, Jonathan Beich, Jyotishman Pathak, and Amit Sheth. 2021. Characterization of Time-variant and Time-invariant Assessment of Suicidality on Reddit Using C-SSRS. *PLoS ONE*, 16(5):e0250448.

Debanjan Ghosh, Avijit Vajpayee, and Smaranda Muresan. 2020a. A Report on the 2020 Sarcasm Detection Shared Task. In *Proceedings of the Second Workshop on Figurative Language Processing*, pages 1–11, Online. Association for Computational Linguistics.

Shalmoli Ghosh, Janardan Misra, Saptarshi Ghosh, and Sanjay Podder. 2020b. Utilizing Social Media for Identifying Drug Addiction and Recovery Intervention. In *2020 IEEE International Conference on Big Data (Big Data)*, pages 3413–3422.

Suchin Gururangan, Ana Marasovi´cmarasovi´c, Swabha Swayamdipta, Kyle Lo, Iz Beltagy, Doug Downey, and Noah A Smith. 2020. Don't Stop Pretraining: Adapt Language Models to Domains and Tasks. In *Proceedings of the 58th Annual Meeting of the Association for Computational Linguistics*, pages 8342–8360.

Ari Z. Klein and Graciela Gonzalez-Hernandez. 2020. An Annotated Data Set for Identifying Women Reporting Adverse Pregnancy Outcomes on Twitter. *Data in Brief*, 32:106249.

Ritesh Kumar, Atul Kr. Ojha, Shervin Malmasi, and Marcos Zampieri. 2018. Benchmarking Aggression Identification in Social Media. In *Proceedings of the First Workshop on Trolling, Aggression and Cyberbullying (TRAC-2018)*, pages 1–11, Santa Fe, New Mexico, USA. Association for Computational Linguistics.

Jinhyuk Lee, Wonjin Yoon, Sungdong Kim, Donghyeon Kim, Sunkyu Kim, Chan Ho So, and Jaewoo Kang. 2019. BioBERT: A Pre-trained Biomedical Language Representation Model for Biomedical Text Mining. *Bioinformatics*.

Gondy Leroy, Yang Gu, Sydney Pettygrove, and Margaret Kurzius-Spencer. 2017. Automated Lexicon and Feature Construction Using Word Embedding and Clustering for Classification of ASD Diagnoses Using EHR BT - Natural Language Processing and Information Systems. pages 34–37, Cham. Springer International Publishing.

Yinhan Liu, Myle Ott, Naman Goyal, Jingfei Du, Mandar Joshi, Danqi Chen, Omer Levy, Mike Lewis, Luke Zettlemoyer, and Veselin Stoyanov. 2019. RoBERTa: A Robustly Optimized BERT Pretraining Approach. *arXiv*, 1907(11692).

Arjun Magge, Ari Z Klein, Antonio Miranda-Escalada, Mohammed Ali Al-Garadi, Ilseyar Alimova, Zulfat Miftahutdinov, Salvador Lima López, Ivan Flores, Karen O'connor, Davy Weissenbacher, Elena Tutubalina, Juan M Banda, Martin Krallinger, and Graciela Gonzalez-Hernandez. 2021. Overview of the Sixth Social Media Mining for Health Applications (#SMM4H) Shared Tasks at NAACL 2021.

Saif Mohammad, Felipe Bravo-Marquez, Mohammad Salameh, and Svetlana Kiritchenko. 2018. SemEval-2018 Task 1: Affect in Tweets. In *Proceedings of The 12th International Workshop on Semantic Evaluation*, pages 1–17, New Orleans, Louisiana. Association for Computational Linguistics.

Dat Quoc Nguyen, Thanh Vu, and Anh Tuan Nguyen. 2020a. BERTweet: A Pre-trained Language Model for English Tweets. In *Proceedings of the 2020 Conference on Empirical Methods in Natural Language Processing: System Demonstrations*, pages 9–14.

Dat Quoc Nguyen, Thanh Vu, Afshin Rahimi, Mai Hoang Dao, Linh The Nguyen, and Long Doan. 2020b. WNUT-2020 Task 2: Identification of Informative COVID-19 English Tweets. In *Online*, pages 314–318. Association for Computational Linguistics (ACL).

Dat Quoc Nguyen, Thanh Vu, Afshin Rahimi, Mai Hoang Dao, Linh The Nguyen, and Long Doan. 2020c. WNUT-2020 Task 2: Identification of Informative COVID-19 English Tweets. In *Proceedings of the 6th Workshop on Noisy User-generated Text*.

Javier Parapar, Patricia Martín-Rodilla, David E Losada, and Fabio Crestani. 2021. eRisk 2021: Pathological Gambling, Self-harm and Depression Challenges. In *Advances in Information Retrieval*, pages 650–656, Cham. Springer International Publishing.

Romain Paulus and Jeffrey Pennington. Script for Preprocessing Tweets.

Daniel Preoţiuc-Pietro, H Andrew Schwartz, Gregory Park, Johannes Eichstaedt, Margaret Kern, Lyle Ungar, and Elisabeth Shulman. 2016. Modelling Valence and Arousal in Facebook Posts. In *Proceedings of the 7th Workshop on Computational Approaches to Subjectivity, Sentiment and Social Media Analysis*, pages 9–15.

A. Sarker, M. Belousov, J. Friedrichs, K. Hakala, S. Kiritchenko, F. Mehryary, S. Han, T. Tran, A. Rios, R. Kavuluru, B. De Bruijn, F. Ginter, D. Mahata, S.M. Mohammad, G. Nenadic, and G. Gonzalez-Hernandez. 2018a. Data and Systems for Medication-Related Text Classification and Concept Normalization From Twitter: Insights From the Social Media Mining for Health (SMM4H)-2017 Shared Task. *Journal of the American Medical Informatics Association*, 25(10).

A. Sarker and G. Gonzalez. 2015a. Portable Automatic Text Classification for Adverse Drug Reaction Detection via Multi-Corpus Training. *Journal of Biomedical Informatics*, 53.

Abeed Sarker, Mohammed Ali Al-Garadi, Yuan-Chi Yang, Sahithi Lakamana, Jie Lin, Sabrina Li, Angel Xie, Whitney Hogg-Bremer, Mylin Torres, Imon Banerjee, and Abeed Sarker. 2020. Automatic Breast Cancer Survivor Detection from Social Media for Studying Latent Factors Affecting Treatment Success. *medRxiv*.

Abeed Sarker, Maksim Belousov, Jasper Friedrichs, Kai Hakala, Svetlana Kiritchenko, Farrokh Mehryary, Sifei Han, Tung Tran, Anthony Rios, Ramakanth Kavuluru, Berry de Bruijn, Filip Ginter, Debanjan Mahata, Saif M Mohammad, Goran Nenadic, and Graciela Gonzalez-Hernandez. 2018b. Data and Systems for Medication-Related Text Classification and Concept Normalization from Twitter: Insights from the Social Media Mining for Health (SMM4H)-2017 Shared Task. *Journal of the American Medical Informatics Association*, 25(10):1274–1283.

Abeed Sarker and Graciela Gonzalez. 2015b. Portable Automatic Text Classification for Adverse Drug Reaction Detection via Multi-Corpus Training. *J. of Biomedical Informatics*, 53(C):196–207.

Rico Sennrich, Barry Haddow, and Alexandra Birch. 2016. Neural machine translation of rare words with subword units. In *Proceedings of the 54th Annual Meeting of the Association for Computational Linguistics (Volume 1: Long Papers)*, pages 1715–1725, Berlin, Germany. Association for Computational Linguistics.

Davy Weissenbacher, Juan Banda, Vera Davydova, Darryl Estrada Zavala, Luis Gasco Sánchez, Yao Ge, Yuting Guo, Ari Klein, Martin Krallinger, Mathias Leddin, Arjun Magge, Raul Rodriguez-Esteban, Abeed Sarker, Lucia Schmidt, Elena Tutubalina, and Graciela Gonzalez-Hernandez. 2022. Overview of the seventh social media mining for health applications (#SMM4H) shared tasks at COLING 2022. In *Proceedings of The Seventh Workshop on Social Media Mining for Health Applications, Workshop & Shared Task*, pages 221–241, Gyeongju, Republic of Korea. Association for Computational Linguistics.

Guangyi Xu. 2022. The dilemma and prospects of deep learning. In *2022 IEEE International Conference on Electrical Engineering, Big Data and Algorithms (EEBDA)*, pages 1196–1199.

Marcos Zampieri, Shervin Malmasi, Preslav Nakov, Sara Rosenthal, Noura Farra, and Ritesh Kumar. 2019. Predicting the Type and Target of Offensive Posts in Social Media. In *Proceedings of NAACL*.

A Appendix

The full details about the benchmarking tasks and classification results are shown in Table 3.

ID	Task	Source	Evaluation metric	TRN	TST	L	IAA
1	ADR Detection (Sarker and Gonzalez, 2015b)	Twitter	P_F_1	4318	1152	2	0.71
2	Breast Cancer (Sarker et al., 2020)	Twitter	P_F_1	3513	1204	2	0.85
3	NPMU characterization (Ali Al-Garadi et al., 2020)	Twitter	P_F_1*	11829	3271	4	0.86
4	WNUT-20-task2 (COVID-19 tweet detection) (Nguyen et al., 2020c)	Twitter	P_F_1	6238	1000	2	0.8
5	SMM4H-17-task1 (ADR detection) (Sarker et al., 2018b)	Twitter	P_F_1	5340	6265	2	0.69
6	SMM4H-17-task2 (medication consumption) (Sarker et al., 2018b)	Twitter	M_F_1	7291	5929	3	0.88
7	SMM4H-21-task1 (ADR detection) (Magge et al., 2021)	Twitter	P_F_1	15578	913	2	-
8	SMM4H-21-task3a (regimen change on Twitter) (Magge et al., 2021)	Twitter	P_F_1	5295	1572	2	-
9	SMM4H-21-task3b (regimen change on WebMD) (Magge et al., 2021)	WebMD	P_F_1	9344	1297	2	-
10	SMM4H-21-task4 (adverse pregnancy outcomes) (Magge et al., 2021)	Twitter	P_F_1	4926	973	2	0.9
11	SMM4H-21-task5 (COVID-19 potential case) (Magge et al., 2021)	Twitter	P_F_1	5790	716	2	0.77
12	SMM4H-21-task6 (COVID-19 symptom) (Magge et al., 2021)	Twitter	M_F_1	8188	500	3	-
13	SMM4H-22-task9 (self-reporting exact age) (Weissenbacher et al., 2022)	Reddit	M_F_1	7165	1000	2	-
14	Suicidal Ideation Detection (Gaur et al., 2021)	Reddit	M_F_1	1695	553	6	0.88
15	Drug Addiction and Recovery Intervention (Ghosh et al., 2020b)	Reddit	M_F_1	2032	601	5	-
16	eRisk-21-task1 (Signs of Pathological Gambling) (Parapar et al., 2021)	Reddit	P_F_1	1511	481	2	-
17	eRisk-21-task2 (Signs of Self-Harm) (Parapar et al., 2021)	Reddit	P_F_1	926	284	2	-
18	Sentiment Analysis (Food Allergy) (Carrillo-de Albornoz et al., 2018)	MedHelp	M_F_1	618	191	3	0.75
19	Sentiment Analysis (Crohn'S Disease) (Carrillo-de Albornoz et al., 2018)	MedHelp	M_F_1	1056	317	3	0.72
20	Sentiment Analysis (Breast Cancer) (Carrillo-de Albornoz et al., 2018)	MedHelp	M_F_1	551	161	3	0.75
21	Factuality Classification (Food Allergy) (Carrillo-de Albornoz et al., 2018)	MedHelp	M_F_1	580	159	3	0.73
22	Factuality Classification (Crohn'S Disease) (Carrillo-de Albornoz et al., 2018)	MedHelp	M_F_1	1018	323	3	0.75
23	Factuality Classification(Breast Cancer) (Carrillo-de Albornoz et al., 2018)	MedHelp	M_F_1	524	161	3	0.75
24	OLID-1 (Zampieri et al., 2019)	Twitter	M_F_1	11916	860	2	-
25	OLID-2 (Zampieri et al., 2019)	Twitter	M_F_1	11916	240	2	-
26	OLID-3 (Zampieri et al., 2019)	Twitter	M_F_1	11916	213	3	-
27	TRAC-1-1 (Kumar et al., 2018)	Facebook	M_F_1	11999	916	3	-
28	TRAC-1-2 (Kumar et al., 2018)	Twitter	M_F_1	11999	1257	3	-
29	TRAC2-1 (Bhattacharya et al., 2020)	Youtube	M_F_1	4263	1200	3	-
30	TRAC2-2 (Bhattacharya et al., 2020)	Youtube	M_F_1	4263	1200	2	-
31	SemEval-2018 Task 1-4 (Mohammad et al., 2018)	Twitter	PRS	1182	938	8	
32	SemEval-2018 Task 1-2-1 (Mohammad et al., 2018)	Twitter	PRS	1701	1002	4	0.9
33	SemEval-2018 Task 1-2-2 (Mohammad et al., 2018)	Twitter	PRS	1616	1105	4	0.91
34	SemEval-2018 Task 1-2-3 (Mohammad et al., 2018)	Twitter	PRS	1533	975	4	0.83
35	SemEval-2018 Task 1-2-4 (Mohammad et al., 2018)	Twitter	PRS	2252	986	4	0.85
36	Valence CLS (Preoţiuc-Pietro et al., 2016)	Facebook	PRS	2066	604	9	0.77
37	Arousal CLS (Preoţiuc-Pietro et al., 2016)	Facebook	PRS	2088	590	9	0.83
38	Sarcasm-FigLang-Reddit (Ghosh et al., 2020a)	Reddit	M_F_1	3960	1800	2	-
39	Sarcasm-FigLang-Twitter (Ghosh et al., 2020a)	Twitter	M_F_1	4500	1800	2	-
40	Airline (sentiment analysis) (Crowdflower, 2016)	Twitter	M_F_1	10493	2957	3	-

Table 3: Details of the classification tasks and the data statistics. P_F_1 denotes the F_1-score for the positive class, M_F_1 denotes the micro-averaged F_1-score among all the classes, and PRS denotes Pearson correlation coefficient. *For NPMU, P_F_1 denotes the F_1-score of the non-medical use class. TRN, TST, and L denote the training set size, the test set size, and the number of classes, respectively. IAA is the inter-annotator agreement, where Task 4 used Fleiss' K, Task 14 used Krippendorff's alpha, Task 18-23 provided IAA but did not mention the coefficient they used, and other tasks used Cohen's Kappa.

Edit Aware Representation Learning via Levenshtein Prediction

Edison Marrese-Taylor[1,2], Machel Reid[2,3], Alfredo Solano[2]
[1]National Institute of Advanced Industrial Science and Technology
[2]The University of Tokyo
[3]Google Research, Brain Team
edison.marrese@aist.go.jp
{machelreid, asolano}@weblab.t.u-tokyo.ac.jp

Abstract

We propose a novel approach that employs token-level Levenshtein operations to learn a continuous latent space of vector representations to capture the underlying semantic information with regard to the document editing process. Though our model outperforms strong baselines when fine-tuned on edit-centric tasks, it is unclear if these results are due to domain similarities between fine-tuning and pre-training data, suggesting that the benefits of our proposed approach over regular masked language-modelling pre-training are limited.

1 Introduction

Editing documents has become a pervasive component of many human activities (Miltner et al., 2019). For example, right before a conference deadline technical papers worldwide are finalized and polished, often involving common fixes for grammar, clarity, and style (Yin et al., 2019). In light of this, it is reasonable to wonder if it would be possible to automatically extract rules from these common edits. This has led researchers to work on the task of learning distributed representations of edits (Yin et al., 2019; Marrese-Taylor et al., 2021; Reid and Neubig, 2022).

Auto-encoding approaches such as the ones proposed by Yin et al. (2019); Marrese-Taylor et al. (2021) have been used previously in the context of representation learning initially in the visual domain, but more recently have been extended to the natural language and video modalities. These approaches largely form the foundation of "self-supervised learning" which enables the learning of representations via objectives which solely require a source datum. An instance of this relevant to Natural Language Processing (NLP) is that of the pre-trained masked language model, BERT (Devlin et al., 2019), in which a source text is initially corrupted with a mask token `[MASK]` and then reconstructed into the original form with a Transformer encoder.

As an alternative to this approach, other works have instead produced representations of edits in an indirect manner, by instead focusing on edit-centric downstream tasks such as edit-based article quality estimation on Wikipedia (Sarkar et al., 2019; Marrese-Taylor et al., 2019), English grammatical error correction (GEC), and machine translation post-editing.

In this paper, differently from existing prior work, we propose a continued pre-training task not based on auto-encoding, which aims at learning distributed representations of natural language edits. In particular, we look at using the Levenshtein algorithm as a form of supervision to encourage a model to learn to convert a given input sequence into a desired output sequence, namely an edit. In particular, we look to answer whether creating a "neural Levenshtein algorithm" is conducive to improved downstream performance on edit-based tasks, given the edit-centricity of the algorithm. In addition to this, we also propose and test two complementary loss functions that help the encoder retain valuable information about the edit.

Our **E**dit **A**ware **R**epresentation **L**earning model, or EARL, is trained in large datasets of edits collected from Wikipedia, and we test it on a selection of edit-centric downstream tasks, including adversarial paraphrasing detection, grammatical error correction and edit-level article quality estimation. Our results show that EARL outperforms strong baselines when fine-tuned on such edit-centric tasks. However, it is unclear if these improvements are due to domain similarities between fine-tuning and pre-training data, suggesting that the benefits of our proposed approach over regular masked language-modelling pre-training are limited. We release[1] our code and trained models to encourage further research in this direction.

[1]github.com/epochx/earl

The Fourth Workshop on Insights from Negative Results in NLP, pages 53–58
May 5, 2023 ©2023 Association for Computational Linguistics

2 Related Work

Our work is primarily related to Yin et al. (2019), who did seminal work in proposing to directly learn distributed representations of edits by means of a task specifically designed for this purpose, based on auto-encoding. The work of Zhao et al. (2019) proposed a similar approach that was specifically tailored at source code. After that, Marrese-Taylor et al. (2021) proposed a variation of this model where a latent variable is introduced as a means to capture properties of natural language edits, which is then tested on a selection or edit-centric tasks.

Our approach is also related to prior work on edit-based generative models, which have utilized semi-autoregressive sequence generation approaches for various tasks. One such example is the work of Guu et al. (2018), who proposed a sentence-level generative model that first samples a prototype sentence and then edits it into a new sentence. Though related, our approach is fundamentally different as in our setting edits are clearly identified by two distinct versions of each item.

In the context of semi-autoregressive language generation, our approach is also related to prior work utilizing the Levenshtein algorithm for such goals. For example, the work of Gu et al. (2019) has explored non-autoregressive methods that use an iterative generation process for machine translation. More recently, the works of Reid and Zhong (2021); Reid and Neubig (2022) have relied on the Levenshtein algorithm to propose edit-based generative approaches for general-purpose tasks. In the former, an iterative edit-based generative model was proposed for the task of style-transfer, where a coarse-to-fine editor transforms text using Levenshtein edit operations similar to ours. In the latter, the authors extend this idea and propose a generic framework to describe the likelihood of multi-step edits, also describing neural models that can learn a generative model of sequences based on these.

Finally, other works have instead produced representations of edits in an indirect manner, by focusing on specific edit-centric downstream tasks. For example, Sarkar et al. (2019) proposed obtaining edit representations that are useful to predict changes in the quality of articles and similarly Marrese-Taylor et al. (2019) proposed to improve quality assessment by jointly predicting the quality of a given edit and generating a description of it in natural language.

3 Levenshtein Prediction

Differently from previous work, here we instead look to see if we can include the Levenshtein objective from a natural language understanding (NLU) perspective. In particular, we look to assess whether Transformer encoder representations can be trained to contain information relevant to an edit, which we hypothesize can be achieved by directly predicting relevant operations and their associated tokens —as produced by an oracle Levenshtein algorithm.

Concretely, we propose a new pre-training task based on self-supervision and look at using the Levenshtein algorithm as a means of pushing a model to learn to convert a given input sequence into a desired output sequence. Let x_- be the original version of an object, and x_+ its form after a change/edit has been applied. We assume that both x_- and x_+ are sequences of tokens such that $x_- = [x_-^1, \dots, x_-^n]$ and $x_+ = [x_+^1, \dots, x_+^m]$. We use a fast implementation of the Levenshtein algorithm to identify spans of tokens that have been replaced, inserted or deleted as a result of the edit, and define token-level edit operation labels to indicate how each token was changed.

To process each edit, we first tokenize the pair (x_-, x_+), then use the Levenshtein algorithm to identify the text spans that have changed, and finally further process this output to assign token-level labels capturing the transformations required to convert x_- into x_+.

Let $x_-^{i:j}$ be the sub-span on x_- that goes from positions i to j, our post-processing works on a case-by-case manner, as follows.

1. When a span has been inserted between positions $x_-^{i:j}$, such that it appears in $x_+^{k:j}$, we label the tokens in the latter as w^+, and also label token x_-^{i-1}, as $+$. We do this to provide the model with context of where the insertion was performed, in terms of x_-.

2. Similarly, if the span $x_-^{i:j}$ has been replaced by the span $x_-^{k:l}$, we label the tokens on the respective spans as $\Leftrightarrow$ and $w^{\Leftrightarrow}$.

3. If the span $x_-^{i:j}$ has been removed from the sequence as a result of the edit, we label each token as $-$.

4. Tokens that have not been involved in the edit are label with an empty tag, denoted as $=$.

[CLS]	My	name	is	John	[SEP]	My	last	name	is	Wayne
$=$	$+$	$=$	$=$	$\Leftrightarrow$	$=$	$=$	w^{+}	$=$	$=$	$w^{\Leftrightarrow}$

Figure 1: Example of model input-output for the edit defined by the sequences "My name is John" and " My last name is Wayne" (using whitespace tokenization), where the label $=$ denotes tokens that have not been directly involved in the edit.

Dataset	Edits	Avg. Len
WIKIATOMICEDITS		
Insertions	13.7M	24.5
Deletions	9.3M	25.1
WIKIEDITSMIX	114K	61.6

Table 1: Details of the data utilized for pre-training.

As a result of our post-processing, each token in both x_- and x_+ is mapped to a single Levenshtein operation label: $\Leftrightarrow$, $w^{\Leftrightarrow}$, $+$ or w^{+}, as shown in Figure 1. The end goal of our task is to predict these token-level Levenshtein operations relevant to transform x_- into x_+.

The input to our model is constructed by first prepending the [CLS] token to x_- and x_+, which are separated using the [SEP] token, whose total length we denote as $l = m + n + 2$. This input is embedded and then fed to a Transformer encoder that returns a sequence of hidden representations $\boldsymbol{h}_0, \ldots \boldsymbol{h}_l$. We add a classification head (a linear classifier) and require the model to predict the corresponding label for each token, ignoring tokens that have not been directly involved in the edit (label $=$), using a cross entropy loss ($\mathcal{L}_{lev}$).

We also consider an additional mechanism to enrich the quality of the learned representations, based on techniques that have proven useful in previous work (Marrese-Taylor et al., 2021). Concretely, we note that the vector associated to the [CLS] token ($\boldsymbol{h}_0$) is frequently used to represent the complete model input when using Transformer models such as ours. Since there is no specific token-level Levenshtein label associated to this token, we encourage its representation to contain information about the overall edit. We do this by requiring our model to predict the set of tokens that have been changed in the edit in an unordered fashion, using a separate model head (again, a simple linear projection) which receives this as input, setting $f = \text{MLP}(\boldsymbol{h}_0) \in \mathbb{R}^{|\mathbb{V}|}$, where $|\mathbb{V}|$ is the vocabulary size.

$$\mathcal{L}_{x_\Delta} := -\log p(x_\Delta | \boldsymbol{h}_0) = -\log \prod_{t=1}^{|x_\Delta|} \frac{\exp(f_{x_t})}{\sum_j^V \exp(f_j)} \quad (1)$$

We then let our model minimize the loss function defined in Equation 1, above, where x_Δ is the set of tokens that have been involved in the change (inserted, replaced or removed).

Finally, given the success of the masked language modelling task in model pre-traning (Devlin et al., 2019; Liu et al., 2019) we also experiment combining the Levenshtein prediction task with masked language modeling. Since our model input has a special structure, we propose a modified procedure to generate masks. Concretely, for each example, we either mask the tokens on x_- or on x_+, with a probability of 50% each. Once one side is chosen, we overall follow the approach by Liu et al. (2019) (RoBERTa) to choose which/how many tokens to mask. However, we require the tokens with the relevant Levenshtein operation labels ($\Leftrightarrow$, $w^{\Leftrightarrow}$, $+$, w^{+} or $-$) to always be masked. Once the locations of the masks have been determined, we require the model to predict the masked tokens using the standard masked language modelling loss $\mathcal{L}_{MLM}$. Finally, the total loss used to train our Edit Aware Representation Learning model is the simple summation of the above introduced losses, $\mathcal{L} = \mathcal{L}_{lev} + \mathcal{L}_{x_\Delta} + \mathcal{L}_{MLM}$.

4 Experimental Setup

Pre-training We leverage large available corpora containing natural language edits in a variety of domains. We specifically rely on two datasets of edits extracted from Wikipedia, WIKIEDITSMIX (Marrese-Taylor et al., 2021) and WIKIATOMICEDITS (Faruqui et al., 2018), from which we use the insertions and deletions portions together. Please see details in Table 1. Since pre-training is computationally very expensive, we first use WIKIEDITSMIX, which is much smaller, as a test-bed and for ablation experiments regarding our proposed $\mathcal{L}_{x_\Delta}$ and $\mathcal{L}_{MLM}$ losses. To evaluate the pre-training phase, we utilize the overall and per-token F1-score.

Downstream Tasks We consider a broad selection of datasets and probe the ability of the model to solve three edit-related downstream tasks.

- Paraphrasing Detection: we measure the ability of our edit encoder to model structure, context, and word order information, by means of using PAWS (Yang et al., 2019), an ad-

Model	WikiEditsMix (F1-score)						PAWS		WikiEdits		GEC	
	$+$	w^+	$\Leftrightarrow$	$w^{\Leftrightarrow}$	$-$	All	ZS	Ft	ZS	Ft	ZS	Ft
$\mathcal{L}_{lev}$	**89.4**	**96.1**	90.6	88.6	93.7	**91.8**	56.8	94.9	56.8	78.1	**49.5**	52.4
$\mathcal{L}_{lev}$+ $\mathcal{L}_{x_\Delta}$	87.8	95.6	89.9	**88.7**	93.5	91.2	**63.8**	94.9	56.7	78.2	48.6	**53.4**
$\mathcal{L}_{lev}$+ $\mathcal{L}_{MLM}$	80.0	94.7	**93.8**	86.3	**95.6**	90.2	60.7	**95.0**	**64.8**	**78.4**	48.8	53.1

Table 2: Results of our ablation experiments on WIKIEDITSMIX.

versarial dataset for paraphrasing detection. Naturally, paraphrases are strongly correlated to edits, as paraphrases are defined as sentences that are semantically similar to each other. PAWS main focus is on sentence pairs that have high lexical overlap but are not paraphrases, with a total of 49,401 pairs for training, and 8K sentences for validation and testing.

- Edit-level Article Quality Estimation: we evaluate the quality of edit representations by means of running a multi-class classification to predict the quality labels on WIKIEDITSMIX (Marrese-Taylor et al., 2021). Concretely, the task is edit-level quality prediction with 4 labels: *spam, vandalism, attack OK*, each corresponding to a different quality of the edit.

- Classification of Grammatical Errors: since grammatical errors consist of many different types, we follow previous work (Marrese-Taylor et al., 2021) and use the WI + LOCNESS (Bryant et al., 2019) dataset for GEC, where each example is labeled into one of 3 CEFR levels (A (beginner), B (intermediate), and C (advanced). We test the ability of the models to classify each edit using a multi-class setting over these three labels.

For evaluation on these downstream tasks, we use accuracy for PAWS, and F1-score for the other datasets. Following previous work, we test our model on two different settings, fine-tuning (Ft) and zero-shot (ZS). For the former, we simply add a new randomly-initialized classification head to our transformer model, and then train all the parameters using a cross-entropy loss based on the labeled data. For the latter, we feed the training examples through our models and extract the vector associated to the [CLS] token ($\boldsymbol{h}_0$) to represent each edit. These representations are then passed through a randomly-initialized MLP to perform classification.

Finally, we compare our model to relevant baselines selected from previous work. On the one hand, we consider the encoder proposed by Yin et al. (2019), but we omit the copy mechanism proposed in the paper in order to make our results comparable. On the other hand, we compare with EVE (Marrese-Taylor et al., 2021), which also uses an auto-encoding loss for training, but does so in variational inference framework. We additionally consider the approach by Guu et al. (2018), but skip their sampling procedure. As our task requires the model to capture structure, context, and word order information, we initialize our model with ROBERTA-base (Liu et al., 2019), which we also adopt as a baseline for downstream experiments.

4.1 Implementation Details

For pre-training, we split WIKIATOMICEDITS into train/valid/testing splits randomly, and use the splits provided by Marrese-Taylor et al. (2021) for WIKIEDITSMIX. For fine-tuning, we respect the original splits for each considered dataset.

Our pre-training is performed using data parallelism to speed up convergence time, but our proposed model can run on single GPUs. We use fairseq (Ott et al., 2019) to implement our model and perform distributed pre-training using 16 NVIDIA V100-16 GB GPUs, and fine-tuning with a single NVIDIA A100-40 GB GPU. We access the former by means of nodes on a large cluster, where each node has four GPUs. For WIKIEDITSMIX we used a single node with a maximum training time of 24 hours (or 100 epochs). on WIKIATOMICEDITS, we used 4 nodes simultaneously, also for a maximum of 24 hours (or 100 epochs).

We use the Adam (Kingma and Ba, 2015) optimizer with a learning rate of 1e-4 during pre-training, and of 1e-3 for fine-tuning on the downstream tasks. Instructions to replicate our experiments and the details of the exact hyper-parameter settings used for pre-training and fine-tuning can be found in our code release.

	Model	PAWS	WikiEditsMix	GEC
ZS	RoBERTa	58.1	63.2	**50.7**
	EARL_{Mix}	**63.8**	56.7	48.6
	$\text{EARL}_{\text{Ins+Del}}$	62.2	**57.0**	47.6
Ft	RoBERTa	94.5	**78.9**	54.0
	Guu (2018)	-	74.3	85.6
	Yin (2019)	-	66.8	83.1
	EVE (2021)	-	77.4	**95.8**
	EARL_{Mix}	**94.9**	78.2	53.4
	$\text{EARL}_{\text{Ins+Del}}$	94.5	78.3	54.5

Table 3: Results of our model on the downstream tasks, compared to our baselines. EARL_{Mix} and $\text{EARL}_{\text{Ins+Del}}$ indicate models that have been pre-trained on WikiEditsMix and WikiAtomicEdits (Insertions+Deletions), respectively.

5 Results

As can be seen in Table 2, all of our models attain excellent performance on the pre-training task, with an overall F1-Score of more than 90%. We believe this shows that EARL is capable of successfully predicting the operations generated by our oracle Levenshtein editor, suggesting that the representations contain information relevant to the changes that are introduced. This would also explain the high performance attained when fine-tuning on PAWS and WikiEditsMix.

Regarding the impact of $\mathcal{L}_{x_\Delta}$, we see that when added, the overall performance of the model decreases slightly on the pre-training task, but leads to improvements downstream, specially on the zero-shot settings. We believe this result is consistent with previous work, validating the contribution of this loss applied to our setting. Finally, we also see that $\mathcal{L}_{MLM}$ further decreases performance on the pre-training task, but again leads to improved performance when fine-tuning on downstream tasks.

Based on the above findings, we use both losses for our final experiments, which are summarized in Table 3, where we also compare to previous work. We see that when fine-tuned, EARL is able to outperform RoBERTa in PAWS, suggesting that the representations induced by our task help the model learn relevant information about edits. We also see that our model struggles to attain good performance on the GEC tasks, falling considerably behind previous work. We surmise this is due to the pre-training domain being too different from the task. We further note that the best performing model in this task (EVE), is pre-trained on a large corpus of unlabeled GEC edits, a fact that supports our domain shift hypothesis.

Since our model is initialized with RoBERTa-base, we further assessed the impact of our pre-training on a standard NLP downstream task and checked whether it leads to catastrophic forgetting. We considered the widely-used GLUE benchmark (Wang et al., 2018) and selected the MNLI dataset (MNLI) as a test-bed. We find that both RoBERTa and EARL obtain the same accuracy of 87.6, suggesting that our training procedure is compatible with masked language modelling pre-training.

Regarding the models pre-trained on different datasets, we observe that the impact of additional training data is marginal, as the performance of models trained on WikiEditsMix and WikiAtomicEdits is similar across downstream tasks. As these results are well-aligned with our findings regarding the GEC tasks, we think this may suggest the results we are observing are due to pre-training/fine-tuning domain similarity, rather than to the effectiveness of our proposed pre-training.

6 Conclusions and Future Work

This paper proposes a novel approach for training a general-purpose edit representation model, which is not based on auto-encoding. Concretely, we propose a predictive task based on token-level Levenshtein operations where the token-level labels encode the set of operations necessary to transform a given input sentence into an output sentence. Our results show the task is effective at capturing edits, but is not substantially better than the masked language modeling task. We think this evidence still supports the idea that creating a neural model that implements the Levenshtein algorithm is conducive to improved downstream performance on edit based tasks, suggesting a potential new path for the future of pre-training.

Acknowlegments

This paper is partially based on results obtained from project AAZ20285R1B at the National Institute of Advanced Industrial Science and Technology (AIST). For large pre-training experiments, computational resources of the AI Bridging Cloud Infrastructure (ABCI) provided by AIST were also used. Finally, we are also grateful to the NVIDIA Corporation, which donated one of the GPUs used for this research.

References

Christopher Bryant, Mariano Felice, Øistein E. Andersen, and Ted Briscoe. 2019. The BEA-2019 Shared Task on Grammatical Error Correction. In *Proceedings of the Fourteenth Workshop on Innovative Use of NLP for Building Educational Applications*, pages 52–75, Florence, Italy. Association for Computational Linguistics.

Jacob Devlin, Ming-Wei Chang, Kenton Lee, and Kristina Toutanova. 2019. BERT: Pre-training of Deep Bidirectional Transformers for Language Understanding. In *Proceedings of the 2019 Conference of the North American Chapter of the Association for Computational Linguistics: Human Language Technologies, Volume 1 (Long and Short Papers)*, pages 4171–4186, Minneapolis, Minnesota. Association for Computational Linguistics.

Manaal Faruqui, Ellie Pavlick, Ian Tenney, and Dipanjan Das. 2018. WikiAtomicEdits: A multilingual corpus of Wikipedia edits for modeling language and discourse. In *Proceedings of the 2018 Conference on Empirical Methods in Natural Language Processing*, pages 305–315, Brussels, Belgium. Association for Computational Linguistics.

Jiatao Gu, Changhan Wang, and Junbo Zhao. 2019. Levenshtein Transformer. In H. Wallach, H. Larochelle, A. Beygelzimer, F. d\textquotesingle Alché-Buc, E. Fox, and R. Garnett, editors, *Advances in Neural Information Processing Systems 32*, pages 11181–11191. Curran Associates, Inc.

Kelvin Guu, Tatsunori B. Hashimoto, Yonatan Oren, and Percy Liang. 2018. Generating Sentences by Editing Prototypes. *Transactions of the Association for Computational Linguistics*, 6:437–450.

Diederik P. Kingma and Jimmy Ba. 2015. Adam: A method for stochastic optimization. In *3rd International Conference on Learning Representations, ICLR 2015, San Diego, CA, USA, May 7-9, 2015, Conference Track Proceedings*.

Yinhan Liu, Myle Ott, Naman Goyal, Jingfei Du, Mandar Joshi, Danqi Chen, Omer Levy, Mike Lewis, Luke Zettlemoyer, and Veselin Stoyanov. 2019. RoBERTa: A Robustly Optimized BERT Pretraining Approach. *arXiv:1907.11692 [cs]*.

Edison Marrese-Taylor, Pablo Loyola, and Yutaka Matsuo. 2019. An Edit-centric Approach for Wikipedia Article Quality Assessment. In *Proceedings of the 5th Workshop on Noisy User-generated Text (W-NUT 2019)*, pages 381–386, Hong Kong, China. Association for Computational Linguistics.

Edison Marrese-Taylor, Machel Reid, and Yutaka Matsuo. 2021. Variational Inference for Learning Representations of Natural Language Edits. *Proceedings of the AAAI Conference on Artificial Intelligence*, 35(15):13552–13560.

Anders Miltner, Sumit Gulwani, Vu Le, Alan Leung, Arjun Radhakrishna, Gustavo Soares, Ashish Tiwari, and Abhishek Udupa. 2019. On the fly synthesis of edit suggestions. *Proceedings of the ACM on Programming Languages*, 3(OOPSLA):143:1–143:29.

Myle Ott, Sergey Edunov, Alexei Baevski, Angela Fan, Sam Gross, Nathan Ng, David Grangier, and Michael Auli. 2019. Fairseq: A Fast, Extensible Toolkit for Sequence Modeling. In *Proceedings of the 2019 Conference of the North American Chapter of the Association for Computational Linguistics (Demonstrations)*, pages 48–53, Minneapolis, Minnesota. Association for Computational Linguistics.

Machel Reid and Graham Neubig. 2022. Learning to Model Editing Processes. In *Findings of the Association for Computational Linguistics: EMNLP 2022*, pages 3822–3832, Abu Dhabi, United Arab Emirates. Association for Computational Linguistics.

Machel Reid and Victor Zhong. 2021. LEWIS: Levenshtein editing for unsupervised text style transfer. In *Findings of the Association for Computational Linguistics: ACL-IJCNLP 2021*, pages 3932–3944, Online. Association for Computational Linguistics.

Soumya Sarkar, Bhanu Prakash Reddy, Sandipan Sikdar, and Animesh Mukherjee. 2019. StRE: Self Attentive Edit Quality Prediction in Wikipedia. In *Proceedings of the 57th Annual Meeting of the Association for Computational Linguistics*, pages 3962–3972, Florence, Italy. Association for Computational Linguistics.

Alex Wang, Amanpreet Singh, Julian Michael, Felix Hill, Omer Levy, and Samuel Bowman. 2018. GLUE: A Multi-Task Benchmark and Analysis Platform for Natural Language Understanding. In *Proceedings of the 2018 EMNLP Workshop BlackboxNLP: Analyzing and Interpreting Neural Networks for NLP*, pages 353–355, Brussels, Belgium. Association for Computational Linguistics.

Yinfei Yang, Yuan Zhang, Chris Tar, and Jason Baldridge. 2019. PAWS-X: A cross-lingual adversarial dataset for paraphrase identification. In *Proceedings of the 2019 Conference on Empirical Methods in Natural Language Processing and the 9th International Joint Conference on Natural Language Processing (EMNLP-IJCNLP)*, pages 3687–3692, Hong Kong, China. Association for Computational Linguistics.

Pengcheng Yin, Graham Neubig, Miltiadis Allamanis, Marc Brockschmidt, and Alexander L. Gaunt. 2019. Learning to Represent Edits. In *Proceedings of the 7th International Conference on Learning Representations*.

Rui Zhao, David Bieber, Kevin Swersky, and Daniel Tarlow. 2019. Neural Networks for Modeling Source Code Edits. In *Proceedings of the 7th International Conference on Learning Representations*.

What changes when you randomly choose BPE merge operations? Not much.

Jonne Sälevä and **Constantine Lignos**
Michtom School of Computer Science
Brandeis University
jonnesaleva, lignos@brandeis.edu

Abstract

We introduce two simple randomized variants of byte pair encoding (BPE) and explore whether randomizing the selection of merge operations substantially affects a downstream machine translation task. We focus on translation into morphologically rich languages, hypothesizing that this task may show sensitivity to the method of choosing subwords. Analysis using a Bayesian linear model indicates that one variant performs nearly indistinguishably compared to standard BPE while the other degrades performance less than we anticipated. We conclude that although standard BPE is widely used, there exists an interesting universe of potential variations on it worth investigating. Our code is available at: https://github.com/bltlab/random-bpe.

1 Introduction and related work

Most neural machine translation (NMT) models assume their inputs to be sequences of units drawn from a fixed vocabulary. While these units were tokens in the early years of NMT (Cho et al., 2014; Sutskever et al., 2014), there has since been a transition to *subword*-level models that learn a vocabulary of "word pieces" which serve as an intermediate representation between words and characters (Mielke et al., 2021). Such representations are attractive because they solve the closed-vocabulary problem of early, word-level NMT (Luong et al., 2015) while also yielding more semantically meaningful units than individual characters.

Well-known subword segmentation algorithms include byte pair encoding (BPE) (Sennrich et al., 2016), SentencePiece Unigram LM (Kudo and Richardson, 2018; Kudo, 2018) and the WordPiece algorithm (Wu et al., 2016; Song et al., 2021). All of them include a hyperparameter that controls the size of the subword vocabulary: SentencePiece and WordPiece do this explicitly with a vocabulary size parameter, whereas BPE specifies the number of *merge operations* which implicitly define the subword vocabulary.

Prior work has addressed the problem of optimally selecting the vocabulary size. Haddow et al. (2018) and Sennrich and Zhang (2019) find that using too large a subword vocabulary can result in low-frequency tokens being represented as atomic units, which makes it difficult to learn proper representations for them. Gowda and May (2020) suggest a heuristic: use as many subwords as possible provided that at least 95% of the subwords have 100 or more examples in the training set. Gutierrez-Vasques et al. (2021) find that around 350 merge operations are enough to generate similar subword distributions across languages.

Subword segmentation algorithms usually build their subword vocabularies by optimizing an objective function that is independent of the downstream task. For instance, SentencePiece employs the probabilities under its unigram language model, while BPE aims to maximize the degree of sequence compression by greedily selecting and merging the symbol pairs that occur most frequently. Others have re-framed this process as finding an "optimal" set of units that maximize more sophisticated probabilistic criteria. Vilar and Federico (2021) introduce an extension of BPE that learns a subword vocabulary by maximizing a likelihood objective over potential subwords. He et al. (2020) introduce a method that treats the segmentation as a latent variable to be marginalized out and seek to find segmentations that maximize the downstream task probability directly.

In this paper, we build upon the concept of stochastic segmentation and conduct neural machine translation experiments on four languages (German, Finnish, Estonian and Uzbek) of varying morphological complexity, using variants of BPE that randomly sample merge operations instead of deterministically choosing the most frequent one.

Our negative result challenges our initial beliefs

The Fourth Workshop on Insights from Negative Results in NLP, pages 59–66
May 5, 2023

that standard BPE would produce the most effective subword representations for translation and that the success of BPE was due to the greedy selection process for learning merge operations. We find that even when merge operations are randomly sampled uniformly, the performance degradation is less than we anticipated. We conclude by discussing how this finding relates to the overall role of subwords in NMT.

2 Byte pair encoding and randomization

We briefly review the BPE training algorithm and introduce our randomized variants. The pseudocode for the algorithm we use can be seen in Algorithm 1. Our presentation is adapted from the BPE algorithm in Vilar and Federico (2021).

Algorithm 1: BPE training algorithm.

```
Input: D: Training corpus. M: Number of merge
       operations to learn.
Output: R: list of learned merges.
def trainBPE (D, M, method):
    R ← []
    while |R| ≤ M do
        C ← countSymbolPairs(D)
        (x, y) ← choosePair(C, method)
        rule ← ⟨(x, y) → xy⟩
        R ← append(R, rule)
        D ← applyRule(D, rule)
    return R
def choosePair (counts, method):
    if method = standard then
        pair ← arg max_{pair∈counts} counts[pair]
    else if method = uniform then
        probs ∝ 1
        pair ← sample(counts, probs)
    else
        probs ← softmax(counts)
        pair ← sample(counts, probs)
    return pair
```

2.1 Standard BPE algorithm

The standard byte pair encoding algorithm (Sennrich et al., 2016) is a greedy algorithm that takes as input a corpus D—typically the training set or another large collection of text—as well an integer M that specifies the number of merge operations to learn. After first segmenting D into space-separated characters, the algorithm counts how many times each pair of symbols occurs in D (`countSymbolPairs`). Based on the counts, the algorithm finds the most frequent symbol pair (`choosePair`) and learns a new merge operation that merges the constituent symbols into a new symbol. After learning the merge operation, the algorithm replaces all occurrences of the symbol pair in D with the new merged symbol (`applyRule`).

While the initial merge operations merge individual characters, during the later iterations larger chunks of words are merged together as well. For example, if the most frequent symbol pair was `(ab, c)`, the algorithm would learn the rule `ab c` → `abc` which replaces all occurrences of `ab c` with `abc`, taking care to not cross word boundaries.

This is repeated for M iterations until a desired number of merge operations is learned, after which the algorithm returns the list of merge operations as output. At test time, the algorithm splits incoming lines of text into individual characters and then applies each of the learned merge operations in order, resulting in text where each space-separated token is an individual subword.

2.2 Randomized BPE variants

To extend BPE to randomized variants, we replace the step of picking the most frequent symbol pair at each iteration with random sampling.

Softmax sampling In our first variant, we assign each symbol pair a probability of being sampled based on how often it occurs in the observed data. We apply a softmax to the observed symbol pair occurrence counts and draw a random symbol pair to merge according to a categorical distribution with the softmax probabilities as its parameters.

Uniform sampling As our second variant, we select each merge operation with uniform probability from the set of observed symbol pairs. Since every symbol pair has equal probability of being sampled, the frequency of each symbol pair is not used in sampling.

3 Experimental setup

Task and data We experiment with translation from English to several morphologically rich languages: Finnish, Estonian, German, and Uzbek. Statistics for each dataset can be found in the Appendix. For all languages except Uzbek, we use the WMT shared task data from He et al. (2020). For Uzbek, we use the Turkic Interlingua corpus (Mirzakhalov et al., 2021).

Tokenization and subword segmentation All of our datasets had previously been tokenized. We performed BPE segmentation on those tokens at the character level using `subword-nmt`, which we

Language	Merges	BLEU			chrF		
		Standard	Random	Uniform	Standard	Random	Uniform
Estonian	2,000	18.08 ± 0.07	18.17 ± 0.06	17.48 ± 0.04	51.01 ± 0.09	51.10 ± 0.09	50.38 ± 0.07
	5,000	17.98 ± 0.11	17.89 ± 0.09	17.43 ± 0.06	50.80 ± 0.14	50.65 ± 0.11	50.48 ± 0.06
	32,000	16.13 ± 0.06	16.13 ± 0.10	16.86 ± 0.06	48.70 ± 0.09	48.65 ± 0.05	50.21 ± 0.09
Finnish	2,000	16.40 ± 0.08	16.20 ± 0.04	15.26 ± 0.14	50.99 ± 0.07	50.90 ± 0.06	49.76 ± 0.12
	5,000	15.77 ± 0.08	16.01 ± 0.04	14.63 ± 0.09	50.64 ± 0.07	50.67 ± 0.06	49.32 ± 0.09
	32,000	13.83 ± 0.09	13.88 ± 0.09	13.28 ± 0.11	48.20 ± 0.11	48.20 ± 0.07	47.92 ± 0.08
German	2,000	24.56 ± 0.05	24.46 ± 0.06	22.54 ± 0.08	55.77 ± 0.03	55.74 ± 0.03	53.41 ± 0.08
	5,000	24.84 ± 0.07	24.79 ± 0.10	22.73 ± 0.04	56.12 ± 0.04	55.98 ± 0.04	53.65 ± 0.05
	32,000	25.49 ± 0.06	25.33 ± 0.05	22.91 ± 0.07	56.60 ± 0.03	56.54 ± 0.04	54.26 ± 0.05
Uzbek	2,000	47.31 ± 0.21	45.82 ± 1.14	37.85 ± 0.24	64.51 ± 0.18	63.24 ± 1.00	57.66 ± 0.23
	5,000	46.77 ± 1.10	45.39 ± 1.46	38.79 ± 0.20	63.78 ± 0.92	62.52 ± 1.31	58.39 ± 0.15
	32,000	48.63 ± 0.75	47.98 ± 0.70	41.73 ± 0.51	64.76 ± 0.56	64.24 ± 0.59	60.43 ± 0.42

Table 1: Mean and standard error of BLEU and chrF scores across target languages, merge operations and BPE segmentation types. All numbers computed over 10 replications with different random seeds.

modified to support randomized subword sampling. All subword vocabularies are learned separately for each language. As the number of merge operations M is a hyperparameter, we experiment with the values 2,000, 5,000, and 32,000. The largest value, 32,000, is taken directly from He et al. (2020); the smaller values of 2,000 and 5,000 are motivated the observation that higher numbers of merges tend to lead to a near-word-level segmentations for which learning good representations may not be feasible (Sennrich and Zhang, 2019).

Model and training Our model is a standard Transformer-based encoder-decoder model, as implemented in the `fairseq` library. Our architecture is similar to `transformer-base`, with 512-dimensional embeddings on both the encoder and decoder side, 2048-dimensional feedforward layers, and 6 stacked Transformer layers with 8 attention heads each in both the encoder and decoder. We train all our models for 10,000 updates using a learning rate of 0.005 and the largest feasible batch size (36K tokens per batch for Finnish and Estonian, 30K tokens per batch for German, and 12K tokens per batch for Uzbek). Each translation experiment is run on a single NVIDIA V100 GPU (24GB). We simulate training on multiple GPUs by accumulating gradients for 16 backward passes before each parameter update. To estimate the variability of our results across random seeds, we perform 10 replications of each experiment.

Evaluation We evaluate all of our models with the `sacrebleu` library (Post, 2018) using BLEU[1] (Papineni et al., 2002) as well as chrF[2] (Popović, 2015) as it is a tokenization-free metric. Both metrics are computed using the default parameters. We use the `sacremoses`[3] detokenizer to create the detokenized versions of our corpora.

4 Results

Our main experimental results are displayed in Table 1 and Figure 1. For most languages translation performance appears to be rather stable across seeds, but in Uzbek standard errors are larger than other languages and they seem to increase with increasing numbers of merge operations. We believe this noisiness is due to the smaller size of the Uzbek dataset rather than any language-specific phenomena.

Initially, we would have expected that standard BPE would perform the best out of all methods and that different BPE variants would produce noticeable performance differences for all languages. Somewhat contrary to our hypothesis, we find that using randomized BPE variants seems to have quite a small average effect with significant variation in the effect size from language to language. Uniform segmentation tends to consistently perform worse than standard BPE and softmax-based sampling, which can be explained by the roughly 3x longer sequences the model produces. Looking across merge operations, the BLEU/chrF differences between the best and worst BPE variants seem to be less than 1.0 and 1.5 points for Estonian

[1]Version string: `nrefs:1|case:mixed|eff:no|tok:13a|smooth:exp|version:2.3.1`

[2]Version string: `nrefs:1|case:mixed|eff:yes|nc:6|nw:0|space:no|version:2.3.1`

[3]`https://github.com/alvations/sacremoses`

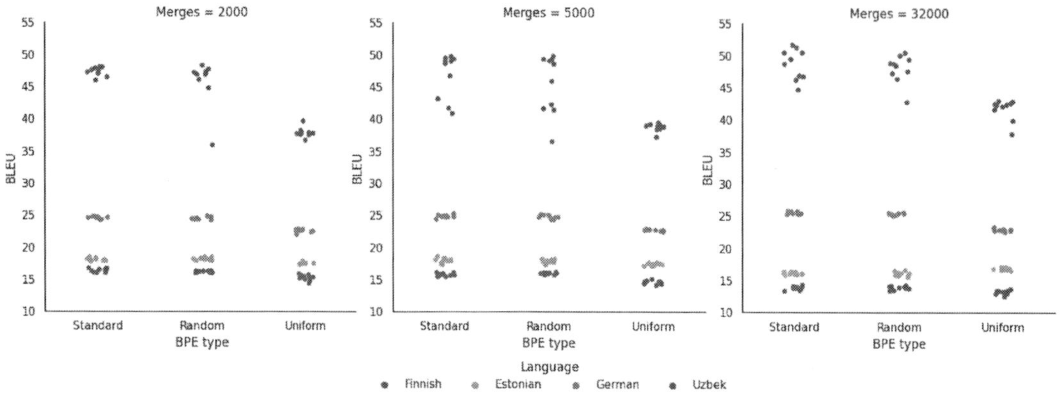

Figure 1: Translation performance (BLEU) across languages and merge operations. A figure showing chrF is provided in the Appendix.

and Finnish, respectively. However, German and Uzbek show a different picture, with BLEU/chrF differences of around 2-2.5 points for German and 4-9 points for Uzbek.

The impact of varying the number of merge operations varies and again bifurcates the set of languages. Finnish and Estonian seem to suffer slightly as the merge operations are increased (approx. -2 to -2.5 points in BLEU/chrF), whereas German and Uzbek seem to benefit from more merge operations (approx. +1 to +2 points in BLEU/chrF). We find this perplexing, as the German and Uzbek datasets are the largest and smallest used in our experiments.

To analyze these results, we fit a hierarchical, Bayesian linear model with language-specific effects for the BPE variant and number of merge operations:

$$\mu = \alpha^{(l)} + \beta_b^{(l)} + \gamma_m^{(l)} + \epsilon$$

where $\alpha^{(l)}$ is an intercept, $\beta_b^{(l)}$ is the effect of using BPE variant b, $\gamma_m^{(l)}$ is the effect of using m merge operations, and ϵ represents residual sampling error. All effects are specific to language l and are drawn from common prior distributions: $\alpha^{(l)} \sim \mathcal{N}(0, \sigma_\alpha^2)$, $\beta_b^{(l)} \sim \mathcal{N}(\bar{\beta}_b, \sigma_{\beta,b}^2)$ and $\gamma_m^{(l)} \sim \mathcal{N}(\bar{\gamma}_m, \sigma_{\gamma,m}^2)$. Since our model is hierarchical, we also infer posteriors for the language-independent effects of using each BPE variant/number of merge operations, $\bar{\beta}_b$ and $\bar{\gamma}_m$, as well as the standard deviations $\sigma_{\beta,b}^2$ and $\sigma_{\gamma,m}^2$ that quantify between-language variation in the BPE and merge effects. We set the priors of the average effects to $\mathcal{N}(0, 1)$ and those of the standard deviations to $\mathcal{N}^+(1)$, except for σ_α^2 for which we use the default $\mathcal{N}^+(s_\alpha)$, $s_\alpha \approx 68$ prior specified by the Bambi modeling library (Capretto et al., 2022) which we use to fit our model. We fit all our models using the No-U-Turn Sampler (Hoffman and Gelman, 2014). We run 4 Markov chains in parallel and draw 1,000 posterior samples from each chain. Prior to sampling, we also run each chain for 1,000 warm-up steps.

Table 2 shows a posterior mean point estimate for each effect of interest and quantifies their uncertainty using a 94% highest density interval (HDI). The effect sizes of randomized BPE variants seem confirm our experimental results. While the language-independent average effect sizes are all modest in magnitude, ranging from -0.97 for uniform BPE to +0.61 for standard BPE, there is substantial variation in the effect sizes when using uniform random sampling: effect sizes ranging from -6.65 for Uzbek to +0.26 for Estonian. Most importantly, the uncertainty intervals include zero for all languages and BPE types except for $\beta_{\text{Uniform, German}}$ and $\beta_{\text{Uniform, Uzbek}}$.

The effects for the number of merges are largely similar, with small average effects and between-language variation in effects on both sides of zero. While effect sizes tend to be very small for 2,000 and 5,000 merge operations, the effect varies with 32K merges. German and Uzbek seem to benefit from using 32K merge operations (posterior means 0.59 and 2.30, respectively). In contrast, Finnish and Estonian have significantly negative effect sizes (-1.83 and -1.31, respectively) with the entire 94% HDI for Finnish below zero as well.

Parameter	Mean	HDI (lower)	HDI (upper)	Incl. zero?
BPE effects (average)				
$\bar{\beta}_{\text{Standard}}$	0.61	-0.71	1.85	✓
$\bar{\beta}_{\text{Uniform}}$	-0.97	-2.57	0.58	✓
$\bar{\beta}_{\text{Random}}$	0.35	-0.92	1.68	✓
BPE effects (language-specific)				
$\beta_{\text{Standard, Estonian}}$	0.45	-1.00	1.86	✓
$\beta_{\text{Standard, Finnish}}$	0.47	-0.98	1.94	✓
$\beta_{\text{Standard, German}}$	0.57	-0.95	1.95	✓
$\beta_{\text{Standard, Uzbek}}$	1.26	-0.38	2.83	✓
$\beta_{\text{Random, Estonian}}$	0.39	-1.13	1.74	✓
$\beta_{\text{Random, Finnish}}$	0.43	-1.00	1.90	✓
$\beta_{\text{Random, German}}$	0.44	-0.92	1.89	✓
$\beta_{\text{Random, Uzbek}}$	0.26	-1.34	1.73	✓
$\beta_{\text{Uniform, Estonian}}$	0.26	-1.18	1.77	✓
$\beta_{\text{Uniform, Finnish}}$	-0.51	-2.05	0.94	✓
$\beta_{\text{Uniform, German}}$	-1.67	-3.04	-0.08	
$\beta_{\text{Uniform, Uzbek}}$	-6.65	-8.29	-5.01	
Merge effects (average)				
$\bar{\gamma}_{2000}$	0.10	-1.06	1.44	✓
$\bar{\gamma}_{5000}$	0.00	-1.24	1.21	✓
$\bar{\gamma}_{32000}$	-0.03	-1.44	1.39	✓
Merge effects (language-specific)				
$\gamma_{2000\text{, Estonian}}$	0.18	-1.11	1.59	✓
$\gamma_{2000\text{, Finnish}}$	0.33	-1.00	1.72	✓
$\gamma_{2000\text{, German}}$	-0.04	-1.40	1.28	✓
$\gamma_{2000\text{, Uzbek}}$	-0.04	-1.43	1.37	✓
$\gamma_{5000\text{, Estonian}}$	0.05	-1.29	1.41	✓
$\gamma_{5000\text{, Finnish}}$	-0.03	-1.39	1.26	✓
$\gamma_{5000\text{, German}}$	0.09	-1.18	1.48	✓
$\gamma_{5000\text{, Uzbek}}$	-0.08	-1.54	1.26	✓
$\gamma_{32000\text{, Estonian}}$	-1.31	-2.67	0.16	✓
$\gamma_{32000\text{, Finnish}}$	-1.83	-3.26	-0.44	
$\gamma_{32000\text{, German}}$	0.59	-0.82	1.96	✓
$\gamma_{32000\text{, Uzbek}}$	2.30	0.79	3.75	

Table 2: Posterior means and 94% posterior highest density intervals for the BLEU model.

5 Discussion

5.1 Limitations and future work

While our results suggest that randomized BPE segmentation algorithms have no consistent deleterious effect on BLEU/chrF across languages, it is possible that further experiments may find differently. There is room for exploration regarding randomization of the BPE algorithm. For example, instead of sampling from the set of observed symbol pairs, merge operations could be chosen by sampling two unigrams independently or using a temperature-augmented sampler.

Although we focus on morphologically rich languages, our experiments still utilize a moderate amount of training data. Many morphologically rich languages that we did not consider may also lack such resources and thus be more impacted by the choice of subword segmentation algorithm. We feel that future work should pay particular attention should to this intersection of morphological complexity and low-resourcedness.

5.2 Conclusion

We introduced two randomized variants of BPE with the expectation that they would have a negative effect on translation performance because the traditional greedy approach should result in better subwords. Instead, our results indicate that subword vocabularies created with randomized BPE yield translation models that perform comparably to those that use subwords created using the standard greedy BPE algorithm. Even when using uniform sampling, performance only degrades substantially for two of the languages we consider. This finding is corroborated by further analysis using a Bayesian linear model which suggests that the effect of uniform sampling is significantly different from zero for only German and Uzbek.

We find this negative result significant, as it suggests that variations on standard BPE can perform reasonably well. We emphasize, however, that it is not clear whether this holds universally, particularly when using Transformer architectures optimized for handling longer sequences or when working with extremely small amounts of training data. We hope that our negative result can motivate further research into the optimal use of subword segmentation algorithms, especially in the context of languages that are both morphologically rich and less-resourced, such as various Indigenous languages.

References

Tomás Capretto, Camen Piho, Ravin Kumar, Jacob Westfall, Tal Yarkoni, and Osvaldo A Martin. 2022. Bambi: A Simple Interface for Fitting Bayesian Linear Models in Python. *Journal of Statistical Software*, 103.

Kyunghyun Cho, Bart van Merriënboer, Caglar Gulcehre, Dzmitry Bahdanau, Fethi Bougares, Holger Schwenk, and Yoshua Bengio. 2014. Learning phrase representations using RNN encoder–decoder for statistical machine translation. In *Proceedings of the 2014 Conference on Empirical Methods in Natural Language Processing (EMNLP)*, pages 1724–1734, Doha, Qatar. Association for Computational Linguistics.

Thamme Gowda and Jonathan May. 2020. Finding the optimal vocabulary size for neural machine translation. In *Findings of the Association for Computa-*

tional Linguistics: EMNLP 2020, pages 3955–3964, Online. Association for Computational Linguistics.

Ximena Gutierrez-Vasques, Christian Bentz, Olga Sozinova, and Tanja Samardzic. 2021. From characters to words: the turning point of BPE merges. In *Proceedings of the 16th Conference of the European Chapter of the Association for Computational Linguistics: Main Volume*, pages 3454–3468, Online. Association for Computational Linguistics.

Barry Haddow, Nikolay Bogoychev, Denis Emelin, Ulrich Germann, Roman Grundkiewicz, Kenneth Heafield, Antonio Valerio Miceli Barone, and Rico Sennrich. 2018. The University of Edinburgh's submissions to the WMT18 news translation task. In *Proceedings of the Third Conference on Machine Translation: Shared Task Papers*, pages 399–409, Belgium, Brussels. Association for Computational Linguistics.

Xuanli He, Gholamreza Haffari, and Mohammad Norouzi. 2020. Dynamic programming encoding for subword segmentation in neural machine translation. In *Proceedings of the 58th Annual Meeting of the Association for Computational Linguistics*, pages 3042–3051, Online. Association for Computational Linguistics.

Matthew D. Hoffman and Andrew Gelman. 2014. The No-U-Turn Sampler: Adaptively Setting Path Lengths in Hamiltonian Monte Carlo. *J. Mach. Learn. Res.*, 15(1):1593–1623.

Taku Kudo. 2018. Subword regularization: Improving neural network translation models with multiple subword candidates. In *Proceedings of the 56th Annual Meeting of the Association for Computational Linguistics (Volume 1: Long Papers)*, pages 66–75, Melbourne, Australia. Association for Computational Linguistics.

Taku Kudo and John Richardson. 2018. SentencePiece: A simple and language independent subword tokenizer and detokenizer for neural text processing. In *Proceedings of the 2018 Conference on Empirical Methods in Natural Language Processing: System Demonstrations*, pages 66–71, Brussels, Belgium. Association for Computational Linguistics.

Thang Luong, Hieu Pham, and Christopher D. Manning. 2015. Effective approaches to attention-based neural machine translation. In *Proceedings of the 2015 Conference on Empirical Methods in Natural Language Processing*, pages 1412–1421, Lisbon, Portugal. Association for Computational Linguistics.

Sabrina J. Mielke, Zaid Alyafeai, Elizabeth Salesky, Colin Raffel, Manan Dey, Matthias Gallé, Arun Raja, Chenglei Si, Wilson Y. Lee, Benoît Sagot, and Samson Tan. 2021. Between words and characters: A brief history of open-vocabulary modeling and tokenization in NLP. *arXiv preprint 2112.10508*.

Jamshidbek Mirzakhalov, Anoop Babu, Aigiz Kunafin, Ahsan Wahab, Bekhzodbek Moydinboyev, Sardana Ivanova, Mokhiyakhon Uzokova, Shaxnoza Pulatova, Duygu Ataman, Julia Kreutzer, Francis Tyers, Orhan Firat, John Licato, and Sriram Chellappan. 2021. Evaluating multiway multilingual NMT in the Turkic languages. In *Proceedings of the Sixth Conference on Machine Translation*, pages 518–530, Online. Association for Computational Linguistics.

Kishore Papineni, Salim Roukos, Todd Ward, and Wei-Jing Zhu. 2002. Bleu: a method for automatic evaluation of machine translation. In *Proceedings of the 40th Annual Meeting of the Association for Computational Linguistics*, pages 311–318, Philadelphia, Pennsylvania, USA. Association for Computational Linguistics.

Maja Popović. 2015. chrF: character n-gram F-score for automatic MT evaluation. In *Proceedings of the Tenth Workshop on Statistical Machine Translation*, pages 392–395, Lisbon, Portugal. Association for Computational Linguistics.

Matt Post. 2018. A call for clarity in reporting BLEU scores. In *Proceedings of the Third Conference on Machine Translation: Research Papers*, pages 186–191, Brussels, Belgium. Association for Computational Linguistics.

Rico Sennrich, Barry Haddow, and Alexandra Birch. 2016. Neural machine translation of rare words with subword units. In *Proceedings of the 54th Annual Meeting of the Association for Computational Linguistics (Volume 1: Long Papers)*, pages 1715–1725, Berlin, Germany. Association for Computational Linguistics.

Rico Sennrich and Biao Zhang. 2019. Revisiting low-resource neural machine translation: A case study. In *Proceedings of the 57th Annual Meeting of the Association for Computational Linguistics*, pages 211–221, Florence, Italy. Association for Computational Linguistics.

Xinying Song, Alex Salcianu, Yang Song, Dave Dopson, and Denny Zhou. 2021. Fast WordPiece tokenization. In *Proceedings of the 2021 Conference on Empirical Methods in Natural Language Processing*, pages 2089–2103, Online and Punta Cana, Dominican Republic. Association for Computational Linguistics.

Ilya Sutskever, Oriol Vinyals, and Quoc V Le. 2014. Sequence to sequence learning with neural networks. In *Advances in Neural Information Processing Systems*, pages 3104–3112.

David Vilar and Marcello Federico. 2021. A statistical extension of byte-pair encoding. In *Proceedings of the 18th International Conference on Spoken Language Translation (IWSLT 2021)*, pages 263–275, Bangkok, Thailand (online). Association for Computational Linguistics.

Yonghui Wu, Mike Schuster, Zhifeng Chen, Quoc V. Le, Mohammad Norouzi, Wolfgang Macherey, Maxim Krikun, Yuan Cao, Qin Gao, Klaus Macherey, Jeff Klingner, Apurva Shah, Melvin Johnson, Xiaobing Liu, Łukasz Kaiser, Stephan Gouws, Yoshikiyo Kato, Taku Kudo, Hideto Kazawa, Keith Stevens, George Kurian, Nishant Patil, Wei Wang, Cliff Young, Jason Smith, Jason Riesa, Alex Rudnick, Oriol Vinyals, Greg Corrado, Macduff Hughes, and Jeffrey Dean. 2016. Google's neural machine translation system: Bridging the gap between human and machine translation. *arXiv preprint 1609.08144*.

A Additional Tables and Figures

Corpus statistics Table 3 shows relevant statistics for each translation dataset, including number of sentences, token and type counts, and type-to-token ratios.

Translation performance Figure 2 shows a visualization of translation performance in terms of BLEU and chrF across languages and number of merge operations.

Language	Split	Sentences	Tokens		Types		Type-to-token ratio	
			English	Non-English	English	Non-English	English	Non-English
Estonian	Train	1,856,236	32,850,284	27,221,588	361,245	713,970	0.01	0.03
	Dev	2,000	45,892	36,333	7,731	12,275	0.17	0.34
	Test	2,000	48,340	38,063	8,085	12,956	0.17	0.34
Finnish	Train	1,754,754	43,898,422	32,012,655	116,620	677,874	0.00	0.02
	Dev	1,500	34,251	24,617	6,251	10,005	0.18	0.41
	Test	1,370	29,183	21,142	5,761	8,958	0.20	0.42
German	Train	4,173,550	99,557,517	94,741,339	881,684	1,805,238	0.01	0.02
	Dev	3,000	67,807	66,412	9,778	12,859	0.14	0.19
	Test	3,003	70,620	66,081	10,607	14,053	0.15	0.21
Uzbek	Train	529,574	11,502,156	9,361,833	120,768	250,629	0.01	0.03
	Dev	2,500	52,963	42,701	8,312	13,847	0.16	0.32
	Test	2,500	54,061	43,945	8,349	13,265	0.15	0.30

Table 3: Counts of sentences, tokens and word types in our corpora.

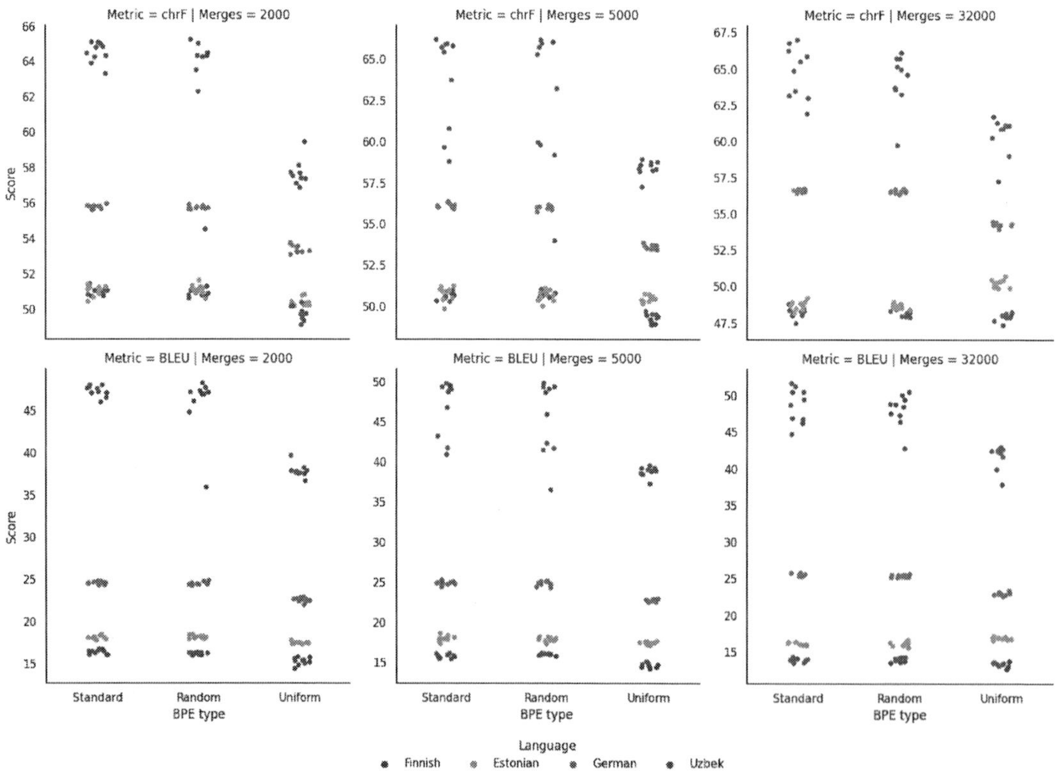

Figure 2: Translation performance across languages and numbers of merges using BLEU (top) and chrF (bottom).

Hiding in Plain Sight: Insights into Abstractive Text Summarization

Vivek Srivastava, Savita Bhat, Niranjan Pedanekar
TCS Research
Pune, Maharashtra, India
{srivastava.vivek2, savita.bhat, n.pedanekar}@tcs.com

Abstract

In recent years, there has been growing interest in the field of abstractive text summarization with focused contributions in relevant model architectures, datasets, and evaluation metrics. Despite notable research advances, previous works have identified certain limitations concerning the quality of datasets and the effectiveness of evaluation techniques for generated summaries. In this context, we examine these limitations further with the help of three quality measures, namely, *Information Coverage*, *Entity Hallucination*, and *Summarization Complexity*. As a part of this work, we investigate two widely used datasets (*XSUM* and *CNN-DM*) and three existing models (*BART*, *PEGASUS*, and *BRIO*) and report our findings. Some key insights are: 1) Cumulative ROUGE score is an inappropriate evaluation measure since few high-scoring samples dominate the overall performance, 2) Existing summarization models have limited capability for information coverage and hallucinate to generate factual information, and 3) Compared to the model-generated summaries, the reference summaries have lowest information coverage and highest entity hallucinations reiterating the need of new and better reference summaries.

ARTICLE: Andros Townsend enjoyed silencing the critics with his wonder strike for England, saying naysayers like Paul Merson provided the perfect motivation for him in Italy. This has been a topsy-turvy season for the 23-year-old, who has yet to reach the heights he scaled when he first burst onto the international scene. Three Lions manager Roy Hodgson has, however, kept faith with the Tottenham winger - belief he paid back in quite exceptional fashion at the Juventus Stadium. Andros Townsend scores England's equaliser in their 1-1 friendly draw with Italy in Turin on Tuesday night . Townsend celebrates his strike with Tottenham Hotspur team-mates Ryan Mason (left) and Kyle Walker .
REFERENCE SUMMARY: Andros Townsend scored the equaliser in England's 1-1 draw with Italy . Townsend tweeted to hit back at Paul Merson for his previous comments . Townsend has been been 'desperate' to silence his critics . Merson had slammed Townsend for his display against Man United .

Figure 1: Example from the CNN-DM dataset. The highlighted sentences in the reference summary contains facts missing from the source article.

1 Introduction

Abstractive text summarization (ATS) is the process of compressing given textual content into short and concise form by paraphrasing or rewriting the most important information from the source. Considering the high-level language understanding, reasoning, and generation capabilities required for ATS, considerable improvements are reported in this field with contributions such as large-scale datasets (Gliwa et al., 2019; Ladhak et al., 2020), use of innovative techniques/architectures (Liu and Liu, 2021), and novel evaluation metrics for effective validation. Recently, significant interest has been observed in examining the quality of summarization datasets (Tejaswin et al., 2021), reliability of evaluation metrics (Fabbri et al., 2021), architectural choices, and overall impact of these on model performance. In this paper, we re-evaluate the quality of textual content from summarization datasets and generated summaries with *Information Coverage*, *Entity Hallucination*, and *Summarization Complexity* as primary dimensions of evaluation.

Popular summarization datasets, XSUM (Narayan et al., 2018) and CNN-DM (Hermann et al., 2015; Nallapati et al., 2016) (see Table 1), are known to have major issues such as factual consistency (Maynez et al., 2020; Tam et al., 2022; Laban et al., 2022), low degree of summarization complexity (Tejaswin et al., 2021), and layout biases (Kryściński et al., 2019). Figure 1 shows an example where the reference summary contains the facts that are missing from the source article. The models trained on these datasets tend to pick up these limitations and thus are unreliable for any real-world application.

Among all reference-free (Vasilyev et al., 2020;

The Fourth Workshop on Insights from Negative Results in NLP, pages 67–74
May 5, 2023 ©2023 Association for Computational Linguistics

Dataset	Train/Val/Test	Description
XSUM	204k/11k/11k	BBC news articles (1 sentence summaries)
CNN-DM	287k/13k/11k	CNN & DailyMail news articles (3-4 sentences summaries)

Table 1: ATS datasets overview.

Gao et al., 2020) and reference-dependant (Zhang et al.; Zhao et al., 2019) metrics proposed to date, ROUGE (Lin, 2004) is preferred owing to its ease of interpretation, usage, and comparison with other baselines even though it misses out several quality evaluation dimensions such as factuality and informativeness (Bhandari et al., 2020; Pagnoni et al., 2021; Goyal et al., 2022; Deutsch and Roth, 2021; Akter et al., 2022).

In this paper, we examine two widely used datasets (XSUM and CNN-DM) and analyze the performance of three ATS models (BART (Lewis et al., 2020), PEGASUS (Zhang et al., 2020), and BRIO (Liu et al., 2022)) on three interpretable quality evaluation dimensions. In contrast to the similar existing works where the human-based evaluation with a very small subset of datasets is considered (Fabbri et al., 2021; Pagnoni et al., 2021), we present a computational framework for these dimensions. We believe that the framework is especially useful in reducing the dependence on human-based evaluation for the quality of the datasets and ATS models.

Model	XSUM			CNN-DM		
	R1	R2	RL	R1	R2	RL
BART	45.14	22.27	37.25	44.16	21.28	40.9
PEGASUS	47.21	24.56	39.25	44.17	21.47	41.11
BRIO	49.07	25.59	40.4	47.78	23.55	44.57

Table 2: Evaluation results on the ROUGE metric.

2 Quality Evaluation Dimensions

In this section, we define three dimensions for quality evaluation. We examine the performance of ATS models over these dimensions. We report the ROUGE-based performance of these models for comparison (see Table 2). We also explore the reference summaries on these dimensions. We denote model-generated zero-shot summary as zs, reference summary as ref, and article as A.

1. **Information coverage**: A high-quality summary highlights the information present in the source document. We explore the information coverage of a summary from two perspectives: topical coverage and key information coverage. In contrast to the naive word overlap between the generated and reference summaries in ROUGE, we consider an informed overlap of the summary with the source article in both formulations.

   Topical coverage (TC): An article usually discusses multiple aspects/topics to present facts and information (see Appendix). The ROUGE-based evaluation fails to measure the topical coverage of the generated summary. To examine this further, we divide the article A into a sequence of topics using the sentence similarity-based topic-segmentation algorithm, C99 (Choi, 2000). We select C99 due to the fast topic segmentation and flexibility to plug and play with different sentence representation models. We use the sentence BERT representations (Reimers and Gurevych, 2019) to segment the article into multiple topics. Each topic contains a sequential list of sentences. We consider a topic T from article A covered by the summary if at least k words from the summary[1] exist in T. Formally,

$$TC(zs, A, k) = 100 * \frac{f_{TC}(zs, A_{topics}, k)}{|A_{topics}|} \quad (1)$$

   where $f_{TC}(.)$ measures the number of topics covered by the summary (constrained by k).

   Key information coverage (KIC): A document summary, by definition, should cover the key information presented in the source document. We identify the key information in the source document using an unsupervised key-phrase extraction tool, YAKE (Campos et al., 2020)[2] (see Appendix). Formally, we define KIC as:

$$KIC(zs, A) = 100 * \frac{f_{KIC}(zs, A_{key-info})}{|A_{key-info}|} \quad (2)$$

   where $f_{KIC}(.)$ measures the number of key-phrases in A that exist in the summary.

2. **Entity hallucination** (EH): In Figure 1 (also see Appendix), we present an example where the summary contains the entities missing from the article A. We consider a model to be entity-hallucinated if it generates an entity missing from the article (Tam et al., 2022). We use an

[1] we preprocess the summary to remove stopwords using the gensim library: https://github.com/RaRe-Technologies/gensim

[2] based on our manual analysis, we set ngram-size as 4, dedup-lim as 0.5 and select the key-phrases with a score less than 0.1

18-class named-entity recognition module from spacy[3] to detect the entities. Formally,

$$EH(zs, A) = 100 * \frac{f_{EH}(zs_{entities}, A)}{|zs_{entities}|} \quad (3)$$

where $f_{EH}(.)$ measures the number of entities in the summary that are missing from the article.

3. **Summarization complexity**: We consider summarization complexity to be correlated with the measure of extractiveness in the samples. This complexity could potentially influence the model's performance. For instance, ATS models with a higher tendency to copy text fragments from the source document could achieve high ROUGE scores on samples where the reference summaries are more extractive. We examine this by using a phrase overlap (PO) based formulation. We define phrase overlap between the model-generated summary and the article as:

$$PO_{article}(zs, A, n) = 100 * \frac{|zs_n \cap A_n|}{|zs_n|} \quad (4)$$

Similarly, PO between the model-generated and reference summary is given as:

$$PO_{ref}(zs, ref, n) = 100 * \frac{|zs_n \cap ref_n|}{|zs_n|} \quad (5)$$

Here, zs_n, A_n, and ref_n denote the phrases containing n-tokens in the zero-shot summary, article, and reference summary respectively.

3 Analysis

In this section, we discuss the insights from each of these dimensions. In all our analyses, we divide the samples in the test set of both datasets into four groups. Each group contains 25% samples from the original test set sorted based on the ROUGE-L score. Group 1 (G1) contains samples with the lowest ROUGE-L score whereas group 4 (G4) contains samples with the highest ROUGE-L score. While reporting the results for the reference summary, we use the groups identified using the ROUGE-L ranking of samples with the BRIO model. We report the average scores for each group (see Tables 3 and 4 for information coverage, Table 5 for entity hallucinations, and Tables 6 and 7 for summarization complexity). Some key observations are:

Models trained on the CNN-DM dataset tends to show higher information coverage. This tendency could also be partially attributed to the longer and more extractive summaries generated with the CNN-DM dataset. The gap for topical coverage between both datasets widens further as we increase the value of k.

k	Model	XSUM				CNN-DM			
		G1	G2	G3	G4	G1	G2	G3	G4
1	BART	**76.47**	**81.04**	**81.82**	**81.97**	88.78	91.62	92.22	92.59
	PEG	73.19	79.47	79.68	80.23	87.25	90.78	91.59	91.73
	BRIO	76.96	80.95	81.42	81.34	**91**	**92.58**	**93.02**	**93.51**
	Ref	71.40	78.80	79.95	80.93	86.98	90.71	91.41	92.45
2	BART	54.19	60.24	61.35	**61.17**	79.65	84.23	85.07	85.99
	PEG	50.26	57.88	57.73	58.52	76.87	82.89	84.20	84.56
	BRIO	**54.52**	**60.08**	**59.88**	60.46	**84.02**	**86.40**	**87.47**	**87.94**
	Ref	47.13	56.36	57.55	59.12	75.66	82.14	84.25	85.61
5	BART	**13.31**	**14.91**	**16.03**	**14.80**	54.68	62.13	64.33	66.19
	PEG	11.24	13.16	13.09	12.79	50.86	59.95	62.77	63.58
	BRIO	13.30	14.79	15.33	14.63	**61.97**	**67.98**	**69.07**	**70.03**
	Ref	7.97	11.71	12.30	13.63	45.67	57.50	61.50	65.30

Table 3: Topical coverage on k = 1, 2, and 5. For each k, we highlight minimum TC and **maximum** TC for a group within a dataset. A higher TC is preferred.

Model	XSUM				CNN-DM			
	G1	G2	G3	G4	G1	G2	G3	G4
BART	11.69	**12.08**	11.82	**11.20**	37.55	42.55	44.11	46.54
PEG	**11.81**	11.79	11.15	10.59	33.95	39.18	41.71	43.88
BRIO	11.66	11.97	**11.91**	10.89	**42.36**	**45.75**	**47.63**	**49.62**
Ref	9.60	10.92	10.93	10.51	24.90	30.36	33.60	38.33

Table 4: Key information coverage. We highlight minimum KIC and **maximum** KIC for a group within a dataset. A higher KIC is preferred.

BART gives tough competition to BRIO. Although BRIO gets the highest TC and KIC score on the CNN-DM dataset, BART performs competitively. On the XSUM dataset, both models perform equally well. PEGASUS has the worst TC among all three models suggesting that the generated summaries with PEGASUS are limited in their capability to cover the overall source document.

We need new reference summaries! It is interesting to note that the reference summaries show worst KIC than all three models suggesting that the ATS model's capability to cover key information is limited due to training on these poor-quality reference summaries. Also, the topical coverage of reference summaries is significantly lower in G1 compared to other groups in both datasets, denoting the need for targeted analysis for this group.

Models trained on the XSUM dataset tend to show higher entity hallucination. EH is more prominent in the models trained on the XSUM dataset due to the inherent nature of the dataset (i.e., very high EH score of reference summaries), which calls for the need to look beyond word overlap-based metrics like ROUGE while training and evaluating the ATS models. Also, the high EH of reference summaries in both datasets is

[3] https://github.com/explosion/spacy-models/releases/tag/en_core_web_sm-3.5.0

concerning since it directly limits the capability of proposed techniques for ATS.

The ROUGE-based bench-marking of ATS models is inadequate. In addition to giving tough competition to BRIO for information coverage, BART consistently shows the least EH than the other two models. PEGASUS and BRIO have a similar degree of EH on both datasets (see class-wise EH distribution in Appendix). Low information coverage and high EH of PEGASUS compared to BART contradicts PEGASUS's superior behavior based on the ROUGE score (see Table 2). It reiterates the need for an alternative bench-marking of the ATS models.

Model	XSUM				CNN-DM			
	G1	G2	G3	G4	G1	G2	G3	G4
BART	36.52	**38.80**	**40.95**	**44.96**	**2.08**	**1.38**	**1.29**	**1.37**
PEG	**34.91**	40.36	45.12	48.22	5.87	5.53	5.49	4.91
BRIO	40.27	43.41	45.84	49.52	6.55	4.42	3.99	3.61
Ref	46.01	46.43	50.54	52.61	15.03	12.37	10.68	7.72

Table 5: Entity hallucinations. We highlight maximum EH and **minimum** EH for a group within a dataset. A lower EH is preferred.

Articles in the CNN-DM dataset are easier to summarize? The models trained on the CNN-DM dataset tend to copy text fragments from the source article, and this behavior is more prominent in high ROUGE scoring samples (i.e., G4). BART shows a very-high tendency to copy content from the article and manages to perform well on the ROUGE-based evaluation. It further highlights the extractive nature of the reference summaries in the CNN-DM dataset that guides the model to learn to copy content from the source document.

The tendency to be more abstractive is costly for BRIO! BRIO-generated summaries are more abstractive in nature, especially in the low ROUGE-scoring group G1. The significantly lower PO_{ref} score in this group compared to other groups results in a lower ROUGE score suggesting that the abstractiveness proves costly for BRIO.

ROUGE score is dominated by a few samples. For both the datasets, all models show a sharp increase in the PO_{ref} score as we move from G1 to G4 (see Table 7), suggesting that only a small proportion of samples contribute heavily towards the overall ROUGE score. The gap between the groups widens as we increase the phrase length.

XSUM and CNN-DM datasets are NOT the benchmark datasets for the ATS task. As discussed earlier, the reference summaries in the CNN-DM dataset are more extractive in nature. It is interesting to note that the extractive text summarization models built on this dataset show comparative performance to the ATS models (An et al., 2022). In contrast, the reference summaries in the XSUM dataset are more abstractive with a higher degree of hallucination, making them unsuitable for effective utilization.

n	Model	XSUM				CNN-DM			
		G1	G2	G3	G4	G1	G2	G3	G4
1	BART	64.94	64.72	64.18	62.28	94.74	94.94	94.77	95.16
	PEG	63.92	62.83	61.18	59.69	89.27	89.92	90.12	90.76
	BRIO	62.80	62.31	61.41	59.76	88.03	89.75	90.51	91.92
	Ref	**52.72**	**54.98**	**55.27**	**55.71**	**75.45**	**79.77**	**82.57**	**86.58**
2	BART	23.61	22.38	21.74	20.23	85.38	85.23	84.91	86.02
	PEG	24.80	21.40	19.34	17.93	74.59	74.59	74.84	77.03
	BRIO	20.99	19.79	19.06	17.86	61.72	65.48	68.05	72.92
	Ref	**11.44**	**13.15**	**13.48**	**14.66**	**32.82**	**38.91**	**44.45**	**54.53**
3	BART	9.82	8.13	7.79	7.18	77.40	76.72	76.07	77.76
	PEG	12.35	8.67	6.74	5.95	64.01	63.17	63.33	66.34
	BRIO	6.75	6.18	5.93	5.52	42.74	46.65	49.92	56.96
	Ref	**2.35**	**3.07**	**3.26**	**4.04**	**16.12**	**20.3**	**25.32**	**36.61**

Table 6: Phrase overlap with the article on n = 1, 2, and 3. For each n, we highlight **minimum** $PO_{article}$ and maximum $PO_{article}$ for a group within a dataset. A higher $PO_{article}$ suggests more extractive summaries.

n	Model	XSUM				CNN-DM			
		G1	G2	G3	G4	G1	G2	G3	G4
1	BART	24.99	37.21	46.74	63.28	22.40	32.11	39.17	51.01
	PEG	25.87	39.97	50.13	**68.43**	25.69	35.70	43.24	**56.23**
	BRIO	**27.46**	**40.64**	**50.50**	67.12	**27.95**	**37.27**	**43.68**	53.89
2	BART	4.81	12.76	22.05	42	5.41	11.01	16.89	30.02
	PEG	5.38	14.81	25.48	**48**	5.98	12.39	18.88	**33.79**
	BRIO	**6.18**	**15.53**	**25.44**	46.37	**7.75**	**13.68**	**19.01**	30.60
3	BART	0.95	4.68	11.28	29.40	1.93	5.11	9.32	20.97
	PEG	1.19	5.80	**13.93**	**35.03**	2.24	5.87	**10.57**	**23.99**
	BRIO	**1.47**	**6.50**	13.68	33.36	**2.86**	**6.35**	10.11	20.09

Table 7: Phrase overlap with the reference summary on n = 1, 2, and 3. For each n, we highlight minimum PO_{ref} and **maximum** PO_{ref} for a group within a dataset. A higher PO_{ref} suggests higher phrase overlap with the reference summary.

4 Conclusion

In this paper, we document our experiments on two widely used ATS datasets and three models trained on these datasets. We evaluate these on three dimensions of quality and demonstrate how the reported progress made in terms of the ROUGE metric is inconclusive. Our analysis shows that BART still shows competing behavior with current state-of-the-art models on various quality dimensions. We also highlight the need to carefully analyze the reference summaries in both datasets. Alternate evaluation metrics are required to account for different quality dimensions such as summarization complexity.

References

Mousumi Akter, Naman Bansal, and Shubhra Kanti Karmaker. 2022. Revisiting automatic evaluation of extractive summarization task: Can we do better than rouge? In *Findings of the Association for Computational Linguistics: ACL 2022*, pages 1547–1560.

Chenxin An, Ming Zhong, Zhiyong Wu, Qin Zhu, Xuanjing Huang, and Xipeng Qiu. 2022. Colo: A contrastive learning based re-ranking framework for one-stage summarization. *arXiv preprint arXiv:2209.14569*.

Manik Bhandari, Pranav Narayan Gour, Atabak Ashfaq, and Pengfei Liu. 2020. Metrics also disagree in the low scoring range: Revisiting summarization evaluation metrics. In *Proceedings of the 28th International Conference on Computational Linguistics*, pages 5702–5711.

Ricardo Campos, Vítor Mangaravite, Arian Pasquali, Alípio Jorge, Célia Nunes, and Adam Jatowt. 2020. Yake! keyword extraction from single documents using multiple local features. *Information Sciences*, 509:257–289.

Freddy YY Choi. 2000. Advances in domain independent linear text segmentation. In *1st Meeting of the North American Chapter of the Association for Computational Linguistics*.

Daniel Deutsch and Dan Roth. 2021. Understanding the extent to which content quality metrics measure the information quality of summaries. In *Proceedings of the 25th Conference on Computational Natural Language Learning*, pages 300–309.

Alexander R Fabbri, Wojciech Kryściński, Bryan McCann, Caiming Xiong, Richard Socher, and Dragomir Radev. 2021. Summeval: Re-evaluating summarization evaluation. *Transactions of the Association for Computational Linguistics*, 9:391–409.

Yang Gao, Wei Zhao, and Steffen Eger. 2020. Supert: Towards new frontiers in unsupervised evaluation metrics for multi-document summarization. In *Proceedings of the 58th Annual Meeting of the Association for Computational Linguistics*, pages 1347–1354.

Bogdan Gliwa, Iwona Mochol, Maciej Biesek, and Aleksander Wawer. 2019. Samsum corpus: A human-annotated dialogue dataset for abstractive summarization. In *Proceedings of the 2nd Workshop on New Frontiers in Summarization*, pages 70–79.

Tanya Goyal, Junyi Jessy Li, and Greg Durrett. 2022. News summarization and evaluation in the era of gpt-3. *arXiv preprint arXiv:2209.12356*.

Karl Moritz Hermann, Tomas Kocisky, Edward Grefenstette, Lasse Espeholt, Will Kay, Mustafa Suleyman, and Phil Blunsom. 2015. Teaching machines to read and comprehend. *Advances in neural information processing systems*, 28.

Wojciech Kryściński, Nitish Shirish Keskar, Bryan McCann, Caiming Xiong, and Richard Socher. 2019. Neural text summarization: A critical evaluation. In *Proceedings of the 2019 Conference on Empirical Methods in Natural Language Processing and the 9th International Joint Conference on Natural Language Processing (EMNLP-IJCNLP)*, pages 540–551.

Philippe Laban, Tobias Schnabel, Paul N Bennett, and Marti A Hearst. 2022. Summac: Re-visiting nli-based models for inconsistency detection in summarization. *Transactions of the Association for Computational Linguistics*, 10:163–177.

Faisal Ladhak, Esin Durmus, Claire Cardie, and Kathleen Mckeown. 2020. Wikilingua: A new benchmark dataset for cross-lingual abstractive summarization. In *Findings of the Association for Computational Linguistics: EMNLP 2020*, pages 4034–4048.

Mike Lewis, Yinhan Liu, Naman Goyal, Marjan Ghazvininejad, Abdelrahman Mohamed, Omer Levy, Veselin Stoyanov, and Luke Zettlemoyer. 2020. Bart: Denoising sequence-to-sequence pre-training for natural language generation, translation, and comprehension. In *Proceedings of the 58th Annual Meeting of the Association for Computational Linguistics*, pages 7871–7880.

Chin-Yew Lin. 2004. Rouge: A package for automatic evaluation of summaries. In *Text summarization branches out*, pages 74–81.

Yixin Liu and Pengfei Liu. 2021. Simcls: A simple framework for contrastive learning of abstractive summarization. In *Proceedings of the 59th Annual Meeting of the Association for Computational Linguistics and the 11th International Joint Conference on Natural Language Processing (Volume 2: Short Papers)*, pages 1065–1072.

Yixin Liu, Pengfei Liu, Dragomir Radev, and Graham Neubig. 2022. Brio: Bringing order to abstractive summarization. In *Proceedings of the 60th Annual Meeting of the Association for Computational Linguistics (Volume 1: Long Papers)*, pages 2890–2903.

Joshua Maynez, Shashi Narayan, Bernd Bohnet, and Ryan McDonald. 2020. On faithfulness and factuality in abstractive summarization. In *Proceedings of the 58th Annual Meeting of the Association for Computational Linguistics*, pages 1906–1919.

Ramesh Nallapati, Bowen Zhou, Cicero dos Santos, Çağlar Gulçehre, and Bing Xiang. 2016. Abstractive text summarization using sequence-to-sequence rnns and beyond. In *Proceedings of the 20th SIGNLL Conference on Computational Natural Language Learning*, pages 280–290.

Shashi Narayan, Shay B Cohen, and Mirella Lapata. 2018. Don't give me the details, just the summary! topic-aware convolutional neural networks for extreme summarization. In *Proceedings of the 2018 Conference on Empirical Methods in Natural Language Processing*, pages 1797–1807.

Artidoro Pagnoni, Vidhisha Balachandran, and Yulia Tsvetkov. 2021. Understanding factuality in abstractive summarization with frank: A benchmark for factuality metrics. In *Proceedings of the 2021 Conference of the North American Chapter of the Association for Computational Linguistics: Human Language Technologies*, pages 4812–4829.

Nils Reimers and Iryna Gurevych. 2019. Sentence-bert: Sentence embeddings using siamese bert-networks. In *Proceedings of the 2019 Conference on Empirical Methods in Natural Language Processing and the 9th International Joint Conference on Natural Language Processing (EMNLP-IJCNLP)*, pages 3982–3992.

Derek Tam, Anisha Mascarenhas, Shiyue Zhang, Sarah Kwan, Mohit Bansal, and Colin Raffel. 2022. Evaluating the factual consistency of large language models through summarization. *arXiv preprint arXiv:2211.08412*.

Priyam Tejaswin, Dhruv Naik, and Pengfei Liu. 2021. How well do you know your summarization datasets? In *Findings of the Association for Computational Linguistics: ACL-IJCNLP 2021*, pages 3436–3449.

Oleg Vasilyev, Vedant Dharnidharka, and John Bohannon. 2020. Fill in the blanc: Human-free quality estimation of document summaries. In *Proceedings of the First Workshop on Evaluation and Comparison of NLP Systems*, pages 11–20.

Jingqing Zhang, Yao Zhao, Mohammad Saleh, and Peter Liu. 2020. Pegasus: Pre-training with extracted gap-sentences for abstractive summarization. In *International Conference on Machine Learning*, pages 11328–11339. PMLR.

Tianyi Zhang, Varsha Kishore, Felix Wu, Kilian Q Weinberger, and Yoav Artzi. Bertscore: Evaluating text generation with bert. In *International Conference on Learning Representations*.

Wei Zhao, Maxime Peyrard, Fei Liu, Yang Gao, Christian M Meyer, and Steffen Eger. 2019. Moverscore: Text generation evaluating with contextualized embeddings and earth mover distance. In *Proceedings of the 2019 Conference on Empirical Methods in Natural Language Processing (EMNLP)*.

Topic 1: The security forces are reported to have used tear gas against stone-throwing protesters.

Topic 2: They also surrounded the hometown of Burhan Wani, 22, who was killed fighting Indian troops last year. Separately seven people are reported to have been killed in shelling across the Line of Control that divides Indian and Pakistani-administered Kashmir. Officials on the Pakistani side told Reuters that five people died in Indian shelling, while Indian officials say two people were killed by Pakistani fire.

Topic 3: There has been an armed revolt in the Muslim-majority region against rule by India since 1989, although violence has waned in recent years. The disputed region is claimed by both India and Pakistan in its entirety. India blames Pakistan for fuelling the unrest, a claim denied by Islamabad.

Topic 4: Burhan Wani is credited with reviving the image of militancy in Muslim-majority Indian-administered Kashmir, becoming a figurehead for young people. Saturday's violence started as people tried to walk to his home in Tral - where he died in a shootout with the army last July. His death led to a wave of protests during which dozens of people were killed.

Topic 5: The Indian authorities imposed heavy restrictions in the Kashmir valley for the anniversary, stopping internet access and sealing off Tral. There have also been reports of army personnel being injured in a militant attack overnight on Friday.

Figure 2: Example from the XSUM dataset. The article is segmented into five topics. Topic 1: Opening remark, Topic 2: Current situation on the incident, Topic 3: Background on India-Pakistan relationship, Topic 4: Background on the incident, Topic 5: Closing remark.

ARTICLE: Four years after becoming the youngest first-class cricketer in county history, Yorkshire's Barney Gibson has retired from the sport. The Leeds-born wicketkeeper entered the record books in 2011 when he lined up against Durham University just 27 days after his 15th birthday. But that match proved to be his only appearance at senior level and he never again progressed from the second XI. Ben Gibson, pictured at the age of 15, has decided to retire from cricket just four years after his debut . The 19-year-old said it was a 'difficult decision' to retire from cricket at such a young age . In his last game for the second string he did not bat or keep wicket, instead sending down 3.3 overs for 29 runs. 'This was a difficult decision to make,' the 19-year-old said. 'I would like to thank the players and staff at Yorkshire for their support. I have been involved with the club since I was 11 and I feel that now is the right time for me to look at a career change. 'The support from my parents has been tremendous and I would like to thank Ralph Middlebrook at Pudsey Congs Cricket Club and England coach Paul Farbrace, who I had close working relationships with.' Yorkshire's director of cricket development Ian Dews, said: 'Everyone at the club wishes Barney well. It is very much his decision. We hope that the next chapter in his life is very successful.'

REFERENCE SUMMARY: Barney Gibson became the youngest first-class cricketer in 2011 . The Yorkshire wicketkeeper made his debut shortly at 15 . Gibson said it was a 'difficult decision' to retire from the game .

KEY-PHRASES: retired from the sport, cricketer in county history, youngest first-class cricketer, first-class cricketer in county, Yorkshire Barney Gibson, Barney Gibson has retired, Pudsey Congs Cricket Club, Durham University, Leeds-born wicketkeeper entered, England coach Paul Farbrace, Ralph Middlebrook at Pudsey, cricket development Ian Dews, lined up against Durham, cricket, wicketkeeper entered the record, entered the record books, difficult decision, Gibson

Figure 3: Example from the CNN-DM dataset. We highlight the key-phrase containing segments in the article. The key-phrases gives an overall idea about the important discussion points in the article.

ARTICLE: The Belgium international, 24, changed the game from the bench but fell awkwardly in injury time. His agent Patrick de Koster initially said De Bruyne would miss six weeks. But, after seeing a specialist, the £55m former Wolfsburg player said: "I'll be out for around 10 weeks." De Bruyne could miss up to 13 league and cup games, including the League Cup final with Liverpool on 28 February, both legs of the Champions League last-16 tie with Dynamo Kiev and the Manchester derby on 20 March. The Belgian is City's second top goalscorer with 12 this season, four behind striker Sergio Aguero. De Koster added: "Kevin told me the only thing he can do is work hard and come back. Kevin is sad. His dream is to always be playing football." De Bruyne scored one goal and set up another to help City to a 4-3 aggregate victory over the Toffees. Everton goalkeeper Joel Robles, who repeatedly tried to lift up De Bruyne as he lay injured, used social media to say sorry. "I would like to apologise to Kevin de Bruyne for my reaction to his injury," said the 25-year-old Spaniard. "In the heat of the moment I didn't realise he was badly hurt. I wish him all the best and a speedy recovery.
REFERENCE SUMMARY: Manchester City midfielder Kevin de Bruyne says he will be out for about 10 weeks after injuring his right knee during Wednesday's League Cup semi-final victory over Everton.

BART: Manchester City midfielder Kevin de Bruyne will be out for at least 10 weeks after injuring his ankle in Tuesday's Champions League win over Everton.

PEGASUS: Manchester City midfielder Kevin de Bruyne will be out for up to 10 weeks with the ankle injury he suffered in Tuesday's Capital One Cup win over Everton.

BRIO: Manchester City midfielder Kevin de Bruyne will be out for around 10 weeks after fracturing a bone in his right foot in the Capital One Cup win over Everton.

Figure 4: Example from the XSUM dataset. We underline the identified entities and highlight the entities with red that are missing from the source article.

	XSUM				CNN-DM			
	BART	PEGASUS	BRIO	Ref	BART	PEGASUS	BRIO	Ref
GPE	**24.34**	26.48	28.12	30.05	**0.58**	1.5	4.25	5.26
PERSON	**63.69**	63.7	66.28	67.32	**1.96**	9.41	24.4	8.44
ORG	**39.09**	40.85	45.66	45.97	**2.05**	8.5	18.39	10.92
DATE	**61.69**	66.06	67.76	76.71	**1.58**	2.88	5.78	18.71
CARDINAL	**42.17**	46.47	49.54	57.35	**0.31**	0.9	1.28	11.1
EVENT	**57.34**	60.21	62.16	58.8	**4.61**	11.45	23.53	17.49
LOC	**32.35**	38.05	44.4	46.74	**1.15**	2.69	15.56	10.36
ORDINAL	**34.57**	41.07	41.19	48.63	**0.63**	1.29	1.09	11.7
WORK_OF_ART	**38.71**	45.97	42.96	46.77	8.36	24.84	-	25.26
NORP	**26.64**	29.18	29.41	34.55	**0.9**	0.93	6.44	9.69
MONEY	**70.78**	72.61	77.07	86.21	**0.91**	1.57	2.79	16.84
PRODUCT	**25.42**	28.07	27.13	36.5	**0.24**	10.29	13.79	11.94
PERCENT	74.74	**67.44**	73.33	84.17	32.4	**25.0**	36.07	73.66
TIME	51.59	**50.0**	56.93	84.3	**3.08**	3.47	8.68	28.29
FAC	**54.79**	60.96	58.89	61.98	**2.97**	20.53	38.46	12.62
QUANTITY	**52.0**	69.23	77.42	94.38	1.38	**0.92**	3.11	20.18
LANGUAGE	12.5	-	12.5	44.44	-	-	27.78	10.1
LAW	66.67	**60.0**	69.05	70.83	**5.43**	34.07	20.0	35.48

Table 8: Class-wise EH distribution. We highlight maximum EH and **minimum EH** for an entity class within a dataset.

Annotating PubMed Abstracts with MeSH Headings using Graph Neural Network

Faizan E Mustafa
QUIBIQ GmbH
faizan.e.mustafa@quibiq.de

Rafika Boutalbi
Universität Stuttgart
boutalbi.rafika@gmail.com

Anastasiia Iurshina
Universität Stuttgart
anastasiia.iurshina@ipvs.uni-stuttgart.de

Abstract

The number of scientific publications in the biomedical domain is continuously increasing with time. An efficient system for indexing these publications is required to make the information accessible according to the user's information needs. Task 10a of the BioASQ challenge aims to classify PubMed articles according to the MeSH ontology so that new publications can be grouped with similar preexisting publications in the field without the assistance of time-consuming and costly annotations by human annotators. In this work, we use Graph Neural Network (GNN) in the link prediction setting to exploit potential graph-structured information present in the dataset which could otherwise be neglected by transformer-based models. Additionally, we provide error analysis and a plausible reason for the substandard performance achieved by GNN. The source code is available on the GitHub.[1]

1 Introduction

Many scientific publications are available on the internet, and the number of publications is continuously increasing with time. The digital library PubMed[2] currently consists of 33 million citations and is based on the medical database MEDLINE. The articles available on PubMed are indexed with concepts that come from the Medical Subject Headings (MeSH) ontology. The human and financial effort needed to keep up with the rapid pace of development is steadily increasing (You et al., 2020). There was a 5% increase in the number of citations in 2018 for MEDLINE. Moreover, these citations are manually indexed with MeSH headings, which cost $9.4 per citation on average.

A large-scale biomedical semantic indexing task (10a) in the BioASQ[3] challenge is designed to help develop systems that can automatically index PubMed publications using headings from the MeSH ontology[4]. The fact that a publication can be assigned more than one MeSH heading makes it a multi-label classification task. Additionally, there are approximately 30k MeSH headings which makes it an extreme multi-label classification task.

GNN has been shown to achieve unprecedented performance on the benchmarks of link prediction and recommender systems (Ying et al.). A considerable amount of real-world datasets contains latent graph-structured information that could be effectively exploited to improve performance by modeling the task as a graph-related task. The models proposed in previous versions of the BioASQ challenge do not formulate the problem as GNN modeling, which can curtail the performance gain due to the omission of crucial graph-structured information present in the dataset.

Task 10a of the BioASQ challenge is to assign MeSH headings to PubMed articles based on the title and abstract of each article. In this work, we work on the following points to solve the problem.

- We formulate the problem as GNN link prediction task to improve the performance by utilizing the information present in the graph structure.
- We provide error analysis and highlight limitations of the GNN model in order to understand the potential reasons for its inability to perform better than the baseline.

2 Literature Review

The methods used for the task in the previous versions of the BioASQ challenge can be classified into three categories (You et al., 2020). The first category named *Binary relevance* consists of models such as MetaLabeler (Tsoumakas et al., 2013)

[1]GitHub Repository
[2]PubMed Website
[3]BioASQ Website
[4]MeSH Tree View

The Fourth Workshop on Insights from Negative Results in NLP, pages 75–81
May 5, 2023

which uses linear SVMs in a one vs all multi-label classification setting to select the most probable MeSH headings. The second category consists of models like DeepMesh (Peng et al., 2016) and MeSH Now (Mao and Lu, 2017) which rely on the widely used Information Retrieval technique named *Learning to Rank* in order to obtain the most relevant MeSH headings. The final category is based on *Deep Learning* e.g. MeSHProbeNet (Xun et al., 2019) and AttentionMeSH (Jin et al., 2018) which uses RNN and attention mechanism to get the most probable MeSH headings.

Most teams in the 2021 version of the BioASQ challenge relied on contextualized language models, such as BERT (Devlin et al., 2019). The top performing model BERTMeSH You et al. (2020) also uses BERT as a foundational model.

3 Methodolgy

Our proposed GNN model is implemented in the link prediction setting consisting of two modules, namely, *Document Embedding Module* and *Link Prediction Module*.

3.1 Document Embedding Module

We use Sentence-BERT Reimers and Gurevych (2019) to create embedding for the abstract of an article (article embedding). Sentence-BERT is used to make embeddings for the MeSH headings (heading embedding) also by using the "Scope Note". An example of the MeSH heading named *Adult* is shown in Figure 1. Both article and heading embeddings can then be used to initialize the GNN model nodes in the *Link Prediction Module*.

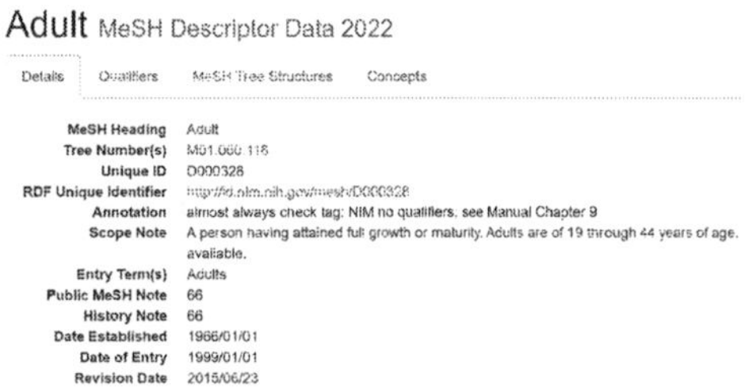

Figure 1: Metadata for heading *Adult*

3.2 Link Prediction Module

Each article is annotated with MeSH headings by the human annotators. The task is to build a model that can predict MeSH headings for new unannotated articles. We formulate the problem as a link prediction between the article and heading nodes in a graph. A GNN model will be used in an inductive setting Veličković et al. (2018) to predict existence/non-existence of links between articles and MeSH headings.

The proposed GNN model consists of an encoder and a decoder. We use SAGEConv layer of the GraphSAGE Hamilton et al. (2017) to create our model. The encoder takes a graph which has two types of nodes, namely, article nodes and the heading nodes initialized by the corresponding embedding obtained from *Document Embedding Module* as described in the previous section. In inductive learning, we need to have three distinct graphs for training, validation, and test sets as described in the section 3.3. The edges in the graph are split into *message-passing* and *supervision* edges. Message-passing edges are used to update the node's embedding using neighborhood aggregation, whereas the existence/non-existence of link should be predicted for supervision edges. The output of the encoder is a graph with new low-dimensional embeddings obtained by using neighborhood aggregation based on message-passing edges. The updated node embedding x'_i for a node i is obtained using neighborhood aggregation as follows

$$x'_i = W_1 x_i + W_2 \cdot \text{mean}_{j \in \mathcal{N}(i)} x_j \qquad (1)$$

Where W_1 and W_2 are trainable parameters, x_i the current node embedding for node i and $\mathcal{N}(i)$ are neighbors of node i.

In order to determine if there is a link between two nodes x_i and x_j as specified by the supervision edges, the decoder uses the inner product between the node's output embeddings followed by a sigmoid activation function.

$$\sigma(x_i \cdot x_j) = \frac{1}{1 + e^{-x_i \cdot x_j}} \qquad (2)$$

The result of sigmoid indicates a presence or absence of a link between two nodes of the supervision edges.

3.3 Graphs Construction

We have described the training, validation and test graphs in Table 1. All graphs have the same number of headings nodes, but they differ in the number of article nodes. An edge between the article and the heading node can be made if the article is annotated with a particular MeSH heading. The edges which are present in the graphs are referred to as positive

Graph	Edge Type	Description
Train	Message-passing	60% of positive train edges
	Supervision	40% of positive train edges + negative edges
Validation	Message-passing	"Borrowed graph" edges
	Supervision	All possible validation edges
Test	Message-passing	"Borrowed graph" edges
	Supervision	All possible test edges

Table 1: Description of edge types for data splits.

edges. We can split the positive edges into message-passing and supervision edges according to some ratio, e.g. 60/40. We split the positive edges for train graph. However, the test set will not have any edges which could be split, as there are no links between articles and MeSH headings. The lack of message-passing edges is problematic because the GNN model needs them for neighborhood aggregation. This could be handled by making edges between all articles and MeSH headings and using them as message-passing and supervision edges. However, the fact that the message-passing edges should be the correct edges and not randomly created will result in a nonrobust model. Therefore, we extract a sub-graph from the train graph named "borrowed graph" by randomly selecting some articles nodes in the train graph. The number of articles nodes to be extracted is treated like a hyper-parameter (40k in our case). As the heading nodes in all the graphs are similar, and we know the correct edges between article and heading nodes in "borrowed graph", we can add it to the test graph so that we have correct edges from "borrowed graph" which could be used as message-passing edges.

In the test graph, the supervision edges are all possible edges between the article nodes of test set and heading nodes. In addition to positive edges in the train graph, supervision edges also contain randomly sampled negative edges, i.e. edges which are not present in the graph. They are included in order to improve the ability of the model in terms of preventing false positive predictions.

4 Dataset

The dataset provided by the organizers of the 2022 version of the BioASQ challenge for task 10a is composed of articles obtained from PubMed. The training dataset consists of 16,218,838 articles and 29,681 distinct MeSH headings. MeSH headings are the concepts that are part of the MeSH ontology, which makes it easy to index and search medical and health-related information. Each article is assigned 12.68 MeSH headings on average. Each human-annotated MeSH heading has a unique ID assigned to it, which needs to be predicted for each article. An example of the MeSH heading named *Adult* is shown in Figure 1 where the heading is described by "Scope Note". The test set provided by the challenge organizers for the first week containing 9659 samples is used for testing.

Figure 2: MeSH hierarchy for *Glucocorticoids*

MeSH headings are categorized into 16 categories, which are further divided into subcategories. Each subcategory has a hierarchical depth of up to 13 where headings are organized from general to specific[5]. One important property of the MeSH hierarchy is that it is a graph instead of a tree. In a tree, each node can have only one parent, which does not hold true in the case of the MeSH hierarchy. Figure 2 shows that the MeSH heading named *Glucocorticoids* has 2 parent nodes, namely *Adrenal Cortex Hormones* and *Hormones*.

5 Experimental Setup

Taking into consideration the large size of the dataset, 70k articles are randomly sampled from the original training set to be used as the training set. Additionally, the validation set of 10k samples is sampled from the original training set. The random sampling of a small subset of articles could lead to a training dataset that has a considerably different distribution than the original dataset, resulting in non-generalizable results. We tried to mitigate that by sampling the training articles using the MeSH ontology, which is described further in Appendix A. However, there was no improvement observed over the random sampling. Therefore, we report results on randomly sampled training data to keep the method intelligible.

[5]MeSH Tree Structures

		P_{micro}	R_{micro}	$F1_{micro}$
BERTMeSH	Val	0.584	0.397	0.473
	Test	0.628	0.399	0.488

Table 2: Results obtained for BERTMeSH

Loss Function	Train	Valid	Test
Binary Cross Entropy	$\begin{bmatrix} 1018551(TN) & 31449(FP) \\ 45900(FN) & 244452(TP) \end{bmatrix}$	$\begin{bmatrix} 2035800 & 74610 \\ 204 & 1086 \end{bmatrix}$	$\begin{bmatrix} 2033029 & 77574 \\ 155 & 942 \end{bmatrix}$
Focal Loss	$\begin{bmatrix} 1041248 & 8752 \\ 116308 & 174044 \end{bmatrix}$	$\begin{bmatrix} 2089116 & 21294 \\ 551 & 739 \end{bmatrix}$	$\begin{bmatrix} 2081154 & 29449 \\ 392 & 705 \end{bmatrix}$

Table 3: Results reported as confusion matrix for GNN

The best-performing model of the 2021 version of BioASQ challenge is used as a baseline model. The model is trained for 5 epochs with an initial learning rate of 1e-5 which is altered using the learning rate scheduling function *get_cosine_schedule_with_warmup* from transformers library (Wolf et al., 2020).

Unlike BERTMeSH, the results on validation and test datasets for GNN are based on only the first 100 articles of both datasets, for computational resource reasons (test graphs for the remaining articles can be made for evaluation as explained in section 3.3). The architecture of GNN is composed of 2 SAGEConv layers where the input, hidden and output dimensions are 768, 256, 128 respectively. GNN is trained with a learning rate of 0.005 and Adam optimizer Kingma and Ba (2015) with the default hyperparameters. Two models are trained using different loss functions, namely, Binary Cross Entropy and Focal Loss. The hyperparameters used for Focal Loss are $\alpha = 0.2$ and $\gamma = 0.2$.

6 Results

Table 2 shows the results obtained for BERTMEsH on micro-averaged precision, recall, and f1 score. The model was able to score 0.488 f1 score. The results for GNN are reported as a confusion matrix in Table 3 because the f1 score is very low and is, therefore, not helpful in understanding the results. When Binary Cross Entropy is used as a loss criterion, the number of FN predictions (155) is considerably low as desired. However, the number of FP predictions is large. In the case of Focal loss, the loss criterion helps to reduce the number of FP predictions from 77574 to 29449 for the test dataset. However, the number of FN predictions increased from 155 to 392 accordingly.

7 Error Analysis

The results obtained using the focal loss indicate that the number of False Positive predictions can be improved using methods that give more importance to hard negatives. The negative edges which are difficult to discern from the positive edges are called hard negatives. Therefore, we assumed that the creation of hard negative samples improves the FP results and used *Dynamic Random Sampling* Zhang et al. (2013) and *mixup* Zhang et al. (2018) to add hard negatives during the training process instead of randomly sampling negative edges.

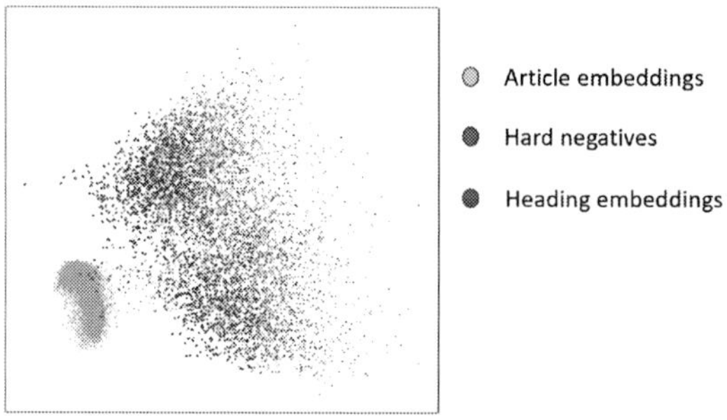

Figure 3: Hard negatives created using Dynamic negative sampling

For Dynamic Random Sampling, we start adding the hard negatives after second epoch. For each article, 5 random negatives and up to 10 hard negatives are added. Negative edges for which the dot product is too high (FP) are ignored in order to avoid the hardest negatives. To this end, negative edges which have dot product between 0.6 and 0.95 are considered hard negatives. The 2-dimensional representation of the embeddings obtained at the output layer of GNN model is shown in Figure 3. It can be observed that the hard negatives are closer to article embeddings in vector space as compared to the embeddings of remaining headings. To empirically verify our observation, we calculated the cosine similarity between the mean of article embeddings and the mean of hard negatives, which turns out to be -0.14. Similarly, a cosine similarity of -0.75 was obtained between the mean of article embeddings and heading embeddings. Although the model correctly selects the hard negatives as indicated by cosine similarity, the results obtained on the evaluation metrics do not surpass the results obtained using Focal Loss only.

The second approach *mixup* uses a linear interpolation of the positive and negative samples to create hard negatives. The following equation is used to linearly interpolate article embedding e_p and heading embedding e_n to create hard negative e_h.

$$e_h = \lambda e_p + (1 - \lambda) e_n \tag{3}$$

We set λ equal to 0.9 for the experimentation. This approach also yields no improvements over the results obtained using Focal Loss only.

8 GNN Limitations

Although GNN has improved performance on many tasks which benefit from graph-structured data, the architecture of GNN has some inherent limitations. One of the problems that Neural Networks has is that the performance is decreased as the number of layers is increased. The vanishing gradient coerces us to limit the number of layers, resulting in a shallow network that is not able to generalize. In addition to the vanishing gradient problem, the GNN model is limited to a small number of layers due to over-smoothing. Li et al. (2018) have shown that the convolution operation of GNN is the source of its predictive power, but is also the cause of its limitation. They proved that the convolution operation of GNN is a kind of Laplacian smoothing, which helps to learn new embedding from the neighboring nodes. However, the repeated application of Laplacian smoothing results in the features of all nodes being identical, which deteriorates the predictive power of the model. As the number of layers increased, the nodes in the graph increasingly have similar neighbors to update their embeddings, resulting in identical nodes.

The architecture of GNN has another limitation, named over-squashing. GNN is less effective on tasks that benefit from long-distance interactions. Equation 1 shows a node update using neighborhood aggregation for a particular layer. It can be seen that as the number of layers increases, the receptive field also grows exponentially. Therefore, the need for the model to encode information from long-distance neighbors creates a bottleneck because the model tries to cram too much information into a single vector. Alon and Yahav (2021) has shown that the information from exponentially growing k-hop neighbors for a k-layer GNN can not be crammed into a single vector representation, which results in low performance for tasks that require long-distance information. Figure 4 illustrates the bottleneck while updating a node's feature representation based on its 3-hop neighbors.

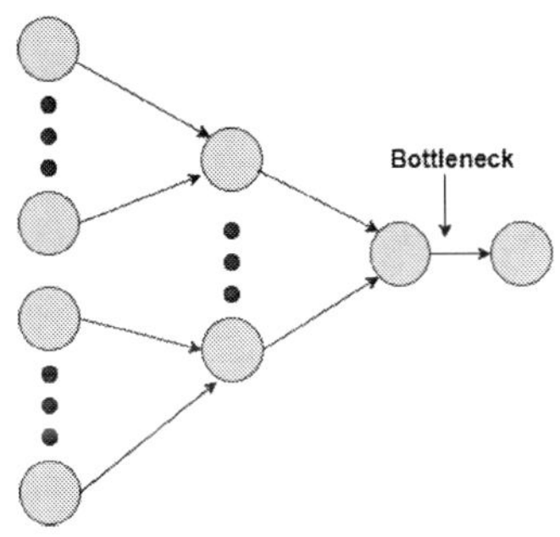

Figure 4: GNN Bottleneck (adapted from Alon and Yahav (2021)). Dots represent arbitrary number of nodes.

Additionally, the degree distribution of our bipartite graph follows a power law and is potentially scale-free graph (Broido and Clauset, 2019). This also forces us to cram a lot of information into high-degree nodes.

Over-smoothing and negative sampling does not seem to be the main cause of low performance in our case. The potential reason for the superior performance of transformer-based models than GNN is the mitigation of the over-squashing problem. BERTMeSH avoids over-squashing by making a unique representation for each label using Multi-label attention instead of making a single vector representation as described in the paper. This allows the model to avoid over-squashing, which leads to improved performance.

9 Conclusion

Taking into consideration, the need for an efficient system to automatically classify MeSH headings, we implemented GNN in the link prediction setting. The use of advanced negative sampling strategies did not yield improved results. We highlighted the limitations of GNN and hypothesized that GNN is not able to generalize due to the over-squashing.

Acknowledgements

This work is part of the Master Thesis done at the Universität Stuttgart. We would like to thank the examiners Roman Klinger and Steffen Staab for the evaluation of the work. We would like to extend our thanks to Felix Weil and QUIBIQ GmbH for sponsoring and their constant support of the work. Finally, we thank Juan G Diaz Ochoa and the reviewers for their valuable feedback.

References

Uri Alon and Eran Yahav. 2021. On the bottleneck of graph neural networks and its practical implications. In *International Conference on Learning Representations*.

Anna Broido and Aaron Clauset. 2019. Scale-free networks are rare. *Nature Communications*, 10.

Jacob Devlin, Ming-Wei Chang, Kenton Lee, and Kristina Toutanova. 2019. BERT: Pre-training of deep bidirectional transformers for language understanding. In *Proceedings of the 2019 Conference of the North American Chapter of the Association for Computational Linguistics: Human Language Technologies, Volume 1 (Long and Short Papers)*, pages 4171–4186. Association for Computational Linguistics.

Will Hamilton, Zhitao Ying, and Jure Leskovec. 2017. Inductive representation learning on large graphs. In *Advances in Neural Information Processing Systems*, volume 30. Curran Associates, Inc.

Qiao Jin, Bhuwan Dhingra, William Cohen, and Xinghua Lu. 2018. AttentionMeSH: Simple, effective and interpretable automatic MeSH indexer. In *Proceedings of the 6th BioASQ Workshop A challenge on large-scale biomedical semantic indexing and question answering*, pages 47–56, Brussels, Belgium. Association for Computational Linguistics.

Diederik P. Kingma and Jimmy Ba. 2015. Adam: A method for stochastic optimization. In *3rd International Conference on Learning Representations, ICLR, Conference Track Proceedings*.

Qimai Li, Zhichao Han, and Xiao-Ming Wu. 2018. Deeper insights into graph convolutional networks for semi-supervised learning. AAAI'18/IAAI'18/EAAI'18. AAAI Press.

Yuqing Mao and Zhiyong Lu. 2017. Mesh now: automatic mesh indexing at pubmed scale via learning to rank. *Journal of Biomedical Semantics*, 8.

Shengwen Peng, Ronghui You, Hongning Wang, ChengXiang Zhai, Hiroshi Mamitsuka, and Shanfeng Zhu. 2016. Deepmesh: deep semantic representation for improving large-scale mesh indexing. *Bioinformatics*, 32:i70 – i79.

Nils Reimers and Iryna Gurevych. 2019. Sentence-BERT: Sentence embeddings using Siamese BERT-networks. In *Proceedings of the 2019 Conference on Empirical Methods in Natural Language Processing and the 9th International Joint Conference on Natural Language Processing (EMNLP-IJCNLP)*, pages 3982–3992. Association for Computational Linguistics.

Grigorios Tsoumakas, M. Laliotis, Nikos Markantonatos, and I. Vlahavas. 2013. Large-scale semantic indexing of biomedical publications at bioasq. *CEUR Workshop Proceedings*, 1094.

Petar Veličković, Guillem Cucurull, Arantxa Casanova, Adriana Romero, Pietro Liò, and Yoshua Bengio. 2018. Graph attention networks. In *International Conference on Learning Representations*.

Thomas Wolf, Lysandre Debut, Victor Sanh, Julien Chaumond, Clement Delangue, Anthony Moi, Pierric Cistac, Tim Rault, Remi Louf, Morgan Funtowicz, Joe Davison, Sam Shleifer, Patrick von Platen, Clara Ma, Yacine Jernite, Julien Plu, Canwen Xu, Teven Le Scao, Sylvain Gugger, Mariama Drame, Quentin Lhoest, and Alexander Rush. 2020. Transformers: State-of-the-art natural language processing. In *Proceedings of the 2020 Conference on Empirical Methods in Natural Language Processing: System Demonstrations*, pages 38–45, Online. Association for Computational Linguistics.

Guangxu Xun, Kishlay Jha, Ye Yuan, Yaqing Wang, and Aidong Zhang. 2019. MeSHProbeNet: a self-attentive probe net for MeSH indexing. *Bioinformatics*, 35(19):3794–3802.

Rex Ying, Ruining He, Kaifeng Chen, Pong Eksombatchai, William L. Hamilton, and Jure Leskovec. Graph convolutional neural networks for web-scale recommender systems. In *Proceedings of the 24th ACM SIGKDD International Conference on Knowledge Discovery & Data Mining, KDD 2018, London, UK, August 19-23, 2018*, pages 974–983. ACM.

Ronghui You, Yuxuan Liu, Hiroshi Mamitsuka, and Shanfeng Zhu. 2020. BERTMeSH: deep contextual representation learning for large-scale high-performance MeSH indexing with full text. *Bioinformatics*, 37(5):684–692.

Hongyi Zhang, Moustapha Cissé, Yann Dauphin, and David Lopez-Paz. 2018. mixup: Beyond empirical risk minimization. *ArXiv*, abs/1710.09412.

Weinan Zhang, Tianqi Chen, Jun Wang, and Yong Yu. 2013. Optimizing top-n collaborative filtering via dynamic negative item sampling. SIGIR '13, page 785–788. Association for Computing Machinery.

A Data Preprocessing

Taking into consideration the large size of the dataset, we randomly filtered articles to train the models efficiently. However, random sampling could result in a dataset subset that has a considerably different distribution than the original dataset. Therefore, we also used the hierarchical structure of MeSH ontology to reduce the number of training articles.

Groups of articles are made by putting the articles into 6749 groups, where 6749 is the number of MeSH headings at depth 3 of the MeSH ontology. Some of the groups along with the number of articles they contain are shown in the table 4.

Groups	No. of articles
Adult	161367
Adolescent_Adult	43519
Treatment Outcome	19234
Adolescent_Adult_Child	17284

Table 4: Groups based on MeSH ontology

As there are numerous shared MeSH headings between articles, the groups overlap with each other. The groups which are made by the combination of two or more MeSH headings have an underscore in their name, e.g. "Adolescent_Adult" is a group that contains articles that are labeled with MeSH labels "Adolescent" and "Adult". The number of articles in the groups follows the distribution of Zipf's law, where a lot of groups have less than 10 articles. Therefore, different percentages of articles are sampled from different groups that are based on the number of articles they contain. For the groups containing articles between 10 and 200. 0.1 percent of the articles are filtered from each group. If a group contains more than 200 articles, then 0.05 percent of the articles are filtered. Finally, 50k groups are randomly sampled from the groups that have less than 10 articles. The number of filtered articles obtained after applying the previously described filtering is 400k articles. Finally, we used the training set to train the model as explained in Section 5.

Do not Trust the Experts:
How the Lack of Standard Complicates NLP for Historical Irish

Oksana Dereza and **Theodorus Fransen** and **John P. McCrae**
University of Galway
Insight Centre for Data Analytics
firstname.lastname@insight-centre.org

Abstract

In this paper, we describe how we unearthed some fundamental problems while building an analogy dataset to evaluate historical Irish embeddings on their ability to detect orthographic, morphological and semantic similarity. Low agreement among field experts and the absence of an editorial standard in available resources make it impossible to build reliable evaluation datasets for computational models and obtain interpretable results. We emphasise the need for a historical text editing standard, particularly for NLP applications, and prompt Celticists and historical linguists to engage in further discussion. We would also like to draw NLP scholars' attention to the role of data and its (extra)linguistic properties in testing new models and evaluation scenarios.

1 Introduction

Historical languages are known to present greater challenges to NLP due to high orthographic variation, diachronic morphological changes and lack of resources (Piotrowski, 2012; Jenset and McGillivray, 2017; Bollmann, 2019). Our initial goal was to compare different embedding architectures and hyperparameters for detecting morphological and spelling variation in historical Irish, but we unearthed some fundamental problems while we were building an evaluation dataset and testing our models on it.

2 Word Embedding Evaluation Scenarios

There are two main strategies for the evaluation of word embeddings: extrinsic and intrinsic (Schnabel et al., 2015; Bakarov, 2018; Torregrossa et al., 2021). Extrinsic evaluation involves using pre-trained embeddings as input vectors in a model solving a downstream NLP task, such as part-of-speech tagging, named entity recognition, or sentiment analysis. The model's performance is believed to reflect the quality of the embeddings it was initialised with. Intrinsic evaluation is focused on assessing linguistic relations within the embedding model itself through solving specially designed mathematical problems: similarity and analogy. The similarity task entails comparing the similarity scores of two words yielded by an embedding model to those calculated based on experts' judgments. The analogy task is a vector proportion, where we ask an embedding model, "What is to b as a' is to a?", and expect b' as an answer.

Generally, task-driven extrinsic evaluation looks more feasible, because it allows the use of already existing evaluation datasets. However, the majority of downstream tasks have not been attempted yet for many minority and historical languages, which leaves us with no available datasets or baselines. As such, constructing a small dataset for intrinsic evaluation seems the best alternative. Both analogy and similarity datasets can be created automatically or semi-automatically by translating an existing dataset from another language, or with the help of a WordNet or a comprehensive dictionary of a language in question in a machine-readable format if there are any. Such a dataset would still require expert proofreading and evaluation, but the amount of manual work would not be as daunting as when a dataset is created from scratch.

3 Early Irish Analogy Dataset

Traditionally, analogy datasets are based on pairwise semantic proportion (Mikolov et al., 2013b), and therefore every question has a single correct answer. Given the high level of variation in historical languages, such a strict definition of a correct answer seems unjustified. Therefore, we follow the creators of the Bigger Analogy Test Set, or BATS (Gladkova et al., 2016). This dataset has highlighted the problems of popular embedding models, such as GloVe, and provided additional proof of the importance of subword information for capturing morphological relations. The origi-

The Fourth Workshop on Insights from Negative Results in NLP, pages 82–87
May 5, 2023 ©2023 Association for Computational Linguistics

nal English BATS has successfully been adapted to Japanese (Karpinska et al., 2018) and Icelandic (Friðriksdóttir et al., 2022). Our Early Irish analogy dataset is not a full-scale adaptation of BATS but draws heavily upon the ideas behind it, providing several correct answers for each analogy question and evaluating the performance with set-based metrics proposed by BATS authors, such as an average of vector offset over multiple pairs (3CosAvg) and a logistic regression cosine similarity (LRCos):

$$b' = \text{argmax}_{b' \in V} \left(\cos\left(b', b + \text{avg\_offset}\right)\right), \quad \text{where avg\_offset} = \frac{\sum_{i=0}^{m} a_i}{m} - \frac{\sum_{i=0}^{n} b_i}{n} \tag{1}$$

$$b' = \text{argmax}_{b' \in V} \left(P_{(b' \in \text{ target\_class })} * \cos\left(b', b\right)\right) \tag{2}$$

The Early Irish analogy dataset consists of four parts: morphological variation, spelling variation, synonyms, and antonyms.

The morphological and spelling variation data was automatically extracted from the eDIL (Toner et al., 2019), a digital historical dictionary of medieval Irish covering the period ca. 700 – 1700. Spelling variants were taken from the headwords, and the morphological variation subset was compiled from the 'Forms' field that covers both inflected forms of a headword and its derivatives. Unlike the original BATS, no division was made between different types of inflection, nor between inflection and derivation, within the morphological variation subset because the structure of eDIL does not allow for obtaining this division automatically. We would also like to point out that the eDIL sometimes lists spelling variants along with inflected forms and derivatives in the 'Forms' section, and we did not filter them out manually. The raw data amounted to 2,370 spelling variation and 9,690 morphological variation questions, from which 100 examples were randomly selected for each of the subsets to be comparable in size with the synonym and antonym subsets.

The synonym and antonym subsets are translations of the correspondent BATS parts proofread by four expert evaluators. The translations for each entry in the synonym subsets L07 (intensity, *cry : scream*) and L08 (exact, *sofa : couch*), and antonym subsets L09 (gradable, *clean : dirty*) and L10 (binary, *up : down*) were obtained by reverse-searching the eDIL. The translations were then organised in synsets, each labelled with an English keyword, which the expert evaluators were asked to review. The evaluators were allowed to consult eDIL but were advised not to rely on provided definitions, if in doubt, but instead to utilise their knowledge of how these words occur in texts. The task description also included the following guidelines:

- words in a synset must express the same concept and be of the same part of speech;
- words in a synset must be used in similar contexts and be of the same part of speech;
- a polysemous word can belong to several synsets;
- the annotators should not distinguish between language periods, i.e. an Old Irish and a Middle Irish word can belong to the same synset.

We obtained 98 entries in the synonym subset and 109 entries in the antonym subset, upon which three or more experts agreed. If a word had multiple spellings in the corresponding eDIL entry, we included all of them in these subsets.

4 Experiment, Evaluation and Epic Fail

Our initial goal was to compare different embedding architectures to measure the effect of leveraging subword information on detecting morphological and spelling variation along with semantic similarity in a diachronic scenario. We also aimed at finding the best embedding size for our low-resource and highly inconsistent data. For this purpose, we trained SkipGram (Mikolov et al., 2013a) and FastText (Bojanowski et al., 2017) models with embedding sizes of 20, 50, 100 and 300 on Old and Middle Irish corpora, as well as on both of them combined. We refer to the combined Old and Middle Irish data as 'Early Irish' for convenience, although this term is usually used to describe a broader period, from Primitive Irish ($4^{th} - 6^{th}$ c. A. D.) to Middle Irish ($10^{th} - 12^{th}$ c. A. D.), according to Stifter and Griffith (2021). More information about the training data for embedding models is provided in Table 1. There was no orthographic normalisation (except lowercasing and sentence-level punctuation removal), lemmatisation, or POS-tagging applied. We then tested these embedding models on our analogy dataset using two different metrics, 3CosAvg (Equation 1) and LRCos (Equation 2), with the help of a Python library Vecto.[1]

[1] https://vecto.space/

Dataset	Source	Period	Tokens	Types	TTR
Old Irish	CELT + St. Gall	$8^{th} - 9^{th}$ c.	400,922	77,754	193.9
Middle Irish	CELT	$10^{th} - 12^{th}$ c.	1,071,640	170,851	159.4
Early Irish	CELT + St. Gall	$8^{th} - 12^{th}$ c.	1,171,439	202,172	172.6

Table 1: Embedding model data, periodisation according to Stifter and Griffith (2021). **CELT** = Corpus of Electronic Texts (Ó Corráin et al., 1997), **St. Gall** = Diplomatic St. Gall Glosses Treebank (Doyle, 2020). TTR scores are calculated as $TTR = \frac{types}{tokens} \times 1000$ according to Schlechtweg et al. (2020).

To our surprise, the scores that our embedding models achieved were low enough to be statistically insignificant regardless of the training corpus, hyperparameters and evaluation metrics: the highest accuracy score in the whole experiment was 0.08, achieved by a Middle Irish FastText model with an embedding size = 100 on the morphological variation subset. We carried out a qualitative evaluation to see if our embedding models really did not learn any linguistic patterns from the data, or if the problem lies somewhere else.

First, we made a few queries to the biggest Early Irish FastText model[2] to see the word vectors nearest to these queries. For example, the closest words to *mainister* 'monastery' were its spelling variants (*mainistear, mainistir, mainisttir*), forms with suffixed demonstratives (*mainistir-si, mainistir-se, mainisttir-si, mainistir-sin*) and compounds (*cédmhainistir* 'early monastery, former monastery', *énmhainistir* 'individual monastery'). The name of a legendary Irish king, *Ailill*, yielded spelling variants (*Ailil, Oilill*), mutated and inflected forms (*hAilill, tAilill, Aililla*)[3] and another personal name, *Ailill Miltenga*. The Early Irish SkipGram model with the same parameters did not capture any morphological or spelling variation but detected semantic associates for personal names from the Early Irish literature.

Then, we used the TensorFlow projector (Smilkov et al., 2016) to see if there are any meaningful clusters in the 3D projection of the vector space of the aforementioned Early Irish FastText model. We found many interesting clusters of different sizes, such as nouns referring to peoples perceived as foreign in the Dat. pl. (*allmurachaib* 'to foreigners', *lochlannachaib* 'to Scandinavians', *saxanachaib* 'to Saxons', *paganachaib* 'to pagans') or verbal nouns ending in *-udh* (*etargnaghudh* 'interpreting, explaining', *cotludh* 'sleeping', *slonnudh* 'naming, mentioning' etc.). It is worth mentioning that the model learned subtle spelling differences: the first cluster mentioned above did not include the later spelling variants with the ending *-aibh*, and in the same way, the second cluster did not include earlier spelling variants ending in *-ud* rather than *-udh*. Moreover, nouns with a suffixed demonstrative *sin* formed two different clusters depending on whether the demonstrative was hyphenated (*fechta-sin, sliabh-sin, caislein-sin* etc.) or not (*ceilgsin, uairsin, curuchsin* etc.).

Thus, we witnessed that our models did learn a significant amount of spelling variation, as well as some inflectional and derivational morphology patterns and a limited quantity of semantic similarities. In this case, what factors may have contributed to the inadequate performance observed?

5 Discussion

5.1 Data Sparsity

The first reason, as one might have expected, is data sparsity combined with high variation. The type-token ratios in our Old, Middle and Early Irish datasets are 193.9, 159.4 and 172.6 respectively. A high TTR score means that a significant amount of words is only attested once or twice in the whole corpus. To put these numbers in context, Schlechtweg et al. (2020) report the TTR of 38.24 for Latin and 47.88 for $18 - 19^{th}$ c. Swedish.

The example of *ulchobchán* 'owl' from Table 2 suggests that there are simply not enough occurrences of this word and its variants in the corpus for the model to learn anything about it: the output we got for this query is completely unrelated to it, the most similar word being a special character for *ocus* 'and'. For the same reason, FastText models learned remarkably less semantic similarity than morphological and orthographic similarity, and SkipGram models could not capture much se-

[2]The hyperparameters of this model are the following: emb_size = 300, min_count = 2, window = 10.

[3]Like other Celtic languages, Irish is notable for initial mutations: sound changes at the beginning of a word happening in a certain grammatical environment. In historical Irish, mutations are marked in spelling in a few different ways and sometimes are not marked at all. The first two examples here demonstrate h-prothesis and t-prothesis.

Subset	Query	Translation	Expected Answer	Answer
Spelling	immairecc	conflict, battle	immairg	**immairec**, immaire, *h-immairecc*, immairi, immaircidi, immaircide
Spelling	ulchobchán	owl	ulchobcán, ulchubchán, ulchubcán, ulcachán	_&_, dhocum, puipli, goirti, disciplina, murruscaib
Morphology	asal	donkey	asaile, assail, asail, asala assail	róuasal, uasal, huasal, asalim, an-uasal, anuasal
Morphology	úasal	high, noble	ūassal, uasal, huasil, huasail, úaisliu, húaisliu, huaisliu, huaisle, huaisli, huaislimem, uasalathair, huasalsacart, huasalfichire, úasal-athraig, huasallieig, huasal-gabáltaid, huasalterchomrictid	**anúasal, ardúasal, úasal-nóeb, róuasal, n-úasal**, asal
Antonyms	dorchae	dark, gloomy	gel, gelbdae, gelmar, gleórach, soillsech, soillside, solus	*dorchatae, dorchai, dorcha, dorchato, dorchadu, dorchatu*
Antonyms	descert	south	túaiscert	*ndescert, descertaig, n-descert, descertach, descertaigi*, **túascert**
Synonyms	fliuch	wet	fliuchaide, uiscemail	imliuch, naliuch, fedliuch, nimliuch, **fliuchaidi**, coiuch
Synonyms	álaind	lovely, beautiful	cáem, cáemdae, cruthach, cruthamail, delbach, delbdae	*hálaind, roálaind, comálaind, n-álaind, com-álaind, fírálaind*

Table 2: Answers of the biggest Early Irish FastText model compared to expected answers. The words in bold are correct answers that were not present in the evaluation dataset; the words in italic are related to the query, but would not have been correct answers to a particular question.

mantic similarity beyond personal names, as qualitative evaluation has shown.

5.2 Lack of Standardisation of Resources

The second reason is a lack of a text editing standard between different resources for the same historical language, or even within the same resource, which is a case of CELT (Ó Corráin et al., 1997). The usual process of editing manuscript texts includes introducing word spacing, expanding contractions and abbreviations, adding punctuation and sometimes even combining different versions of a text from different manuscripts for linguistic clarity. However, the extent of these changes as well as the use of notation, such as brackets, may differ dramatically from editor to editor. For example, the digital corpora of historical Irish that came out in recent years, St. Gall Priscian Glosses Database (Bauer et al., 2017), Diplomatic St. Gall Glosses Treebank (Doyle, 2020) and CorPH (Stifter et al., 2021), all separate words by different linguistic standards.[4] The digitised versions of old paper text editions usually include some updates and corrections but still reflect the original editor's ideas of what the text should look like. Moreover, this kind of variation is not reflected in the metadata, and you have to be familiar with each editor's practice to be able to take it into account. Therefore, it is usually almost impossible to use both text and metadata, such as manuscript datings or language periods (Old Irish, Middle Irish etc.), out-of-the-box for NLP applications. These issues have been discussed in Doyle et al. (2018, 2019) in more detail.

How did this lack of standard manifest in our data? About 65 % of morphological and spelling variation subsets, retrieved from eDIL, were not present in the entire Early Irish corpus retrieved from CELT, on which the biggest model was trained. As for synonym and antonym subsets, ca. 30 % are missing in the corpus (see Table 3 for more detail). In other words, a historical dictionary covering mostly Old and Middle Irish periods contains a very high percentage of forms that do not

[4]However, some steps are being made to initiate a standard as far as tokenisation is concerned: thus, the electronic edition of Würzburg glosses (Doyle, 2018) is deliberately tokenised to the same standard as the St. Gall Glosses Treebank.

Dataset	OIr	MIr	EIr	CELT
Morphology (full)	78.7	72.4	69.3	65.4
Morphology (100)	66.2	58.1	54.7	48.5
Spelling (full)	76.7	70.4	68.2	64.0
Spelling (100)	76.5	69.7	66.7	62.6
Synonyms	42.9	36.0	33.3	28.8
Antonyms	45.8	38.2	35.4	30.9

Table 3: The % of missing words from different parts of the analogy dataset (based on eDIL) in the texts from CELT that served as training data for embedding models. **OIr** = Old Irish, **MIr** = Middle Irish, **EIr** = Early Irish (Old + Middle Irish), **CELT** = all Irish texts from CELT, from Old Irish up to Early Modern Irish, including Classical Modern Irish.[5]

occur in real [edited] Old and Middle Irish texts. This also works in the opposite direction: many forms and spellings from the corpus are not listed in the dictionary and, therefore, did not make their way to the evaluation dataset. Such a discrepancy between the corpus on which they were trained and the historical dictionary, which became the source for the evaluation dataset, seriously affected the performance. Table 2 shows that the model often gives reasonable answers, but they are just not among the expected ones. For example, *anúasal, ardúasal, úasal-nóeb, róuasal* are derivatives of *úasal* 'high, noble', and *n-úasal* is its mutated form; thus, they should have been considered correct answers to a morphological similarity question.

5.3 Lack of Agreement between Experts

In addition to the inherent disagreement on fundamental linguistic questions, such as "What is a word?", and on editorial policies ("To what extent should we edit texts? What should the standard for normalisation be?"), scholars do not concur with each other on more specific tasks either.

All the experts who participated in the evaluation are actively working with Early Irish in their research and/or teaching. In addition to that, they were asked to evaluate their knowledge of Early Irish on a scale from 1 ("I did an introductory course") to 5 ("I am experienced in editing Early Irish texts and/or teaching Early Irish") before completing the task. Three of the participants answered with a 4, and one chose a 3, which suggests a profound level of expertise.

Despite that, the highest pairwise inter-annotator agreement score between experts, measured using Cohen's kappa, was 0.35, which constitutes only "fair agreement" according to Viera et al. (2005). The Fleiss' kappa score between all four annotators was as low as 0.17, which corresponds to "slight agreement" in Viera et al.'s classification.

6 Conclusion

We discussed an attempt at building an analogy dataset to evaluate historical Irish embeddings on their ability to learn orthographic, morphological and semantic similarity. However, the performance of our models was extremely poor regardless of the architecture, hyperparameters and evaluation metrics, while the qualitative evaluation revealed positive tendencies. Several factors have contributed to it, including a low agreement between experts on fundamental lexical and orthographic issues, and the lack of a unified editorial standard for the language.

These problems are by no means caused by poor scholarly practice. Each of the electronic resource creators pursues a particular, perfectly justifiable editorial approach that dictates their choices. However, the necessity of a text editing standard, especially for NLP applications, has not been properly debated and investigated by the historical Irish academic community. We suspect that this may be the problem of historical languages in general. Through this paper, we would like to highlight this issue and invite Celticists and historical linguists to engage in further discussion.

7 Acknowledgements

This publication has emanated from research in part supported by the Irish Research Council under grant number IRCLA/2017/129 (CARDAMOM – Comparative Deep Models of Language for Minority and Historical Languages). It is co-funded by Science Foundation Ireland (SFI) under Grant Number SFI/12/RC/2289 P2 (Insight 2). We would also like to thank Dr. Elisa Roma, Dr. Eystein Thanisch and Adrian Doyle who took part in the evaluation task together with Dr. Theodorus Fransen.

References

Amir Bakarov. 2018. A survey of word embeddings evaluation methods. *arXiv:1801.09536*.

[5]Classical Modern Irish is a strict, highly formalised version of Irish used in bardic poetry, which has developed throughout the Middle Irish period and was fixed around the beginning of the 13th century (McManus, 2005).

Bernhard Bauer, Rijcklof Hofman, and Pádraic Moran. 2017. St. Gall Priscian Glosses, version 2.0. Accessed: 19-02-2023.

Piotr Bojanowski, Edouard Grave, Armand Joulin, and Tomáš Mikolov. 2017. Enriching word vectors with subword information. *Transactions of the association for computational linguistics*, 5:135–146.

Marcel Bollmann. 2019. A Large-Scale Comparison of Historical Text Normalization Systems. In *Proceedings of the 2019 Conference of the North American Chapter of the Association for Computational Linguistics*, pages 3885–3898.

Adrian Doyle. 2018. Würzburg Irish Glosses. Accessed: 19-02-2023.

Adrian Doyle. 2020. Diplomatic St. Gall Glosses Treebank. Accessed: 19-02-2023.

Adrian Doyle, John P McCrae, and Clodagh Downey. 2018. Preservation of original orthography in the construction of an Old Irish corpus. *Sustaining Knowledge Diversity in the Digital Age*, pages 67–70.

Adrian Doyle, John Philip McCrae, and Clodagh Downey. 2019. A character-level LSTM network model for tokenizing the Old Irish text of the Würzburg glosses on the Pauline Epistles. In *Proceedings of the Celtic Language Technology Workshop*, pages 70–79.

Steinunn Rut Friðriksdóttir, Hjalti Daníelsson, Steinþór Steingrímsson, and Einar Sigurdsson. 2022. Ice-BATS: An Icelandic Adaptation of the Bigger Analogy Test Set. In *Proceedings of the Thirteenth Language Resources and Evaluation Conference*, pages 4227–4234.

Anna Gladkova, Aleksandr Drozd, and Satoshi Matsuoka. 2016. Analogy-based detection of morphological and semantic relations with word embeddings: what works and what doesn't. In *Proceedings of the NAACL Student Research Workshop*, pages 8–15.

Gard B Jenset and Barbara McGillivray. 2017. *Quantitative historical linguistics. A corpus framework*, volume 26. Oxford University Press.

Marzena Karpinska, Bofang Li, Anna Rogers, and Aleksandr Drozd. 2018. Subcharacter information in Japanese embeddings: When is it worth it? In *Proceedings of the Workshop on the Relevance of Linguistic Structure in Neural Architectures for NLP*, pages 28–37.

Damian McManus. 2005. Irish Literature [3]. Classical Poetry. In John Thomas Koch, editor, *Celtic Culture: A Historical Encyclopedia*, pages 1003–1005. abc-Clio.

Tomáš Mikolov, Kai Chen, Greg Corrado, and Jeffrey Dean. 2013a. Efficient estimation of word representations in vector space. In *1st International Conference on Learning Representations, ICLR 2013, Scottsdale, Arizona, USA, May 2-4, 2013, Workshop Track Proceedings*.

Tomáš Mikolov, Wen-tau Yih, and Geoffrey Zweig. 2013b. Linguistic regularities in continuous space word representations. In *Proceedings of the 2013 conference of the north american chapter of the association for computational linguistics: Human language technologies*, pages 746–751.

Michael Piotrowski. 2012. *Natural language processing for historical texts*, volume 5 of *Synthesis lectures on human language technologies*. Morgan & Claypool Publishers.

Dominik Schlechtweg, Barbara McGillivray, Simon Hengchen, Haim Dubossarsky, and Nina Tahmasebi. 2020. SemEval-2020 Task 1: Unsupervised lexical semantic change detection. In *Proceedings of the Fourteenth Workshop on Semantic Evaluation*, pages 1–23, Barcelona (online).

Tobias Schnabel, Igor Labutov, David Mimno, and Thorsten Joachims. 2015. Evaluation methods for unsupervised word embeddings. In *Proceedings of the 2015 Conference on Empirical Methods in Natural Language Processing*, pages 298–307, Lisbon.

Daniel Smilkov, Nikhil Thorat, Charles Nicholson, Emily Reif, Fernanda B Viégas, and Martin Wattenberg. 2016. Embedding projector: Interactive visualization and interpretation of embeddings. In *Proceedings of the Workshop on Interpretable Machine Learning in Complex Systems @ NIPS 2016*.

David Stifter, Bernhard Bauer, Fangzhe Qiu, Elliott Lash, Nora White, Siobhán Barret, Aaron Griffith, Romanas Bulatovas, Francesco Felici, Ellen Ganly, Truc Ha Nguyen, and Lars Nooij. 2021. Corpus PalaeoHibernicum (CorPH). Accessed: 19-02-2023.

David Stifter and Aaron Griffith. 2021. Lecture notes in Old Irish. Accessed: 19-02-2023.

Gregory Toner, Sharon Arbuthnot, Máire Ní Mhaonaigh, Marie-Luise Theuerkauf, and Dagmar Wodtko. 2019. eDIL 2019: An Electronic Dictionary of the Irish Language, based on the Contributions to a Dictionary of the Irish Language (Dublin: Royal Irish Academy, 1913-1976). Accessed: 19-02-2023.

François Torregrossa, Robin Allesiardo, Vincent Claveau, Nihel Kooli, and Guillaume Gravier. 2021. A survey on training and evaluation of word embeddings. *International Journal of Data Science and Analytics*, 11(2):85–103.

Anthony J Viera, Joanne M Garrett, et al. 2005. Understanding interobserver agreement: the kappa statistic. *Fam med*, 37(5):360–363.

Donnchadh Ó Corráin, Hiram Morgan, Beatrix Färber, Gregory Toner, Benjamin Hazard, Emer Purcell, Caoimhín Ó Dónaill, Hilary Lavelle, Seán Ua Súilleabháin, Julianne Nyhan, and Emma McCarthy. 1997. CELT: Corpus of Electronic Texts. Accessed: 19-02-2023. Data downloaded: 15-03-2021.

Exploring the Reasons for Non-generalizability of KBQA systems

Sopan Khosla[+]
AWS AI Labs
sopankh@amazon.com

Ritam Dutt[*+]
Carnegie Mellon University
rdutt@andrew.cmu.edu

Vinayshekhar Bannihatti Kumar
AWS AI Labs
vinayshk@amazon.com

Rashmi Gangadharaiah
AWS AI Labs
rgangad@amazon.com

Abstract

Recent research has demonstrated impressive generalization capabilities of several Knowledge Base Question Answering (KBQA) models on the GrailQA dataset. We inspect whether these models can generalize to other datasets in a zero-shot setting. We notice a significant drop in performance and investigate the causes for the same. We observe that the models are dependent not only on the structural complexity of the questions, but also on the linguistic styles of framing a question. Specifically, the linguistic dimensions corresponding to explicitness, readability, coherence, and grammaticality have a significant impact on the performance of state-of-the-art KBQA models. Overall our results showcase the brittleness of such models and the need for creating generalizable systems.

1 Introduction

The task of Question Answering over Knowledge Bases (KBQA) involves answering a natural language question by querying a predefined knowledge base (KB). While progress in KBQA research has addressed several challenges like answering complex questions, multi-hop reasoning (Lan and Jiang, 2020; Ren et al., 2021), conversational QA (Kacupaj et al., 2021), and multi-lingual KBQA (Zhou et al., 2021), most of the prior work in this field has been restricted to an i.i.d. setting (Yih et al., 2016; Talmor and Berant, 2018a).

In a real-world setting, a KBQA system should be well-equipped to handle users' queries that were unseen during training. To motivate research along this front, Gu et al. (2021a) proposed a dataset (GrailQA) with an associated leaderboard to benchmark the generalizability of KBQA methods to new compositions, and unseen schema items (Zero-shot). Multiple state-of-the-art models (Ye et al., 2021; Yu et al., 2022; Gu and Su, 2022; Shu et al., 2022) have achieved remarkable performance on the Zero-shot split giving the impression that KBQA generalization might be a solved problem.

However, a cross-dataset evaluation of the models trained on GrailQA reveals that they do not transfer well even for the more simpler one or two-hop questions. We observe that while these models achieve impressive performance on the GrailQA Zero-shot (GrailQA Z) split, they fail to generalize to questions from other datasets like WebQSP (Yih et al., 2016), GraphQ (Su et al., 2016), and ComplexWebQuestions (Talmor and Berant, 2018b) even though they are built upon the same Knowledge Base (i.e. Freebase). In this work we closely inspect the reasons for this drop. We analyse the structural and linguistic differences between questions from the different publicly available KBQA benchmark datasets.

We observe that while structural complexity somewhat explains the performance variations across questions within the same dataset, it does not explain the performance drop when testing on other datasets. Our analysis shows that the linguistic differences like explicitness and length of questions, grammaticality, readability, and coherence account for the degradation in performance. Although WebQSP and GrailQA share the same underlying KB, the substantial differences in the annotation process manifests as samples having different linguistic properties. We find that these linguistic variations act as an additional dimension for evaluating the generalizability and real-world usefulness of KBQA systems.

2 Datasets

In order to understand the zero-shot efficacy of the state-of-the-art KBQA models, we look at their performance on the following datasets:

GrailQA (Gu et al., 2021b) contains questions across 86 domains and covers more than 3500 Free-

[*]Work conducted during an internship at Amazon.
[+] denotes equal contribution

The Fourth Workshop on Insights from Negative Results in NLP, pages 88–93
May 5, 2023 ©2023 Association for Computational Linguistics

RP-Code	RP Instances	Question
RP-0	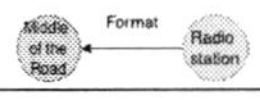	"what radio station uses the middle of the road format?"
RP-1	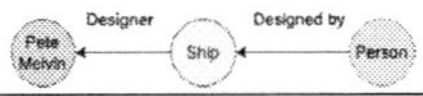	"what ship designer designed a ship that is designed by pete melvin?"
RP-2	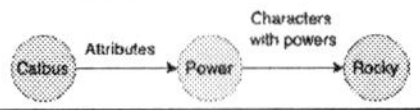	"which powers do both catbus and rocky the flying squirrel have?"
RP-3	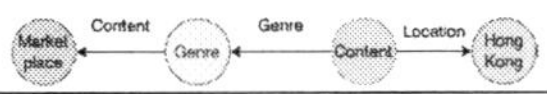	"genres of marketplace can be found in what broadcast content in hong kong?"
RP-4	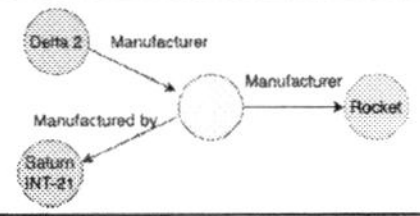	"what other rocket did the manufacturer of saturn int-21 and delta 2 create?"
RP-5	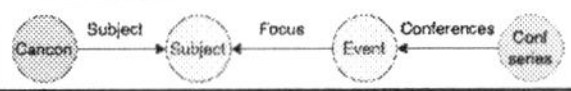	"can-con has which conference series that focuses on it?"

Table 1: Example natural-language questions from GrailQA dev-set and their corresponding RP (relation path) categories. Red and green nodes in the graph correspond to the constraints (entities and literals), and the answer respectively.

base relations. It's development and test sets have three splits to independently measure the i.i.d, compositional and zero-shot capabilities of KBQA systems. We leverage their publicly available training and dev sets for our experiments.

WebQSP (Yih et al., 2016) contains question-answer pairs from non-experts collected using the Google Suggest API, and uses Amazon Mechanical Turk to get the answers for the obtained questions.

GraphQ (Su et al., 2016) has varying question characteristics that include complexity along the semantic structure, qualitative analysis over answer space, topic of the question, and the number of possible answers for the questions.

ComplexWebQuestions (CWQ) (Talmor and Berant, 2018a) builds on top of WebQSP and automatically creates complex questions that include phenomena such as function composition, conjunctions, superlatives and comparatives.

We consider these datasets for our experiments as all of them use Freebase as their underlying KB.

Creating zero-shot splits: We categorize questions in the test/dev splits of the corresponding dataset into (i) Non Zero-shot (I.I.D. + Compositional) and (ii) Zero-shot similar to the categories proposed by Gu et al. (2021a). Specifically, zero-shot instances have at least one schema item (class or relation) that were not seen during training in the original GrailQA dataset. We note the criteria to be a bit lenient for relations whose corresponding inverse relation occurred during training (ex: inventors.inventions as opposed to inventions.invented_by). Consequently, we update the zero-shot criterion to exclude questions where either the relation or it's corresponding inverse relation was observed during training.

	GrailQA		GraphQ		WebQSP		CWQ	
RP	All	Z	All	Z	All	Z	All	Z
RP-0	4950	2809	976	292	892	239	0	0
RP-1	1179	559	503	237	343	177	1188	602
RP-2	349	135	185	33	53	6	965	468
RP-3	128	18	70	31	14	3	1680	1347
RP-4	93	61	39	39	190	136	0	0
RP-5	62	22	33	33	1	0	856	608

Table 2: Data statistics. Distribution of different reasoning paths over the entire test/dev set (All) and the Zero-shot split (Z) for the different datasets.

Reasoning Paths: We characterize the complexity of the questions for different datasets based on the notion of reasoning paths as defined in Das et al. (2022). A reasoning path (hereforth RP) represents the sequence of actions (specifically relations traversed from the starting constraint(s) in the query graph) to reach the final answer. They provide a unified way to measure the complexity in terms of the number of hops and the number of constraints (examples shown in Table 1). Table 2 presents the most salient reasoning paths that occur in the dev split of the original GrailQA dataset and we thus restrict our analysis to these specific RPs on the other datasets. We further note the distribution of these RPs for the different datasets in Table 2.

3 Performance on Other KBQA Datasets

Experimental Setup: In this work, we explore the generalizability of four semantic-parsing based systems. These include (i) RNG-KBQA (Ye et al.,

	GrailQA				GraphQ				WebQSP				CWQ			
Model	EM	F1	EM(Z)	F1(Z)	EM	F1	EM(Z)	F1(Z)	EM	F1	EM(Z)	F1(Z)	EM	F1	EM(Z)	F1(Z)
RNG-KBQA	83.4	86.7	83.5	86.0	61.9	69.3	44.4	55.8	34.6	39.9	22.6	29.0	20.5	35.8	18.4	33.4
ArcaneQA	80.3	84.6	76.7	80.6	45.7	56.2	30.4	45.1	12.4	17.6	8.0	14.2	14.2	30.2	11.2	26.6
BERT-Ranker	66.7	72.2	69.6	74.4	43.9	50.1	32.3	40.1	35.7	43.9	25.0	37.1	13.3	28.3	10.3	25.0
BERT-Transducer	50.6	53.8	42.5	44.9	21.3	24.9	15.6	19.0	15.5	19.5	10.5	13.0	1.8	6.1	1.0	4.7

Table 3: EM and F1 scores for different KBQA baselines for the different KBQA datasets built on top of Freebase KB (with gold entities). Z refers to the Zero-shot subset.

RP	RP-instance	GrailQA Z					GraphQ Z					WebQSP Z					CWQ Z				
		EM	F1	#Z	#W	#N	EM	F1	#Z	#W	#N	EM	F1	#Z	#W	#N	EM	F1	#Z	#W	#N
RP-0	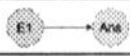	87.1	88.0	2.9	10.6	4.3	41.8	53.8	2.0	8.9	2.9	31.4	38.3	2.0	6.8	2.1	-	-	-	-	-
RP-1		81.9	85.1	4.5	14.3	6.1	54.8	59.7	3.7	10.1	3.5	9.6	14.7	4.0	6.2	1.8	52.5	57.7	3.1	13.3	2.9
RP-2		74.8	86.2	4.7	15.7	6.2	63.6	87.9	5.0	12.3	3.3	0.0	38.3	2.6	8.2	2.6	25.0	45.6	3.2	12.5	2.3
RP-3		5.6	44.8	5.2	19.1	7.6	48.4	98.9	5.5	12.3	3.9	0.0	13.3	5.2	7.7	2.3	9.2	29.4	5.0	12.6	2.3
RP-4	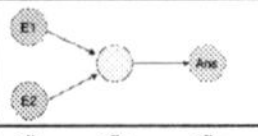	9.8	47.6	7.0	13.0	3.6	17.9	32.7	4.9	12.9	4.5	25.7	31.1	5.3	7.2	2.6	-	-	-	-	-
RP-5		0.0	1.5	5.5	10.6	4.2	0.0	0.0	3.6	11.5	4.1	-	-	-	-	-	0.0	9.0	4.8	14.0	2.9

Table 4: EM and F1 scores for RNG-KBQA, and the mean # zero-shot items (#Z), # words (#W), # common nouns (#N) per question on the zero-shot splits of GrailQA, GraphQ, WebQSP, and CWQ.

2021), (ii) ArcaneQA (Gu and Su, 2022), (iii) BERT-Ranker (Gu et al., 2021a), and (iv) BERT-Transducer. We follow the exact inference setting mentioned in their Github repositories, and evaluate them in terms of EM and F1 scores. All experiments are carried out on a single RTX-1080Ti GPU with 12GB RAM. We use gold entities to control for the confounding caused by entity linking errors.

Overall Results: As shown in Table 3, both RnG-KGQA and ArcaneQA achieve F1 scores of more than 80% on GrailQA zero-shot split with gold entities. We observe that this comes from the near perfect performance on the simpler (RP-0,1,2) questions that make up more than 98% of GrailQA Z. BERT-Ranker also achieves a respectable F1 score of 74.4%, while BERT-Tranducer performs poorly with an F1 of 44.9%.

However, we observe that all models significantly suffer while transferring to other datasets. This is true for both zero-shot and non zero-shot splits, as the overall performance drops by more than half even for samples that do not contain any zero-shot schema items (Table 3). For the simpler 1-hop (RP-0) zero-shot questions, RnG-KGQA's F1 drops by more than 30% (Table 4). ArcaneQA, a seq2seq model, suffers even more. For 2-hop questions (RP-1), while RnG-KGQA scores a respectable 60% F1 on GraphQ Z, its performance on WebQSP Z is severely low (below 15% F1). Overall, we find that the state-of-the-art KBQA models trained on GrailQA are not able generalize to other datasets, despite the presence of gold entities, even though they are built on the same KB.

Number of zero-shot schema items (#Z): Previous works (Gu et al., 2021a; Ye et al., 2021) have shown a degradation in performance of KBQA systems when exposed to unseen schema items. We thus compare the number of zero-shot schema items in the questions across the datasets.

We observe that the zero-shot splits of the diferent datasets contain similar or fewer zero-shot schema items than GrailQA Z across the different reasoning paths (Table 4, 5). For example, the mean for WebQSP Z lies between 2 and 5 for the different RPs. Compare this with GrailQA Z, where this goes as high as 7 (RP-4). GraphQ Z is closer to GrailQA Z with an overall mean of 3.2, and with its bias towards more complex questions CWQ Z has a mean of 4.0 zero-shot items.

Controlling for RPs, none of the other datasets have significantly more zero-shot items than GrailQA Z, suggesting that these questions are not necessarily *more difficult*, and the non-generalizability of the evaluated systems cannot be solely attributed to this factor.

4 Analyzing Linguistic Variation

In this section, we explore whether the regression in performance can be explained via the linguistic variation among the different KBQA datasets. We analyze the questions in these datasets using the dimensions discussed below:

Dimension	GrailQA		GraphQ		WebQSP		CWQ	
	All	Z	All	Z	All	Z	All	Z
# Zero-shot items	1.87 ± 1.72	3.3 ± 0.97	1.46 ± 1.77	3.19 ± 1.67	1.65 ± 0.93	3.41 ± 0.76	2.95 ± 1.09	4.0 ± 0.72
# Words	10.96 ± 4.08	11.41 ± 3.58	9.35 ± 3.00	10.03 ± 2.94	6.64 ± 1.55	6.71 ± 1.61	13.19 ± 3.16	13.00 ± 3.12
# Common Nouns	4.32 ± 1.84	4.72 ± 1.75	3.22 ± 1.30	3.39 ± 1.30	2.12 ± 1.00	2.17 ± 1.00	2.6 ± 1.24	2.6 ± 1.25
Grammaticality	0.71 ± 0.45	0.7 ± 0.46	0.85 ± 0.36	0.83 ± 0.38	0.68 ± 0.47	0.73 ± 0.44	0.78 ± 0.41	0.75 ± 0.43
Complexity	0.02 ± 0.13	0.01 ± 0.11	0.01 ± 0.07	0.00 ± 0.00	0.00 ± 0.00	0.00 ± 0.00	0.00 ± 0.05	0.01 ± 0.08
Coherency	-5.96 ± 0.90	-5.99 ± 0.90	-5.54 ± 1.00	-5.54 ± 1.00	-5.7 ± 1.00	-5.65 ± 1.00	-4.96 ± 0.92	-5.04 ± 0.94
Formality	0.14 ± 0.24	0.16 ± 0.26	0.12 ± 0.23	0.13 ± 0.25	0.01 ± 0.02	0.01 ± 0.02	0.99 ± 0.08	0.99 ± 0.09
Readability	65.34 ± 30.91	60.46 ± 26.85	66.46 ± 31.4	71.85 ± 25.71	79.75 ± 23.89	77.23 ± 25.19	74.03 ± 22.57	71.57 ± 21.60

Table 5: Mean and std. dev. scores for All and Zero-shot (Z) questions across different KBQA datasets on the various analysis dimensions.

Sentence Length (#W): Firstly, we compare the length of the natural language questions in each dataset. We find that WebQSP seems to have the shortest questions (Table 4, 5). WebQSP questions consistently contain 6-8 words regardless of the complexity of the reasoning path. Compare this to GrailQA that contains more than double of that (19 words) in its RP-3 questions. Furthermore, CWQ that was built by combining different WebQSP samples also contains longer question statements.

Common Nouns (#N): We also investigate the frequency of common nouns across the dataset questions. We use NLTK's POS-tagger and consider words corresponding to "NN" and "NNS" tags as common nouns. We compute the mean distrbution of common nouns (#N) across the datasets.

We observe that #N is twice as large in GrailQA compared to WebQSP and CWQ (Table 4, 5). While this phenomenon is seen for very simple questions (RP-0,2), it is magnified more for questions with hidden nodes (RP-1,3). We attribute this difference to the explicit language used in GrailQA, where hidden classes in the graph query are also sometimes mentioned in the question statement.

Grammaticality & Complexity: Linjordet and Balog (2022) demonstrates a significant drop in performance of KBQA models in presence of more natural questions. The authors measure "naturalness" of questions along the lines of grammaticality, fluency, and complexity. We thus investigate whether the different datasets are similar in distribution along these aforementioned dimensions.

We use the BLIMP (Warstadt et al., 2020) and COLA corpora (Warstadt et al., 2019) to fine-tune a BERT-base-uncased model to detect grammaticality. We observe high scores for WebQSP and CWQ and low for GraphQ and GrailQA which ties in with previous findings. We also analyse whether the questions in the different datasets have varying degrees of complexity, for which we use the dataset of Iavarone et al. (2021). We observe that none of the four datasets are very complex, with GrailQA All achieving the highest mean score of 0.02.

Readability: We use the Flesch-reading score to characterize how easy it is to comprehend a given question in each of these datasets. We observe that GraphQ has a very similar score to GrailQA in that they are less readable, whereas WebQSP and CWQ have much higher readability (Table 5).

Formality: To quantify the formality in the writing style, we pass the questions through a RoBERTa based classifier trained on GYAFC and take the softmax outputs as the formality score. We find that WebQSP questions have the least mean formality (0.01) while CWQ questions have the highest (0.99). GrailQA and GraphQ questions are also on the informal side (Table 5).

Coherency: To measure the differences in the coherency, we use a reference free metric called CTRLEval (Ke et al., 2022). We observe that GrailQA is not as coherent as WebQSP (Table 5). We hypothesize this to be the case because of the mention of the hidden classes in GrailQA question statements. On the other hand, WebQSP questions are more natural as they are scrapped from the Google Suggest API. We also observe that both CWQ and GraphQ have much higher coherency scores when compared to both GrailQA and WebQSP.

5 Discussion

Overall, our results show that systems trained on GrailQA seem to transfer the best to GraphQ which has similar linguistic properties to GrailQA i.e., higher sentence lengths and number of common nouns, medium formality scores, and lower readablity. This is inline with the similarity in their

https://huggingface.co/s-nlp/roberta-base-formality-ranker

annotation processes that requires annotators to refer to a query graph to arrive at a NL question, which might bias them to include hidden nodes in the reasoning path. The questions in GrailQA are more explicit (highest #N) than GraphQ.

Compare this with the extremely poor performance on WebQSP, which can be explained by the stark differences in the language used in this dataset i.e., lesser (i) number of words in question sentences, (ii) number of common nouns and (iii) formality, and higher readability. This follows from WebQSP containing real-world non-expert queries collected from a search engine.

Finally, despite CWQ having longer questions like GrailQA, it does not contain as many #N suggesting that the annotators do not rely on introducing hidden classes in the NL question while merging the simpler WebQSP questions. Higher formality, readability, and coherency scores for CWQ show that the paraphrasing step used by the authors creates more *natural* and *readable* questions, as compared to GrailQA. We believe that these linguistic differences atleast partially explain the drop in performance for models when tested on CWQ.

We posit that the higher explicitness of GrailQA questions might provide some additional signal to KBQA systems during training that helps them in deciding the best relations/ nodes among the possible options. Systems' over-reliance on this signal might not transfer well to other datasets (as shown in this work) thus rendering them less useful.

6 Conclusion

Recent KBQA systems have demonstrated impressive performance on the GrailQA leaderboard that evaluates them for their zero-shot genearlizability. In this work, we show that these systems that are trained on GrailQA do not transfer to other KBQA datasets built on top of the same KB. Our analysis shows that despite controlling for structural complexity of the questions, there is a drop in performance across datasets. We observe that this can be explained by the difference in annotation processes and the resulting variations in the linguistic properties of these questions. Our work showcases that linguistic variation is an important dimension for evaluating the generalizability of KBQA systems in real-world scenarios.

References

Rajarshi Das, Ameya Godbole, Ankita Naik, Elliot Tower, Manzil Zaheer, Hannaneh Hajishirzi, Robin Jia, and Andrew Mccallum. 2022. Knowledge base question answering by case-based reasoning over subgraphs. In *Proceedings of the 39th International Conference on Machine Learning*, volume 162 of *Proceedings of Machine Learning Research*, pages 4777–4793. PMLR.

Yu Gu, Sue Kase, Michelle Vanni, Brian Sadler, Percy Liang, Xifeng Yan, and Yu Su. 2021a. Beyond iid: three levels of generalization for question answering on knowledge bases. In *Proceedings of the Web Conference 2021*, pages 3477–3488.

Yu Gu, Sue Kase, Michelle Vanni, Brian Sadler, Percy Liang, Xifeng Yan, and Yu Su. 2021b. Beyond iid: three levels of generalization for question answering on knowledge bases. In *Proceedings of the Web Conference 2021*, pages 3477–3488.

Yu Gu and Yu Su. 2022. Arcaneqa: Dynamic program induction and contextualized encoding for knowledge base question answering. *arXiv preprint arXiv:2204.08109*.

Benedetta Iavarone, Dominique Brunato, and Felice Dell'Orletta. 2021. Sentence complexity in context. In *Proceedings of the Workshop on Cognitive Modeling and Computational Linguistics*, pages 186–199, Online. Association for Computational Linguistics.

Endri Kacupaj, Joan Plepi, Kuldeep Singh, Harsh Thakkar, Jens Lehmann, and Maria Maleshkova. 2021. Conversational question answering over knowledge graphs with transformer and graph attention networks. In *Proceedings of the 16th Conference of the European Chapter of the Association for Computational Linguistics: Main Volume*, pages 850–862, Online. Association for Computational Linguistics.

Pei Ke, Hao Zhou, Yankai Lin, Peng Li, Jie Zhou, Xiaoyan Zhu, and Minlie Huang. 2022. Ctrleval: An unsupervised reference-free metric for evaluating controlled text generation. *arXiv preprint arXiv:2204.00862*.

Yunshi Lan and Jing Jiang. 2020. Query graph generation for answering multi-hop complex questions from knowledge bases. In *Proceedings of the 58th Annual Meeting of the Association for Computational Linguistics*, pages 969–974, Online. Association for Computational Linguistics.

Trond Linjordet and Krisztian Balog. 2022. Would you ask it that way? measuring and improving question naturalness for knowledge graph question answering. In *Proceedings of the 45th International ACM SIGIR Conference on Research and Development in Information Retrieval*, SIGIR '22, page 3090–3098, New York, NY, USA. Association for Computing Machinery.

Hongyu Ren, Hanjun Dai, Bo Dai, Xinyun Chen, Michihiro Yasunaga, Haitian Sun, Dale Schuurmans, Jure Leskovec, and Denny Zhou. 2021. Lego: Latent execution-guided reasoning for multi-hop question answering on knowledge graphs. In *International Conference on Machine Learning*, pages 8959–8970. PMLR.

Yiheng Shu, Zhiwei Yu, Yuhan Li, Börje F Karlsson, Tingting Ma, Yuzhong Qu, and Chin-Yew Lin. 2022. Tiara: Multi-grained retrieval for robust question answering over large knowledge bases. *arXiv preprint arXiv:2210.12925*.

Yu Su, Huan Sun, Brian Sadler, Mudhakar Srivatsa, Izzeddin Gür, Zenghui Yan, and Xifeng Yan. 2016. On generating characteristic-rich question sets for qa evaluation. In *Proceedings of the 2016 Conference on Empirical Methods in Natural Language Processing*, pages 562–572.

Alon Talmor and Jonathan Berant. 2018a. The web as a knowledge-base for answering complex questions. In *Proceedings of the 2018 Conference of the North American Chapter of the Association for Computational Linguistics: Human Language Technologies, Volume 1 (Long Papers)*, pages 641–651, New Orleans, Louisiana. Association for Computational Linguistics.

Alon Talmor and Jonathan Berant. 2018b. The web as a knowledge-base for answering complex questions. In *North American Chapter of the Association for Computational Linguistics*.

Alex Warstadt, Alicia Parrish, Haokun Liu, Anhad Mohananey, Wei Peng, Sheng-Fu Wang, and Samuel R. Bowman. 2020. BLiMP: A benchmark of linguistic minimal pairs for English. In *Proceedings of the Society for Computation in Linguistics 2020*, pages 409–410, New York, New York. Association for Computational Linguistics.

Alex Warstadt, Amanpreet Singh, and Samuel R. Bowman. 2019. Neural network acceptability judgments. *Transactions of the Association for Computational Linguistics*, 7:625–641.

Xi Ye, Semih Yavuz, Kazuma Hashimoto, Yingbo Zhou, and Caiming Xiong. 2021. Rng-kbqa: Generation augmented iterative ranking for knowledge base question answering. *arXiv preprint arXiv:2109.08678*.

Wen-tau Yih, Matthew Richardson, Chris Meek, Ming-Wei Chang, and Jina Suh. 2016. The value of semantic parse labeling for knowledge base question answering. In *Proceedings of the 54th Annual Meeting of the Association for Computational Linguistics (Volume 2: Short Papers)*, pages 201–206, Berlin, Germany. Association for Computational Linguistics.

Donghan Yu, Sheng Zhang, Patrick Ng, Henghui Zhu, Alexander Hanbo Li, Jun Wang, Yiqun Hu, William Wang, Zhiguo Wang, and Bing Xiang. 2022. Decaf: Joint decoding of answers and logical forms for question answering over knowledge bases. *arXiv preprint arXiv:2210.00063*.

Yucheng Zhou, Xiubo Geng, Tao Shen, Wenqiang Zhang, and Daxin Jiang. 2021. Improving zero-shot cross-lingual transfer for multilingual question answering over knowledge graph. In *Proceedings of the 2021 Conference of the North American Chapter of the Association for Computational Linguistics: Human Language Technologies*, pages 5822–5834, Online. Association for Computational Linguistics.

An Empirical Study on Active Learning for Multi-label Text Classification

Mengqi Wang
wangmengq@deakin.edu.au

Ming Liu
m.liu@deakin.edu.au

Abstract

Active learning has been widely used in the task of text classification for its ability to select the most valuable samples to annotate while improving the model performance. However, the efficiency of active learning in multi-label text classification tasks has been under-explored due to the label imbalanceness problem. In this paper, we conduct an empirical study of active learning on multi-label text classification and evaluate the efficiency of five active learning strategies on six multi-label text classification tasks. The experiments show that some strategies in the single-label setting especially in imbalanced datasets.

1 Introduction

Active Learning (AL) has been applied in many Natural Language Processing (NLP) tasks due to its efficiency in improving model performance with limited annotation cost. Most works in AL have focused on developing strategies for single-label text classification (Tong and Koller, 2001; Hoi et al., 2006), Named Entity Recognition (Tomanek and Hahn, 2009; Shen et al., 2004, 2017) and Neural Machine Translation (Zhang et al., 2018; Peris and Casacuberta, 2018; Zhao et al., 2020). More recently, multi-label text classification (Liu et al., 2017; Pant et al., 2019; Liu et al., 2021) has received considerable attention since many text classification tasks are multi-labeled, i.e., each document can belong to more than one category. Take news classification as an example, a news article talking about the effect of the Olympic games on the tourism industry might belong to the following topic categories: *sports*, *economy* and *travel*. The challenge of multi-label text classification lies in three aspects: (i) heavily imbalanced labels, i.e. only a small amount of labels have high frequency while others exhibit extremely low frequency; (ii) sparse label correlation, where some labels may be correlated with others, but the correlation is weak; and (iii) hierarchical label structures, this is prevalent in many scientific document indexing, e.g. arXiv or PubMed (Lu, 2011).

Given the above challenges, we raise the research questions: Are the commonly used strategies in single-label text classification still applicable for the multi-label setting? Will they always benefit classification performances? To answer these questions, We conducted an empirical study to evaluate the effectiveness of five AL strategies on six prevalent multi-label text classification datasets. Our experiments show that the strategies commonly used in single-label text classification can have some effectiveness under multi-label settings. However, their performance is not consistent and highly dependent on the label distribution of the datasets. The main findings of our work are as follows:

- **The common AL strategies used in the single label classification are not robust for all multi-label setting.**
- **Diversity strategies consistently outperform other strategies across different dataset sizes and models.**
- **Larger and imbalanced dataset will heavily degrade the performance of common active learning strategies**

2 Active Learning on Multi-label Text Classification

We consider multiple widely-used AL strategies to investigate their different performance on multi-label text classification, including **Least Confidence (LC)** (Culotta and McCallum, 2005), **KMeans** (Kang et al., 2004), **Max Entropy** (Lewis and Gale, 1994), **Deep Bayesian Active Learning(BALD)** (Houlsby et al., 2011), **Monte Carlo (MC) Dropout** (Gal et al., 2017) and **Coreset** (Geifman and El-Yaniv, 2017; Sener and Savarese,

The Fourth Workshop on Insights from Negative Results in NLP, pages 94–102
May 5, 2023 ©2023 Association for Computational Linguistics

Algorithm 1 Pool-based multi-label active learning

Input: Initial labeled set L, unlabeled set U, query budget $\mathcal{B}$, model parameter Θ, annotation cost per round b, query strategy Q

Output: The final classifier $\hat{\Theta}$

Initialize Θ_0 with L
for $t \in 1, \ldots,$ **do**
  $\{(\mathrm{x}_i, y_i)_{i=1}^{b}\}^t \leftarrow \text{Query}(U, Q, \Theta_{t-1})$ ▷ Use strategy Q to select b examples
  $L \leftarrow L + \{(x_i, y_i)_{i=1}^{b}\}^t$
  $U \leftarrow U - \{(x_i, y_i)_{i=1}^{b}\}^t$
  $\Theta_t \leftarrow \text{retrainModel}(\Theta_{t-1}, L)$
  if $b * t > B$ **then** ▷ If budget exhausted
    $\hat{\Theta} \leftarrow \Theta_t$; **break**
return $\hat{\Theta}$

2018). **Random Sampling**, also known as passive learning, randomly selects instances for annotation and serves as a baseline for comparison with other AL strategies. **LC** is one of the most common approach to select queries in active learning, in which it uses the probability to measure how uncertain the model is towards the instances. **KMeans** clustering unlabeled data samples based on their feature representations, and then selecting the samples closest to the cluster centres for labeling. This strategy can help improve the efficiency and effectiveness of the active learning process by focusing on the most representative samples in each cluster. **Max Entropy** measures the confidence of the model using entropy (Shannon, 2001). It ranks all instances in U by the posterior class entropy under the model $H_\theta = -\sum P_\theta(Y \mid X) \log P_\theta(Y \mid X)$, and selects the top unlabelled instances to be labelled by the expert. **BALD** (Houlsby et al., 2011) is another commonly used uncertainty-based AL strategy, which maximizes the mutual information between the predictions and model posterior to achieve maximum information gain. **MC Dropout** selects samples based on their representativeness. As its name, it uses the MC dropout on inference circles, where the uncertainty is measured by the fraction of models across MC samples that disagree with the most popular choice (Siddhant and Lipton, 2018). **Coreset** (Geifman and El-Yaniv, 2017; Sener and Savarese, 2018), is one of the most popular diversity-based querying criteria, which selects the best representation of the dataset using the farthest-first traversal algorithm.

Algorithm 1 shows the pseudo code of our AL loop, given a fixed budget and an initial labeled set L, we try each strategy for the multi-label text classification tasks. In each AL iteration, we acquire b labelled examples, this process is repeated until the budget is exhausted.

3 Experiments

Datasets

Table 1 shows the statistics of the benchmarking datasets that used in the experiments. The datasets vary in size and cover both news and scientific documentation. We took the summary textual context and the corresponding labels for each data set to be the final classification target. All data sets are long-tailed distributed, i.e., only a small portion of labels frequently appear, majority of the label rarely appears in the data. **Web of Science (WOS)** (Kowsari et al., 2017), contains 46,985 documents with 134 categories includes 7 parents categories. All the documents are the published papers from the Web of Science[1] which is a publisher-independent global citation database. All three versions of WOS have been used in this work: WOS-46985, WOS-11967 and WOS-5736. **Arxiv Academic Paper Dataset (AAPD)**[2] (Yang et al., 2018) consists of 55,840 papers abstracts from arXiv[3] in the field of computer science, along with their corresponding subjects. Each paper may have multiple subjects, with a total of 54 subjects included in the dataset. The objective is to predict the appropriate subjects for an academic paper based on the content of its abstract. **Reuters-21578**[4] (Thoma, 2017), is a collection 10,369 news articles appeared on Reuters newswire in 1987. **Yelp Review**[5] is a modified version of the Yelp reviews dataset, consisting of reviews extracted from the Yelp Dataset Challenge 2017. In this dataset, the business label and rating label together are considered as the multi-label for each review.

AL Process

As shown in Figure. 1, we randomly select a tiny portion of initialized data from each dataset to warm-start the classification model. The portion

[1] `https://www.webofknowledge.com/`
[2] `https://github.com/lancopku/SGM`
[3] `https://arxiv.org/`
[4] `http://kdd.ics.uci.edu/databases/reuters21578/reuters21578.html`
[5] `https://github.com/rnyati/Yelp-Dataset-Classification-`

Dataset	*Size*	*Initial*	*Labels*
WOS5736	5736	1%	11
WOS11967	11967	1%	35
WOS46985	46985	5%	134
AAPD	54840	1%	54
Reuters-21578	10788	1%	168
Yelp Review	208869	5%	466

Table 1: Multi-label text classification datasets.

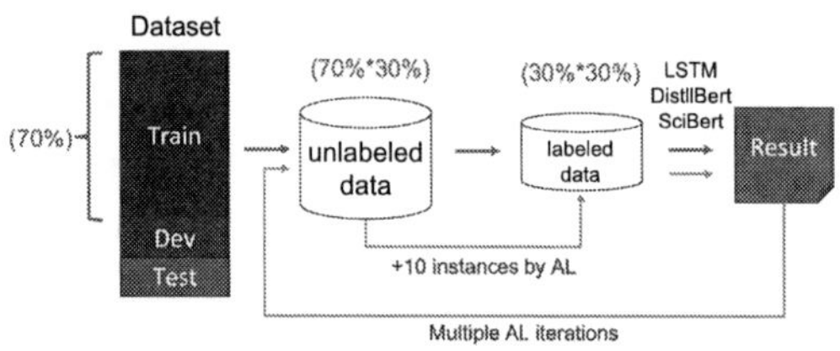

Figure 1: The AL Process in the experiment. Every dataset is divided into three subsets: train, dev, and test. The training data comprises approximately 70% of all samples in the dataset, while the remaining 30% is deemed as unlabeled data. AL strategies are employed to select a few (i.e. 10) instances from the unlabeled data pool, and their labels are then used as the results of the 'human-annotation' process. Multiple rounds of selection are performed until the budget is exhausted.

of initialized random samples ranges between 1%-5% of the 70% training data (see Table 1). We then take the remaining 69% of training data as the unlabeled data pool, which different active learning strategies can actively query. Considering the varying sizes of different datasets, we choose different sizes of annotation budgets, which represents the total number of instances we queried from the selection process. The instances in the unused budget pool will be randomly divided into equal-sized batches to ensure comparable results. The number of selected samples is equally split during each iteration. For each iteration, a batch of samples was identified, and the model was retrained for 20 epochs. The batch size for each dataset is set to 50 follows (Gui et al., 2021). The active querying process stops when all budgets of queried instances are used. Therefore, the batch size setting for different active strategies will be the same for each dataset. We run each strategy on all six datasets 10 times and report the average as the experiment results for evaluation.

Experiment Setup

We conduct the experiment in batch mode, following the traditional pool-based AL scenario(Settles, 2009). To include the popular Bert-based model in our comparison, we adapt the AL strategies following (Ein-Dor et al., 2020). We use **LSTM**(Hochreiter and Schmidhuber, 1997), **DistilBert**(Sanh et al., 2019) and **SciBert**(Beltagy et al., 2019) models. The experiment was implemented by modifying the previous work of large-scale multi-label text classification[6] and incorporating AL settings.

Evaluation Metrics

We use the most representative evaluation metrics for multi-label text classification: Micro-F1 (Huang and Zhou, 2013; Gao et al., 2016; Yu et al., 2020). Micro-F1 score is also known as the micro-averaging of F1 score or simply 'the accuracy' of the multi-label classification problems. It measures the proportion of correctly classified data samples out of all data. As the Micro-F1 score increases, the performance of multi-label text classification improves.

Results

We present the results for all mentioned AL strategies in Section 2. Figure 2 , Figure 3 and Figure 4 show the performance of all strategies on different datasets. We observed that only part of AL strategies improve the accuracy of multi-label text classification among different datasets. The only very promising dataset is Reuters, where all AL strategies outperformed the random baseline on all three models. In most datasets, the random baseline was outperformed by other strategies, even when the baseline performs well, such as in WOS5736.

From a model perspective, AL strategies adapted to DistilBert and SciBert are more robust than those adapted to LSTM. With the boost of the two versions of Bert model, AL strategies can be effective on more datasets in both news and scientific domains. However, AL strategies on the LSTM model provide negative results in both domains. This suggests that without suitable pre-trained models, the AL strategies cannot provide promising results. This can be an important insight for future work, as AL's ability to actively query the most informative samples can better leverage pre-trained models.

[6]https://keras.io/examples/nlp/multi_label_classification/

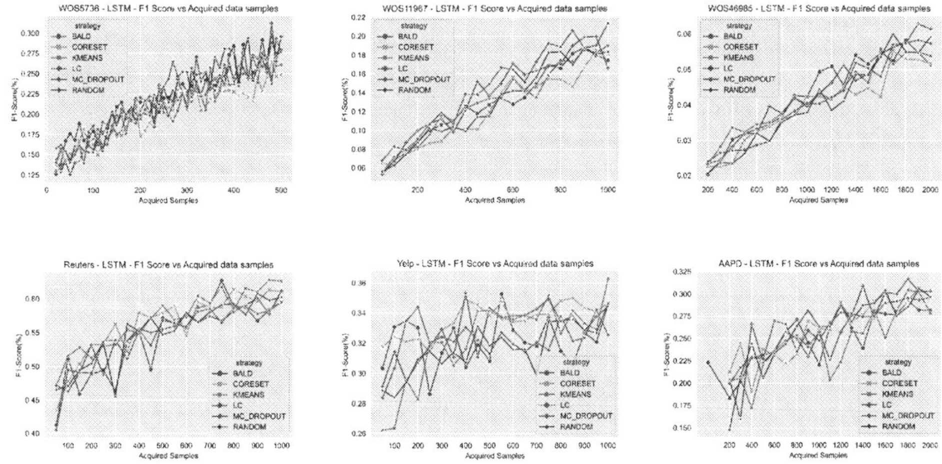

Figure 2: AL Strategies on LSTM

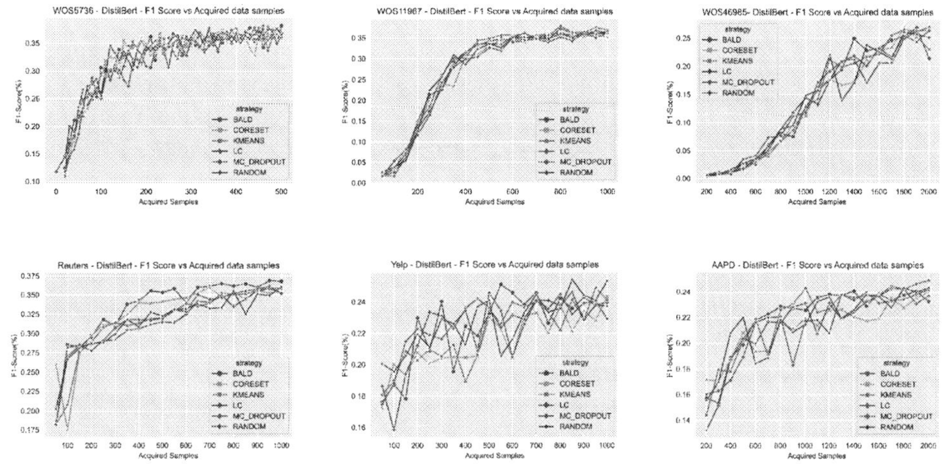

Figure 3: AL Strategies on DistilBert

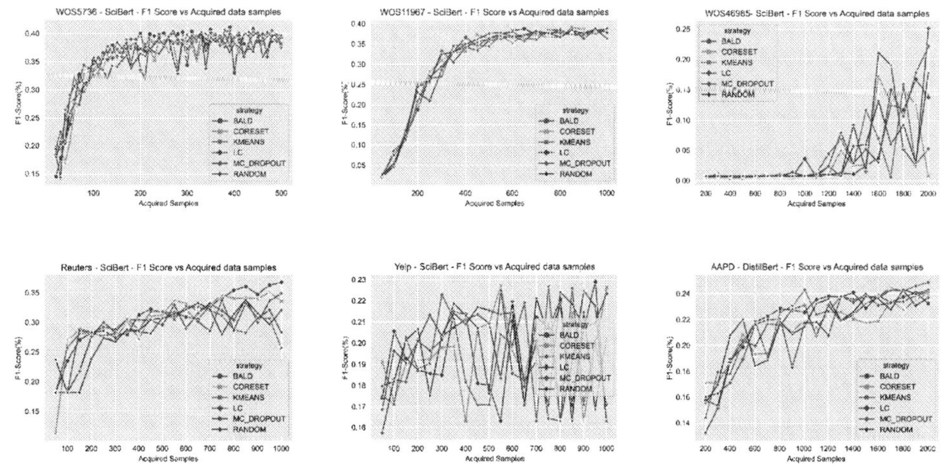

Figure 4: AL Strategies on SciBert

While AL strategies can outperform the Random baseline in multi-text classification using DistilBert and SciBert, there is no single strategy that consistently outperforms all others. For example, BALD in AAPD and Reuters underperforms compared to random. It is natural that no single strategy can outperform all others on all datasets due to the diversity and representativeness of the queried instances, which heavily impacts the effectiveness of AL (Aggarwal et al., 2014; Ren et al., 2021). When the label structure of the original dataset is complex, it is hard for AL strategies to capture both features in the queried instances.The KMEANS strategy achieves the best performance in the larger WOS46985 and AAPD Review datasets. However, in Yelp dataset, it remain comparable to the randombaseline.

Additionally, we do a study to compare the impacts of data sizes on AL performance, the result is presented in the Appendix: Figure 5. We compared the F1-score of three different models, all with the powerful BALD AL strategy, on WOS5736, WOS11978, and WOS46985. In the smaller datasets, WOS5736 and WOS11978, it can be easily observed that BALD effectively improves the F1-score in DistilBert and SciBert after the first ten rounds of actively querying. However, for the larger dataset, WOS46985, BALD only works for DistilBert after ten rounds and takes 20 rounds for SciBert. For all datasets, BALD does not show any effectiveness in all models, as no sudden increase of F1-score can be observed.

We also find that the imbalanced label distribution has an impact on the effectiveness of AL strategies. As shown in Figure 6, the dataset WOS11967, which has the least imbalanced label distribution, has all AL strategies perform better than the other WOS datasets. The accuracy of multi-label text classification with AL improved by over 50% with only one-third of the entire dataset. We plan to conduct a future study to further investigate how label imbalance affects the effectiveness of AL strategies. This research is significant as unbalanced data acquisition can lead to fairness issues that may affect the reliability and validity of machine learning models.

After conducting our initial analysis, we dived deep into the label distribution of the acquired data samples for the WOS dataset in more detail, , the result is presented in the Appendix: Figure 6. We find that the labels in each dataset exhibit an imbalanced distribution, which motivated us to further explore the relationship between AL strategies and the balance of selected data samples in future study. This inquiry is crucial, as unbalanced data acquisition may lead to fairness issues that can significantly affect the validity and reliability of machine learning models.

We also measured and compared the average runtime of one selection iteration for different strategies on all datasets. However, the differences between the runtimes are less than one second. This is understandable, as the different strategies are waiting for the same features from the model's prediction results to decide on the selected samples.

4 Conclusion

In this paper, we explored different Active Learning strategies and its performance on multi-label text classification using a basic neural network model. Our goal is to understand if the popular active learning strategies can prove effective in a multi-label text classification tasks under AL setting. To the best of our knowledge, our work presented the first systematic and comparative study in this context. We observed that unlike single-label text classification, not all strategies can outperform the random baseline. In future work, we plan to perform a deeper analysis of the fairness issue for multi-label text classification under AL setting while exploring more strategies recently published.

References

Charu C Aggarwal, Xiangnan Kong, Quanquan Gu, Jiawei Han, and S Yu Philip. 2014. Active learning: A survey. In *Data Classification*, pages 599–634. Chapman and Hall/CRC.

Iz Beltagy, Kyle Lo, and Arman Cohan. 2019. SciBERT: A pretrained language model for scientific text. In *Proceedings of the 2019 Conference on Empirical Methods in Natural Language Processing and the 9th International Joint Conference on Natural Language Processing (EMNLP-IJCNLP)*, pages 3615–3620, Hong Kong, China. Association for Computational Linguistics.

Aron Culotta and Andrew McCallum. 2005. Reducing labeling effort for structured prediction tasks. In *AAAI*, volume 5, pages 746–751.

Liat Ein-Dor, Alon Halfon, Ariel Gera, Eyal Shnarch, Lena Dankin, Leshem Choshen, Marina Danilevsky, Ranit Aharonov, Yoav Katz, and Noam Slonim. 2020. Active Learning for BERT: An Empirical Study. In *Proceedings of the 2020 Conference on Empirical*

Methods in Natural Language Processing (EMNLP), pages 7949–7962, Online. Association for Computational Linguistics.

Yarin Gal, Riashat Islam, and Zoubin Ghahramani. 2017. Deep bayesian active learning with image data. In *International Conference on Machine Learning*, pages 1183–1192. PMLR.

Nengneng Gao, Sheng-Jun Huang, and Songcan Chen. 2016. Multi-label active learning by model guided distribution matching. *Frontiers of Computer Science*, 10(5):845–855.

Yonatan Geifman and Ran El-Yaniv. 2017. Deep active learning over the long tail. *arXiv preprint arXiv:1711.00941*.

Xiaoqiang Gui, Xudong Lu, and Guoxian Yu. 2021. Cost-effective batch-mode multi-label active learning. *Neurocomputing*, 463:355–367.

Sepp Hochreiter and Jürgen Schmidhuber. 1997. Long short-term memory. *Neural computation*, 9(8):1735–1780.

Steven CH Hoi, Rong Jin, and Michael R Lyu. 2006. Large-scale text categorization by batch mode active learning. In *Proceedings of the 15th international conference on World Wide Web*, pages 633–642.

Neil Houlsby, Ferenc Huszár, Zoubin Ghahramani, and Máté Lengyel. 2011. Bayesian active learning for classification and preference learning. *arXiv preprint arXiv:1112.5745*.

Sheng-Jun Huang and Zhi-Hua Zhou. 2013. Active query driven by uncertainty and diversity for incremental multi-label learning. In *2013 IEEE 13th international conference on data mining*, pages 1079–1084. IEEE.

Jaeho Kang, Kwang Ryel Ryu, and Hyuk-Chul Kwon. 2004. Using cluster-based sampling to select initial training set for active learning in text classification. In *Advances in Knowledge Discovery and Data Mining: 8th Pacific-Asia Conference, PAKDD 2004, Sydney, Australia, May 26-28, 2004. Proceedings 8*, pages 384–388. Springer.

Kamran Kowsari, Donald E Brown, Mojtaba Heidarysafa, Kiana Jafari Meimandi, Matthew S Gerber, and Laura E Barnes. 2017. Hdltex: Hierarchical deep learning for text classification. In *2017 16th IEEE International Conference on Machine Learning and Applications (ICMLA)*, pages 364–371.

David D Lewis and William A Gale. 1994. A sequential algorithm for training text classifiers. In *SIGIR'94*, pages 3–12. Springer.

Hui Liu, Danqing Zhang, Bing Yin, and Xiaodan Zhu. 2021. Improving pretrained models for zero-shot multi-label text classification through reinforced label hierarchy reasoning. *arXiv preprint arXiv:2104.01666*.

Jingzhou Liu, Wei-Cheng Chang, Yuexin Wu, and Yiming Yang. 2017. Deep learning for extreme multi-label text classification. In *Proceedings of the 40th international ACM SIGIR conference on research and development in information retrieval*, pages 115–124.

Zhiyong Lu. 2011. Pubmed and beyond: a survey of web tools for searching biomedical literature. *Database*, 2011.

Pooja Pant, A Sai Sabitha, Tanupriya Choudhury, and Prince Dhingra. 2019. Multi-label classification trending challenges and approaches. *Emerging Trends in Expert Applications and Security*, pages 433–444.

Álvaro Peris and Francisco Casacuberta. 2018. Active learning for interactive neural machine translation of data streams. *arXiv preprint arXiv:1807.11243*.

Pengzhen Ren, Yun Xiao, Xiaojun Chang, Po-Yao Huang, Zhihui Li, Brij B Gupta, Xiaojiang Chen, and Xin Wang. 2021. A survey of deep active learning. *ACM Computing Surveys (CSUR)*, 54(9):1–40.

Victor Sanh, Lysandre Debut, Julien Chaumond, and Thomas Wolf. 2019. Distilbert, a distilled version of bert: smaller, faster, cheaper and lighter. *arXiv preprint arXiv:1910.01108*.

Ozan Sener and Silvio Savarese. 2018. Active learning for convolutional neural networks: A core-set approach. In *International Conference on Learning Representations*.

Burr Settles. 2009. Active learning literature survey.

Claude Elwood Shannon. 2001. A mathematical theory of communication. *ACM SIGMOBILE mobile computing and communications review*, 5(1):3–55.

Dan Shen, Jie Zhang, Jian Su, Guodong Zhou, and Chew Lim Tan. 2004. Multi-criteria-based active learning for named entity recognition. In *Proceedings of the 42nd annual meeting of the Association for Computational Linguistics (ACL-04)*, pages 589–596.

Yanyao Shen, Hyokun Yun, Zachary C Lipton, Yakov Kronrod, and Animashree Anandkumar. 2017. Deep active learning for named entity recognition. *arXiv preprint arXiv:1707.05928*.

Aditya Siddhant and Zachary C. Lipton. 2018. Deep Bayesian active learning for natural language processing: Results of a large-scale empirical study. In *Proceedings of the 2018 Conference on Empirical Methods in Natural Language Processing*, pages 2904–2909, Brussels, Belgium. Association for Computational Linguistics.

Martin Thoma. 2017. The reuters dataset.

Katrin Tomanek and Udo Hahn. 2009. Reducing class imbalance during active learning for named entity annotation. In *Proceedings of the fifth international conference on Knowledge capture*, pages 105–112.

Simon Tong and Daphne Koller. 2001. Support vector machine active learning with applications to text classification. *Journal of machine learning research*, 2(Nov):45–66.

Pengcheng Yang, Xu Sun, Wei Li, Shuming Ma, Wei Wu, and Houfeng Wang. 2018. SGM: sequence generation model for multi-label classification. In *Proceedings of the 27th International Conference on Computational Linguistics, COLING 2018, Santa Fe, New Mexico, USA, August 20-26, 2018*, pages 3915–3926.

Guoxian Yu, Xia Chen, Carlotta Domeniconi, Jun Wang, Zhao Li, Zili Zhang, and Xiangliang Zhang. 2020. Cmal: Cost-effective multi-label active learning by querying subexamples. *IEEE Transactions on Knowledge and Data Engineering*.

Pei Zhang, Xueying Xu, and Deyi Xiong. 2018. Active learning for neural machine translation. In *2018 International Conference on Asian Language Processing (IALP)*, pages 153–158. IEEE.

Yuekai Zhao, Haoran Zhang, Shuchang Zhou, and Zhihua Zhang. 2020. Active learning approaches to enhancing neural machine translation. In *Findings of the Association for Computational Linguistics: EMNLP 2020*, pages 1796–1806, Online. Association for Computational Linguistics.

A Appendix

A.1 Data Size.

We performed an exhaustive analysis of the entire dataset by employing three prominent machine learning models, namely Long Short-Term Memory (LSTM), DistilBERT, and SciBERT, in conjunction with three distinct active learning strategies, namely RANDOM, KMeans, and BALD. We systematically augmented the number of acquired samples and meticulously evaluated the resulting changes in F1-score to gain insights into the performance of each model and strategy. This comprehensive evaluation enabled us to identify the most effective combination of model and active learning strategy for optimal performance.

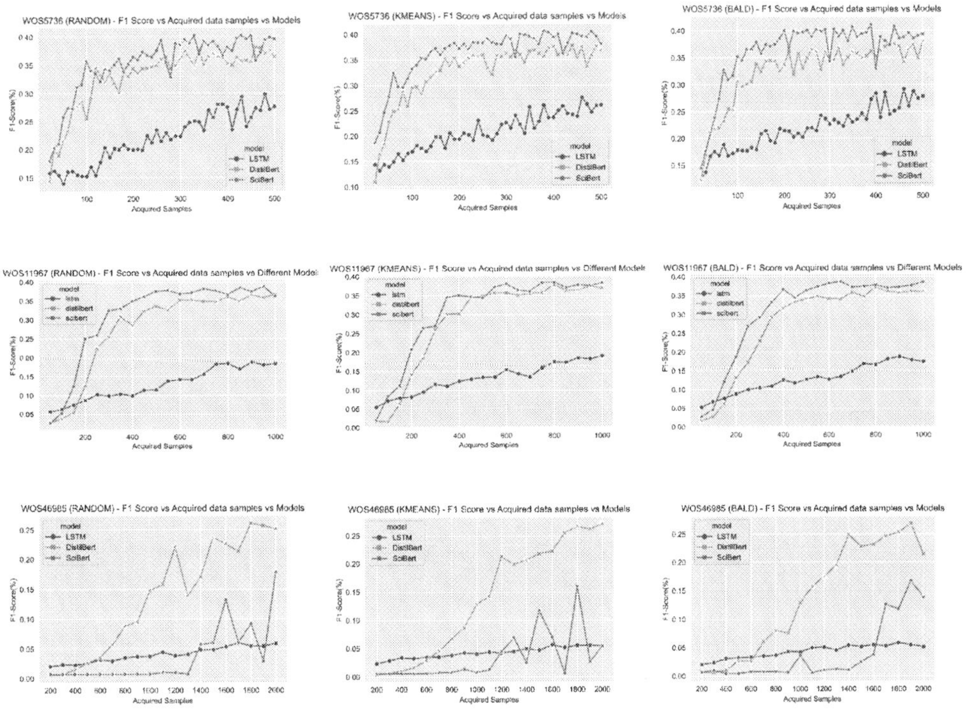

Figure 5: AL strategies on various data sizes and models

A.2 Distribution

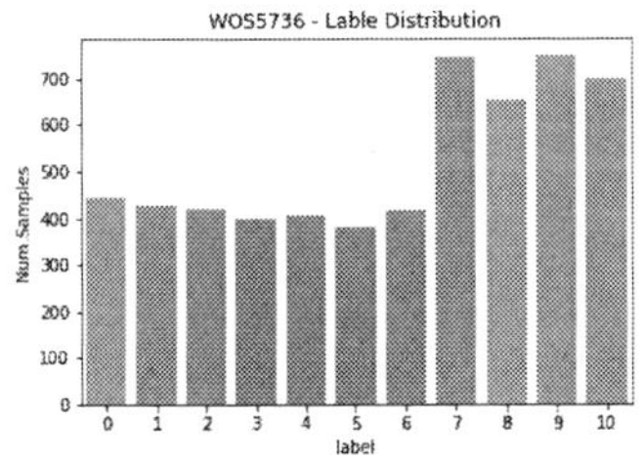

((a)) WOS5736 label distribution

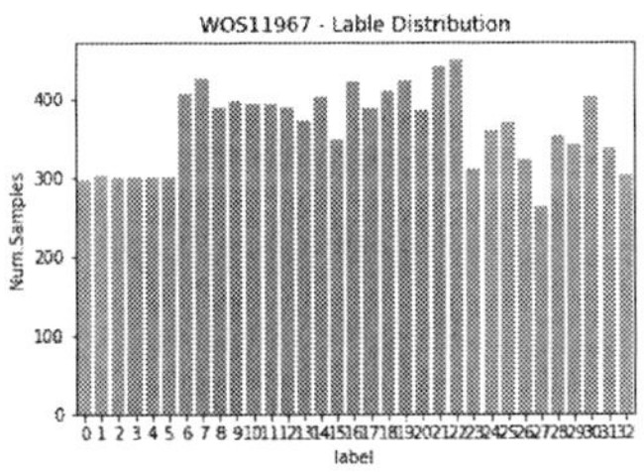

((b)) WOS11967 label distribution

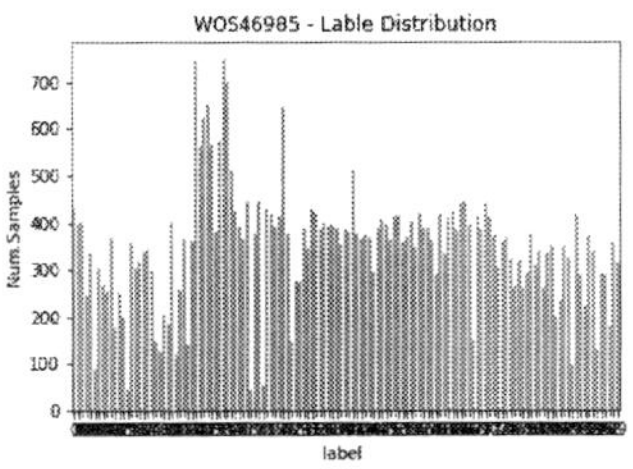

((c)) WOS46985 label distribution

Figure 6: Label distribution for three WOS dataset

After conducting our initial analysis, we dived deep into the label distribution of the acquired data samples for the WOS dataset in more detail, as shown in Figure 6. We find that the labels in each dataset exhibit an imbalanced distribution, which motivated us to further explore the relationship between active learning strategies and the balance of selected data samples in future study. This inquiry is crucial, as unbalanced data acquisition may lead to fairness issues that can significantly affect the validity and reliability of machine learning models.

Author Index

Association for Computational Linguistics
209 N. Eighth Street
Stroudsburg, Pennsylvania 18360

ISBN 978-1-7138-7383-9

CURRAN ASSOCIATES INC.
proceedings.com